lonely planet

Discover
# London

Experience the best
of London

This edition written and researched by

Damian Harper,
Steve Fallon, Emilie Filou,
Vesna Maric, Sally Schafer

# Discover
# London

## The West End (p47)

Where your London adventure begins.

**Don't Miss**: Westminster Abbey, British Museum, Buckingham Palace, Houses of Parliament

## The City (p93)

Almost two millennia of history plus many of London's must-see sights.

**Don't Miss**: Tower of London, St Paul's Cathedral

## The South Bank (p119)

The roll-call of riverside sights includes Shakespeare's Globe and Millennium Bridge.

**Don't Miss**: Tate Modern

## Kensington & Hyde Park (p141)

Superb museums and beautiful parks in a high-class setting.

**Don't Miss**: Victoria & Albert Museum

## Clerkenwell, Hoxton & Spitalfields (p163)

Great food and an even better night out.

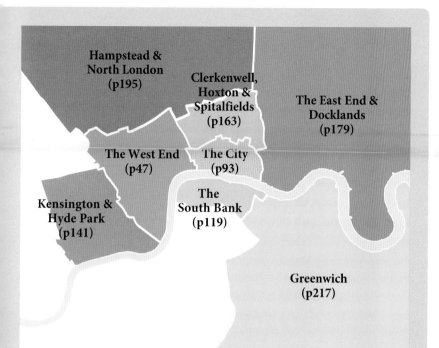

Hampstead &
North London
(p195)

Clerkenwell,
Hoxton &
Spitalfields
(p163)

The East End &
Docklands
(p179)

The West End
(p47)

The City
(p93)

Kensington &
Hyde Park
(p141)

The
South Bank
(p119)

Greenwich
(p217)

### The East End & Docklands (p179)

This diverse neighbourhood is undergoing massive regeneration courtesy of the Olympic Games.

### Hampstead & North London (p195)

Wild expanses of heath and bustling markets guarantee a glorious day out.

**Don't Miss**: British Library

### Greenwich (p217)

The home of world time is steeped in maritime history.

**Don't Miss**: Royal Observatory & Greenwich Park

# Contents

# Welcome to London

The British capital is a buzzing byword for variety and entertainment – its iconic sights are outstanding, its royal splendour and historic grandeur are unmatched, and its nightlife is second to none. London's energy and dynamism can be felt on every street corner.

**London is a city everyone seems to know before visiting.** Its instantly recognisable icons – the red postboxes, the double-decker buses, the guards at Buckingham Palace – are all present and very correct, but the city usually surprises first-time visitors by being anything but the stuffy, ordered capital of popular rumour. Instead, an exciting metropolis with rich veins of culture, art and commerce awaits exploration. A tireless innovator, London is a city of ideas and the imagination, with a stimulating backdrop of creativity and modernity.

**For sightseeing, it's often hard to know where to start.** Sights are largely jammed together centrally, so you could virtually spin a bottle and take your pick. The Roman-founded square mile known as the City of London is a natural choice, home to the imposing Tower of London, historic St Paul's Cathedral, numerous ancient churches, cobbled side streets and hidden treasures.

**The West End is London's contemporary heart.** It will have sightseers doing cartwheels, shoppers in seventh heaven and gastronomes not far behind. Royal Mayfair and political Westminster next door are the playgrounds of the city's elite, packed with impressive stately homes and the world's most famous parliament building.

**Find time for the little things that make London great.** A pint in a pub, a plate of fish and chips by the river, a day out with friends in one of London's expansive wooded parks, a rocking night out in Shoreditch or Soho or a canal-side walk in north London. This is one of the world's great cities and your only problem may be wishing you had time to see it all.

> 66
> London's energy and dynamism can be felt on every street corner
> 99

Traditional red phone booths near the Houses of Parliament (p58)

KMIRAGAYA/DREAMSTIME ©

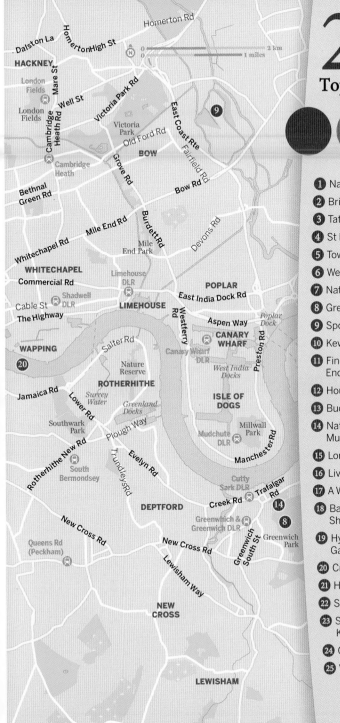

# 25

## Top Experiences

# 25 London's Top Experiences

# National Gallery (p75)

This superlative collection of (largely premodern) art in the heart of London is one of the world's largest and a roll-call of some of the world's most outstanding artistic compositions. With highlights including work by Leonardo da Vinci, Michelangelo, Gainsborough, Constable, Turner, Monet, Renoir and Van Gogh, it's a bravura performance and one not to be missed. On-site restaurants and cafes are also exceptional, rounding out a terrific experience and putting the icing on an already eye-catching cake.

## ② British Museum (p54)

With five million visitors trooping through its doors annually, the British Museum in literary Bloomsbury is London's most popular tourist attraction. It's a vast and hallowed collection of artefacts, art and age-old antiquities; you could spend a lifetime here and still make daily discoveries (admission is free, so you could do just that, if so inclined). Otherwise, join everyone else on the highlights tours (or eyeOpener tours) for a precis of the museum's treasures.

# Tate Modern (p124)

A favourite of Londoners (and, quite possibly, the world), this modern and contemporary art collection enjoys a triumphant position right on the River Thames. Housed in the former Bankside Power Station, the Tate Modern is a vigorous statement of modernity, architectural renewal and accessibility for art lovers of all denominations. The permanent collection is free, but make sure you enter down the ramp into the Turbine Hall, where the gallery's standout temporary exhibitions push the conceptual envelope and satisfy more cerebral art-hunters.

## The Best...
## Modern Architecture

**AQUATICS CENTRE**
Striking and dramatic masterpiece of the Olympic Park. (p187)

**30 ST MARY AXE**
Colloquially dubbed 'the Gherkin', this is the city's most iconic modern edifice. (p108)

**THE SHARD**
A crystalline spike over London Bridge. (p123)

**LLOYD'S OF LONDON**
Richard Rogers' inside-out London masterpiece. (p108)

**LONDON EYE**
Unsurprisingly visible from many remote parts of town. (p128)

13

# The Best...
# Royal Sights

**TOWER OF LONDON**
Castle, tower, prison, medieval execution site and home of the dazzling Crown Jewels. (p98)

**BUCKINGHAM PALACE**
The Queen Mother of all London's royal palaces, with lovely gardens and the Changing of the Guard. (p56)

**HAMPTON COURT PALACE**
Splendid Tudor palace with beautiful grounds, on the Thames (p234).

**KENSINGTON PALACE**
Princess Diana's former home, this stately and recently restored royal palace is the highlight of Kensington Gardens. (p154)

## St Paul's Cathedral (p102)

Wren's 300-year-old masterpiece became a striking symbol of London's dogged resilience during the Blitz, when fire-fighters fought off a conflagration threatening to consume it. Today, the sublime City landmark is as rewarding inside as it is iconic outside. Climb the marvellous dome for superb views of London, and explore the cathedral's astonishing interior and crypt.

## Tower of London (p98)

Few parts of the UK are as steeped in history, or as impregnated with legend and superstition, as this fabulous fortress. The tower is not only an architectural odyssey – there's a diamond almost as big as the Ritz, free tours run by magnificently attired 'beefeaters', and a dazzling array of armour and weaponry. Because there is so much to see, get here early. You will need at least half a day (probably more) to explore it.

## Westminster Abbey (p52)

Fans of medieval ecclesiastical architecture will be in seventh heaven at this sublime abbey and hallowed place of coronation. Almost every nook and cranny has a story attached to it, but few sights in London are as beautiful or well preserved as the Henry VII chapel. Elsewhere there's UK's oldest door, Poet's Corner, the Coronation Chair, 14th-century cloisters, royal sarcophagi and much more.

## Natural History Museum (p153)

With its thunderous animatronic Tyrannosaurus rex, towering diplodocus skeleton, magical Wildlife Garden, outstanding Darwin Centre and architecture straight from a Gothic fairy tale, this museum is quite simply a work of great imagination. Kids are the target audience but, when you look around, adults are equally mesmerised. Popular sleepovers in the museum have young ones snoozing alongside the diplodocus, while winter brings its own magic, as the glittering ice rink by the east lawn swarms with skaters.

# Greenwich Meridian (p222)

It's an oddly satisfying feeling, placing yourself on the Greenwich meridian and knowing that everyone on earth is setting their watches in relation to where you stand. Add to that the neighbouring cluster of classical buildings and the surrounding Greenwich Park and the result is a fascinating excursion from central London. A few steps away is one of London's best vantage points for fantastic views over the stately sights of Greenwich, all of which can be explored in a day.

## The Best...
## Art Galleries

**TATE MODERN**
A breathtaking collection of modern and contemporary art in a power station setting right on the South Bank. (p124)

**NATIONAL GALLERY**
Stupendous collection of more than 2000 pre-20th-century paintings housed in fabulous premises in the heart of London. (p75)

**TATE BRITAIN**
Works by JMW Turner are the standout pieces in this excellent museum that hosts the annual Turner Prize. (p65)

**NATIONAL PORTRAIT GALLERY**
Celebrated British people creatively captured by equally famous artists over 500 years. (p69)

## Sporting London (p187)

The eye-catching, state-of-the-art facilities in the Olympic Park encapsulate the sporting zeitgeist, but there's much more, from watching first-round matches at Wimbledon (p41), cheering runners at the London Marathon (p40) or hopping on a Barclays bike (p283). You may not land tickets to the FA Cup Final at Wembley Stadium or front-row seats for the men's 100m finals at Olympic Stadium, but there are plenty of ways to enjoy sport in London. Wimbledon

# The Best...
# Restaurants

**PROVIDORES & TAPA ROOM**
Fusion food at its absolute best. (p81)

**WAPPING FOOD**
A perfect East End recipe: industrial decor meets haute cuisine. (p191)

**GORDON RAMSAY**
Three Michelin stars and a celebrity chef; say no more. (p158)

**GAUCHO GRILL**
Fabulous restaurant specialising in succulent Argentinian beef. (p210)

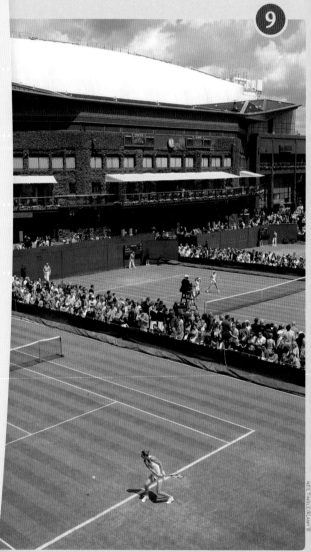

NEIL TINGLE/AL...

## Kew Gardens (p161)

Where else in London can you size up an 18th-century 10-floor Chinese pagoda and a Japanese gateway in one of the world's most outstanding botanical collections? Kew Gardens is loved by Londoners for its 19th-century palm house, Victorian glasshouses, conservatories, tree canopy walkway, architectural follies and mind-boggling plant variety. You'll need a day to do it justice, and you could find yourself heading back for more.

## Fine Dining in the West End (p77)

One of the joys of eating out in London is the sheer profusion of choice. No matter where you go, London rewards foodies with unexpected flavours and culinary discoveries, but it's the West End that delivers the highest concentration of variety and quality. Whatever you are hunting for – Chinese, Indian, Korean, Moroccan or British – you won't have to travel far to find it. It's not the cheapest part of town, but it's the most central.

Yauatcha (p79)

## Houses of Parliament (p58)

There's nothing quite as magnificent or more London than the sublime view of Big Ben and the Houses of Parliament from the River Thames, especially when the sun is shining on its instantly recognisable Gothic facade. The secrets of the Houses of Parliament (also called the Palace of Westminster) can be explored on guided tours, but visitors can also watch debates in both the House of Commons and the House of Lords.

## Buckingham Palace (p56)

There are few more bizarre experiences than paying to snoop around a section of the Queen's lodgings, but for royal enthusiasts it's a superlative highlight. That the hoi polloi can breach this imperious, blue-blooded bastion is remarkable enough and there's nowhere else quite like it in town. The royal household is only open from late July to late September, but get your ticket from Buckingham Palace, have it stamped, and you get a repeat visit.

# National Maritime Museum (p225)

This shipshape museum is not just a first-rate lesson in seamanship and England's rich maritime traditions, but also an occasion to come to Greenwich and soak up its riverine charms. The museum is an inspiring flick through the brine-soaked pages of English history and kids are well catered for, with ample hands-on stuff to keep young salty sea dogs occupied.

## The Best...
## Theatre

**NATIONAL THEATRE**
Cutting-edge theatrical productions in a choice of three theatres. (p138)

**SHAKESPEARE'S GLOBE**
For the authentic open-air Elizabethan effect. (p138)

**ROYAL COURT THEATRE**
Constantly innovative and inspirationally driven Sloane Sq theatre. (p159)

# The Best...
## Views

**ST PAUL'S CATHEDRAL**
Climb up into London's
largest ecclesiastical
dome for awe-inspiring
views of town. (p102)

**LONDON EYE**
Gently rotating, tip-top
views of London – but
choose a fair-weather day.
(p128)

**PARLIAMENT HILL**
Skyscraping views across
London from Hampstead
Heath. (p205)

**GREENWICH PARK**
Clamber up to the statue
of General Wolfe for su-
perlative views. (p222)

15

## London Eye (p128)

You may have eyed up London from altitude as you descended into Heathrow, but your pilot won't have lingered over the supreme views that extend in every direction from London's great riverside Ferris wheel. The queues move as slowly as the Eye rotates (there are ways to fast-track your way on), but that makes it even more rewarding once you've lifted off and London unfurls beneath you. Avoid grey days – although with London's notoriously overcast skies that may be a tall order. London Eye, designed by David Marks and Julia Barfield

TOP: DIEGO LEZAMA/LONELY PLANET IMAGES © LEFT: NEIL SETCHFIELD/LONELY PLANET IMAGES ©

## Live Music in Camden (p213)

16

The South Bank, the West End and Kensington have a monopoly on quality classical music performances but if you want music with more bite and attitude, head to Camden. The edgy North London neighbourhood has traditionally nurtured a plethora of indie and rock bands through its grungy galaxy of clubs and live music venues. Big-ticket names also play here so whatever your taste, you should find a band to fit your musical persuasion. Lenny Kravitz performing at Koko (p214)

17

## A West End Show (p87)

A trip to London is incomplete without seeing a West End show. Whether it's world-class drama or smash-hit musicals, you'll find it in this irrepressibly glitzy theatreland. There's always something new drawing accolades from press critics and an enthusiastic public alike, alongside the filler of long-run hits. Watch Hollywood stars keep it real, or discover something more experimental on the fringe in the world's most famous concentration of theatres.

CHRISTER FREDRIKSSON/LONELY PLANET IMAGES ©

# Bar Hopping in Shoreditch (p175)

Thread your way from bar to bar through hip Shoreditch for a taste of the neighbourhood's trendy watering holes. Many also serve top-notch food, so you can build an entire night's entertainment in boozers without breaking stride to find a restaurant. Many bars only shut up in the early hours at weekends, while a bevy of cutting-edge clubs adds to the late-night buzz. Bricklayers Arms

## The Best...
## Live Music

### PROUD CAMDEN
Leading North London bar with foot-stomping live music and a superb terrace. (p212)

### ROYAL ALBERT HALL
The UK's most iconic concert venue and home to the Proms. (p155)

### 606 CLUB
Get into the subterranean swing of things at this atmospheric, world-famous jazz club. (p160)

### ROYAL FESTIVAL HALL
Smashing acoustics and an excellent program of music across the aural spectrum. (p129)

## Hyde Park & Kensington Gardens (p152)

**19**

London's urban parkland is *the* place to see locals at ease and in their element. Hyde Park alone ranges across a mighty 142 hectares; throw in Kensington Gardens (p154) and you have even more room to roam and everything you could want: a central London setting, a royal palace, extravagant Victoriana, boating opportunities, open-air concerts, an art gallery, magnificent trees, and a thoughtful and tasteful granite memorial to Princess Diana. Hyde Park

OLIVER STREWE/LONELY PLANET IMAGES ©

# The Best...
# Parks, Gardens & Heaths

**HAMPSTEAD HEATH**
Woods, hills, meadows and top scenic views, all rolled into one sublime sprawl. (p205)

**HYDE PARK**
Grand gardens, lovely lawns, a head-turning variety of trees and inviting expanses of greenery. (p152)

**ST JAMES'S PARK**
Feast on sublime views in one of London's most attractive royal parks. (p61)

**KEW GARDENS**
A botanist's paradise, huge gardens and a great day out with the kids. (p161)

CHRISTER FREDRIKSSON/LONELY PLANET IMAGES ©

## 20 Cruising the Thames (p283)

Cleaving the British capital into north and south and pumping through a riveting panorama of both urban and bucolic shades, London's tidal river begs for your attention. For such a great maritime city, it's no surprise that many of London's most iconic sights lie dotted along the riverbank. A cruise along the River Thames is a chance to see the city's riverine magnificence unfold before you at a relaxed pace.

Millennium Bridge, designed by Norman Foster and Anthony Caro

## Historic London Pubs (p116)

London without pubs would be like Paris *sans* cafes or Beijing shorn of its charming *hutong*. Pub culture is part of London's DNA and pubs are the place to be if you want to see local people in their hops-scented element. Longer hours have only cemented the pub's reputation as the cornerstone for a great night out. Mix your ale-drinking with history in one of London's age-old pubs, starting with the magnificent Ye Olde Cheshire Cheese.

## Shakespeare's Globe (p138)

Few London experiences can beat a Bard's-eye view of the stage. It's even fun to get a ticket to stand (Elizabethan style) as one of the all-weather 'groundlings' in the open-air yard before the stage, taking whatever the London skies deliver. But if you want a comfortable perspective on Shakespeare, pay a bit extra and grab one of the seats in the galleries. If you've a soft spot for Shakespeare, architecture and the English climate, you'll have an absolute ball.

## Shopping in Knightsbridge (p160)

Whether you spend the day exploring the phenomenon of Harrods and Harvey Nichols or you have your eye on the top names of Sloane St and Brompton Rd, Knightsbridge has something for every credit card–holding fashionista. In terms of mileage, a trawl through the department stores and boutiques is a day out in itself, where window-shopping and people-watching stylishly go hand in hand.

## The Best...
## Bars & Pubs

**JERUSALEM TAVERN**
Tiny but delightful, with original beers from a Norfolk brewery. (p174)

**BOOK CLUB**
A modern temple to good times, with great offbeat events. (p175)

**PROUD CAMDEN**
Great drinks, music and fun in Camden's old stables. (p213)

**GREENWICH UNION**
Championing drinks from local microbreweries. (p228)

## Camden Market (p205)

A foray into trendy North London is a crucial part of the London experience. Camden's market – actually four markets in one great melange – may be a hectic and tourist-oriented attraction, but snacking on the go from the international food stalls is a great way to enjoy browsing the merchandise. Camden's terrific dining scene, throbbing nightlife and well-seasoned pub culture is well known to night owls citywide.

# The Best...
## Shops

**SILVER VAULTS**
The world's largest collection of silver, from cutlery to jewellery. (p117)

**HARRODS**
Garish, stylish, kitsch yet perennially popular department store. (p160)

**JOHN SANDOE BOOKS**
A treasure trove of literary gems, and excellent staff recommendations. (p161)

**SISTER RAY**
A top independent music shop that has an ever-changing collection of vinyl and CDs. (p90)

(25)

# Victoria & Albert Museum (p146)

You could spend your entire trip in this museum and still be astounded by its variety and depth. The world's leading collection of decorative arts has something for everyone, from imposing 19th-century architecture to antique Chinese ceramics, Islamic textiles, a beautiful collection of jewellery and the revolutionary Sony Walkman (plus other modern design classics).

# Top Days in
London

# The West End & the South Bank

*On your first day plunge into the heart of the West End for some of London's top sights. This itinerary also spans the River Thames to the South Bank, taking in Trafalgar Square, Buckingham Palace, Westminster Abbey, the Houses of Parliament and the London Eye.*

**DAY 1**

## ① Trafalgar Square (p68)

Start your first day in Trafalgar Square and explore the excellent National Gallery (p75).

TRAFALGAR SQUARE ➲ BUCKINGHAM PALACE
🏃 Walk down the Mall.

## ② Buckingham Palace (p56)

Peer through the gates, go on a tour or, if you have made it here early, catch the Changing of the Guard. Take time to savour St James's Park (p61).

BUCKINGHAM PALACE ➲ WESTMINSTER
🏃 Wander across stately St James's Park.

## ③ Westminster Abbey (p52)

Make a beeline for astonishing Westminster Abbey to steep yourself in British history. The far smaller St Margaret's Church next door is also worth a look.

WESTMINSTER ABBEY ➲ HOUSES OF PARLIAMENT
🏃 Cross the road to the Houses of Parliament.

## ④ Houses of Parliament (p58)

Across the square is the Palace of Westminster and possibly London's ultimate sight, Big Ben.

HOUSES OF PARLIAMENT ➲ LONDON EYE
🏃 Cross Westminster Bridge.

## ⑤ London Eye (p128)

Hop on the London Eye for a 'flight' above town. Pre-book tickets online to help shorten queues, or shell out for a fast-track ticket.

LONDON EYE ➲ ANCHOR & HOPE
🏃 Walk to York Rd, turn right onto Waterloo Rd around Waterloo Station then turn left onto The Cut.

## ⑥ Dinner at the Anchor & Hope (p135)

It's well worth the detour for dinner at this famous gastropub. To tie up the day, consider a play at the National Theatre (p138) or the nearby Old Vic (p139) for a taste of London drama.

Trafalgar Square (p68)

## Ancient Heritage to Funky Art

*Your second day has more top sights in store, on a route either side of the
river once more. You'll visit the British Museum in Bloomsbury, climb the
dome of St Paul's Cathedral, explore the Tower of London and admire modern
art at the Tate Modern.*

## ① British Museum (p54)

Begin in Bloomsbury with a visit to the peerless British Museum and ensure you tick off the must-see highlights of this magnificent collection.

BRITISH MUSEUM ➲ ST PAUL'S CATHEDRAL

🔄 Take the Central Line from Holborn or Tottenham Court Rd to St Paul's.

## ② Lunch at St Paul's Cathedral (p102)

Devour some lunch at the Restaurant at St Paul's (p114) before exploring the cathedral. Don't miss climbing the Dome for its astounding London views, but save plenty of time for visiting the fascinating crypt.

ST PAUL'S CATHEDRAL ➲ TOWER OF LONDON

🚌 Hop on bus 15 from St Paul's Cathedral to the Tower of London or 🏃 wander through the narrow streets of the City of London towards the Tower.

## ③ Tower of London (p98)

The millennium of history contained within the Tower of London, including the Crown Jewels, Traitors Gate and the White Tower, deserves a couple of hours to fully explore.

TOWER OF LONDON ➲ TOWER BRIDGE

🏃 Walk down Tower Bridge Approach from the Tower of London to Tower Bridge.

## ④ Tower Bridge (p104)

Cross the River Thames by elegant Tower Bridge, popping into the exhibition en route. If possible, try to coincide your visit with the raising of the bridge!

TOWER BRIDGE ➲ SHAKESPEARE'S GLOBE

🏃 Walk west along the river or 🚌 hop on bus RV1 from the Tower Bridge/City Hall stop to the Southwark Bridge Rd stop.

## ⑤ Shakespeare's Globe (p138)

Either admire the Globe theatre from the outside, or pop in to join a tour of this fascinatingly authentic Elizabethan theatre.

SHAKESPEARE'S GLOBE ➲ OXO TOWER RESTAURANT & BRASSERIE

🏃 Keep walking west; about 500m past the Tate Modern you'll find this restaurant.

## ⑥ Dinner at the Oxo Tower Restaurant & Brasserie (p135)

Stop for an evening meal at this iconic tower restaurant, which rewards you with excellent food and mouth-watering views.

OXO TOWER RESTAURANT & BRASSERIE ➲ TATE MODERN

🏃 Backtrack 500m to the Tate Modern.

## ⑦ Tate Modern (p124)

Round out the day at this erstwhile power station, now a powerhouse to modern and contemporary art. It's open late on Fridays and Saturdays (on other days, you'll have to pop in before dinner). Make sure you experience the Turbine Hall for the latest art installations and avail yourself of the panoramic views from the Tate Modern Restaurant on Level 7.

# Kensington Museums, Knightsbridge Shopping & the West End

*Passing through some of London's best-looking, well-heeled neighbourhoods, this route takes in some of the city's best museums and world-famous department stores before delivering you to the bright lights of the West End.*

DAY
**3**

# 1 Kensington (p148)

Start your first day in South Kensington, home to many of the best museums in the city – take your pick from the Victoria & Albert Museum (p146), the Natural History Museum (p153) and the Science Museum (p148).

**SOUTH KENSINGTON ◯ KENSINGTON GARDENS & HYDE PARK**

🏃 Walk north up Exhibition Rd to Kensington Gardens.

# 2 Kensington Gardens & Hyde Park

Follow the museums with an exploration of Kensington Gardens (p154) and Hyde Park (p152). Make sure you take a look at the Albert Memorial (p155) and the Royal Albert Hall (p155), take a peek inside Kensington Palace (p154) and stroll along the Serpentine (p152).

**KENSINGTON GARDENS & HYDE PARK ◯ ZUMA**

🏃 Stroll through Hyde Park to Zuma, tucked away in Raphael St between Knightsbridge and Brompton Rd.

# 3 Lunch at Zuma (p157)

Dine on tremendous Japanese food in good looking and stylish surrounds at this signature Knightsbridge restaurant. With more than 40 types of sake at the bar, drinkers will find themselves in capable hands.

**ZUMA ◯ HARRODS**

Cross Brompton Rd to reach Harrods.

# 4 Harrods, Knightsbridge (p160)

A visit to Harrods is both fun and fascinating, even if you don't plan to buy anything. Pop into chic Harvey Nichols (p161) for more glamorous displays and window-shop your way down exclusive Sloane St.

**KNIGHTSBRIDGE ◯ PICCADILLY CIRCUS**

⊖ Take the Piccadilly Line three stops from Knightsbridge to Piccadilly Circus.

# 5 Piccadilly Circus (p64)

Jump off the tube at this hectic intersection to have a look at 'Eros' and then wander around boho Soho and aromatic Chinatown (p64).

**PICCADILLY CIRCUS ◯ BOCCA DI LUPO**

🏃 Walk up Shaftesbury Ave, turn left onto Great Windmill St, then take the first right to Archer St and Bocca di Lupo.

# 6 Dinner at Bocca di Lupo (p79)

For winning Italian cuisine in a very competitive market, Bocca di Lupo is a natural choice – both a delicious and delightful way to spend the early evening.

**BOCCA DI LUPO ◯ EXPERIMENTAL COCKTAIL CLUB**

🏃 Walk from Archer St back to Shaftesbury Ave; walk east to Macclesfield St and turn right down to Gerrard St.

# 7 Drinks at Experimental Cocktail Club (p83)

Ease further into the evening with drinks at this super-stylish Chinatown speakeasy with a stunning cocktail menu. It's worth booking ahead as it's very popular.

Piccadilly Circus (p64)

PHOTOGRAPHER: SBURES/DREAMSTIME ©

SHEPHERD ✦ PATENTEE
53 LEADENHALL ST LONDON

GALVANO-MAGNETIC CLOCK

DAY
4

## Greenwich to Camden

*You don't want to neglect the sights further afield and this itinerary makes a big dent in what's on offer. Good-looking Greenwich has a whole raft of stately sights; then you'll explore ancient churches, the East End, trendy Shoreditch, and Camden to develop a real feel for London.*

## ① Greenwich (p224)

Start the day in royal Greenwich and make sure you visit Greenwich Park and the Royal Observatory (p222), checking out the National Maritime Museum (p225), beautiful Queen's House (p224) and other stately sights. Greenwich Market (p227) always turns up surprises, while a walk by the river is lovely.

**GREENWICH ● THE CITY**

Take the DLR from Cutty Sark station to Bank station.

## ② The City (p104)

The area of the City not far from Bank station has a host of historic churches, including St Mary Woolnoth (p109), St Stephen Walbrook (p109) and St Mary-le-Bow (p110). Afterwards, walk to Monument (p105) for excellent views of the City.

**MONUMENT ● TAYYABS**

Take the District Line from Monument station to Whitechapel station then walk west down Whitechapel Rd to Tayyabs on Fieldgate St.

## ③ Lunch at Tayyabs (p189)

Dip into the East End's famed multicultural culinary heritage at this classic Punjabi restaurant. After your meal, wander around Whitechapel, soaking up its atmosphere and visiting the local sights including the Whitechapel Gallery (p184) and the Whitechapel Bell Foundry (p184).

**TAYYABS ● SPITALFIELDS**

Walk north from Whitechapel Rd up Brick Lane to Spitalfields.

## ④ Explore Spitalfields

Wander along Brick Lane (p172) and explore absorbing Georgian Spitalfields (p169) before browsing through Spitalfields Market (p177). The best days for the market are Thursday, Friday and Sunday.

**SPITALFIELDS ● SHOREDITCH**

Walk from Spitalfields Market along Commercial St to Great Eastern St or take bus 135 from Primrose St stop.

## ⑤ Have a drink in Shoreditch

Sample the edgy, creative and offbeat Shoreditch/Hoxton atmosphere by dropping in on a local bar. Check out Book Club (p175), a standout bar in an old Victorian warehouse, or the Queen of Hoxton (p176).

**SHOREDITCH ● CAMDEN**

Jump on a northern line tube from Old St station to Camden Town.

## ⑥ Dinner in Camden

Conclude the day in North London by browsing the stalls of Camden Market (p205), if it's still open, and dining at the excellent Market (p207) before turning to the riveting choice of local bars, pubs and live music venues in this invigorating neighbourhood.

Clock on the Royal Observatory, Greenwich Park (p222)

PHOTOGRAPHER: DOUG MCKINLAY/LONELY PLANET IMAGES ©

# Month by Month

## January

**New Year's Celebration**

On 31 December, the famous countdown to midnight in Trafalgar Square is met with terrific fireworks and massive crowds.

**London Art Fair**

Over 100 major galleries participate in this contemporary art fair (www.londonartfair.co.uk), one of the largest in Europe, with thematic exhibitions, special events and the best emerging artists.

## February

**Chinese New Year**

In late January or early February, Chinatown fizzes, crackles and pops in this colourful street festival, which includes a Golden Dragon parade, eating and partying.

## March

**Head of the River Race**

Some 400 crews take part in this annual boat race (www.horr.co.uk) held over a 7km course on the Thames, from Mortlake to Putney.

**St Patrick's Day**

Top festival for the Irish in London, held on the Sunday closest to 17 March, with a colourful parade through central London and other festivities in and around Trafalgar Square.

## April

**London Marathon**

Some 35,000 runners – most running for charity – pound London in one of the world's biggest road races (www.virginlondonmarathon.com), from Greenwich Park to the Mall.

**Oxford & Cambridge Boat Race**

Crowds line the banks of the Thames to watch the country's two most famous universities go oar-to-oar from Putney to Mortlake. Dates vary, so check www.theboatrace.org.

## May

**Chelsea Flower Show**

The world's most renowned horticultural event (www.rhs.org.uk) attracts the cream of London's green-fingered and flower-mad gardeners.

## June

**Royal Academy Summer Exhibition**

Beginning in June and running through August, this exhibition (www.royalacademy.org.uk) showcases works submitted by artists from all over Britain.

Lord Mayor's Show
BETTINA STRENSKE/IMAGEBROKER ©

### ⊛ Trooping the Colour

The Queen's official birthday is celebrated with parades, pageantry and flyovers. (www.trooping-the-colour.co.uk)

### ✈ Wimbledon Lawn Tennis Championships

For two weeks a year Wimbledon falls under a sporting spotlight as the world's best tennis players gather to battle for the championship (www.wimbledon.com).

## July

### ⊛ Pride London

The gay community paints the town pink in this annual extravaganza (www.pridelondon.org), with a morning parade and a huge afternoon event on Trafalgar Square (locations frequently change).

### ⊛ BBC Promenade Concert (the Proms)

Two months of outstanding classical concerts (www.bbc.co.uk/proms) at various prestigious venues, centred on the Royal Albert Hall (p155).

## August

### ⊛ Notting Hill Carnival

Europe's biggest outdoor carnival (www.thecarnival.

tv) is a celebration of Caribbean London, featuring music, dancing and costumes over the summer bank holiday weekend.

## September

### ⊛ The Mayor's Thames Festival

Celebrating the River Thames, this cosmopolitan festival (www.thamesfestival.org) features fairs, street theatre, music, food stalls, fireworks and river races culminating in the superb Night Procession.

### ◉ London Open House

For a weekend in late September, the public is invited into over 700 heritage buildings that are normally off-limits (p259).

## October

### ⊛ Dance Umbrella

London's annual festival of contemporary dance (www.danceumbrella.co.uk) features five weeks of performances by British and international dance companies at venues across London.

### ⊛ London Film Festival

The city's premier film event (www.lff.org.uk) attracts big names and you can catch over 100 films before their cinema

release. Masterclasses are given by world-famous directors.

## November

### ⊛ Guy Fawkes Night (Bonfire Night)

Bonfire Night commemorates Guy Fawkes' foiled attempt to blow up Parliament in 1605. Bonfires and fireworks light up the night on 5 November. Primrose Hill, Highbury Fields, Alexandra Palace, Clapham Common and Crystal Palace Park have the best firework displays.

### ⊛ Lord Mayor's Show

In accordance with the Magna Carta of 1215, the newly elected Lord Mayor of the City of London travels in a state coach from Mansion House to the Royal Courts of Justice to take an oath of allegiance to the Crown. The floats, bands and fireworks that accompany the mayor were added later (www.lordmayorsshow.org).

## December

### ⊛ Lighting of the Christmas Tree & Lights

A celebrity is normally carted in to switch on the festive lights that line Oxford, Regent and Bond Sts, and a towering Norwegian spruce is set up in Trafalgar Square.

# What's New

*For this new edition of* Discover London, *our authors have hunted down the fresh, the transformed, the hot and the happening. These are some of our favourites. For up-to-the-minute recommendations, see lonelyplanet.com/London.*

## 1 OLYMPIC PARK

Begun in 2008, the huge Olympic Park in Stratford has seen the conversion of a neglected and forgotten part of East London into a shimmering sporting development for the 2012 Olympic Games and beyond. Stand-out design highlights include the stunning Aquatics Centre, the Olympic Stadium and the state-of-the-art Velodrome. The entire park will be rebranded the Queen Elizabeth Olympic Park upon its reopening after the Games in 2013, in a bid to make the park a top destination for visitors and residents after the 2012 Games. (p187)

## 2 BARCLAYS CYCLE HIRE SCHEME

London's enthusiastic, tousle-haired mayor Boris Johnson spearheaded this immensely popular bike-hire scheme, with the affectionately named 'Boris bikes' dotting the capital since 2010. All you need to hire a bike is your debit or credit card, a reasonably fit pair of legs and lungs, plus a basic sense of direction. There are over 400 well-marked docking stations around London and short trips are free! (p283)

## 3 WESTFIELD STRATFORD CITY

Europe's largest urban shopping centre opened next to the Olympic Park in autumn 2011, with an astonishing 300 stores, 70 restaurants, a 17-screen cinema, three hotels, a bowling alley and the UK's largest casino.

## 4 LONDON BRIDGE QUARTER PROJECT

In a costly development, London Bridge station and the surrounding district is receiving a facelift, including erection of the already iconic Shard, set to glitter high above South London in 2012.

## 5 BRITISH MUSEUM EXTENSION

The World Conservation and Exhibitions Centre is currently undergoing construction at the British Museum, with a late 2013 target completion date. The extension will house a new exhibition space plus conservation and science facilities.

## 6 NEW ROUTEMASTER BUSES

Phased out (except for a few heritage routes) and sorely missed by both Londoners and visitors, London's classic Routemaster buses (hop-on, hop-off double-decker buses) are being resurrected in a modern and more environmentally friendly guise. A fleet of buses is expected to be routemastering the capital's streets from 2012.

## 7 LEICESTER SQUARE

This famously underwhelming epicentral square has long punched way beneath its weight and is undergoing a revamp in preparation for a 2012 relaunch.

# Get Inspired

##  Books

○ **Oliver Twist** (Charles Dickens) Dickens' classic and melodramatic tale of grinding Victorian London poverty is stuffed with vivid social detail.

○ **The Buddha of Suburbia** (Hanif Kureishi) This hilarious account of Asian life in the 1970s London suburbs is a firm London favourite.

○ **London Fields** (Martin Amis) A grippingly dark tale of London lowlife in the 1980s; one of the first great postmodernist novels.

○ **Journal of the Plague Year** (Daniel Defoe) Powerfully descriptive fictional account of one man's harrowing experiences of 1665 London.

## Films

○ **The King's Speech** A verbally challenged Colin Firth sets about conquering his demons; partly filmed in London.

○ **28 Days Later** Gore-flecked horror set in London with striking shots of an empty capital, revisited in a shocking sequel.

○ **Bridget Jones's Diary** Everyone's favourite chick flick, set in and around London's South Bank.

## Music

○ **Alright, Still** (Lily Allen) This upbeat album of London life became an instant classic.

○ **Back to Black** (Amy Winehouse) Milestone second album from the tragic North London chanteuse.

○ **Abbey Road** (The Beatles) The ultimate London album.

○ **London Calling** (The Clash) A 1979 call to arms by the legendary London band.

## Websites

○ **Transport for London** (www.tfl.gov.uk) Check the best routes, time journeys and keep up to date with frequent engineering works.

○ **Visit London** (www. visitlondon.com) London's official tourism website is packed with useful information.

○ **Streetmap** (www. streetmap.co.uk) Find any street in London with this excellent website.

## Short on time?

This list will give you an instant insight into the city.

**Read** An evocatively colourful, thematically arranged history of the city, *London: The Biography* (Peter Ackroyd) is a modern classic.

**Watch** The massively offbeat classic comedy *Withnail and I* is set partly in Camden in the closing years of the '60s.

**Listen** Adele's *Hometown Glory* is an exquisite celebration of West Norwood from the Tottenham-born songstress.

**Log On** All the latest London news, gossip and listings can be found in the *Evening Standard* (www. thisislondon.co.uk).

St Paul's Cathedral (p102)
STUART MONK/DREAMSTIME ©

# Need to Know

**Language**
English

**Visas**
Not required for US, Canadian, Australian, New Zealand or South African visitors for stays up to six months. European Union nationals can stay indefinitely.

**Money**
ATMs widespread. Major credit cards accepted everywhere.

**Mobile Phones**
Buy local SIM cards for European and Australian phones. Set other phones to international roaming.

**Time**
London is on GMT; from late March to late October, it is one hour ahead of GMT.

**Wi-Fi**
In most hotels and cafes.

**Tipping**
In restaurants 10% to 15% is standard; 10% or round up to nearest £1 for black cabs.

For more information, see Survival Guide (p280).

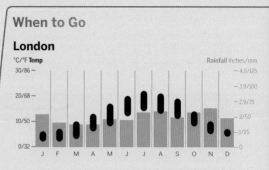

## When to Go

### London

**Summer** is peak season: days are long, festivals are afoot, but it's busy and crowded.

**Spring and autumn** are cooler, but delightful.

**Winter** is cold but quiet, with the possibility of snow.

## Advance Planning

**Three months** Book weekend performance of top shows; dinner at renowned restaurants; tickets for must-see exhibitions; a room at a popular hotel.

**One month** Check listings on entertainment sites such as www.timeout.com for fringe theatre, live music, festivals and then book your tickets.

**A few days** Check the weather on www.tfl.gov.uk/weather.

## Your Daily Budget

### Budget under £60

- Dorm beds £10-30
- Supermarkets, markets, lunchtime specials for food
- Loads of free or cheap museums and sights
- Reduced-price standby tickets or bargain cinema tickets
- Barclays Cycle Hire Scheme (p283)

### Midrange £60-150

- Double room £100
- Two-course dinner with glass of wine £30
- Theatre ticket £10-50

### Top End over £150

- Four-star/boutique hotel room £200
- Three-course dinner in top restaurant with wine £80-100
- Black cab trips £30
- Best-seat theatre tickets £65

## Arriving in London

**Heathrow Airport** Trains, London Underground (tube) and buses to central London 5.25am to midnight (night buses run later), £5-17; taxi £45-65.

**Gatwick Airport** Trains to central London 4.30am to 1.35am, £7-18; buses run to central London hourly 6am to 9.45pm, £7.50-10; taxi £90.

**Stansted Airport** Trains run to central London 5.30am to around midnight, £21. Buses to central London run around the clock, £9-10.50; taxi £90.

**Luton Airport** Trains run to central London 7am to 10pm, £12.50. Buses run to central London around the clock, £10-16; taxi £90.

**London City Airport** Trains run to central London 5.30am to 12.30am Monday to Saturday, 7am to 11.30pm Sunday £4; taxi £30.

**St Pancras International Train Station** In central London (for Eurostar train arrivals from Europe) and connected by many underground lines to other parts of the city.

For much more on Arrival, see p280.

## Getting Around

Prepaid Oyster cards can be used across London's transport network, offering the cheapest fares. Buy one (and top up) at most tube stations, train stations and many newsagents.

o **Underground (tube)** The quickest way to get around; trains run 5.30am to 12.30am (7am to 11.30pm Sunday).

o **Bus** Slow going but ace views from double-deckers. Large number of night buses.

o **Train** Mostly useful for outlying areas such as Hampton Court.

o **Bicycle** The Barclays Cycle Hire Scheme (p283) is excellent value; free for short hops.

o **Taxi** Black cabs can be hailed on the street when the yellow light is lit.

o **Boat** Good for such destinations as Hampton Court Palace and Kew Gardens, but slow.

o **Walking** A lot of central sightseeing is best done on foot.

o **Car Hire** Generally better to use a combination of the above; if you drive, beware the congestion charge.

o For much more on Getting Around, see p282.

## Sleeping

Hanging your hat in London can be expensive and as the city is busy at the best of times, you'll need to book your room well in advance to secure your top choice.

Decent, centrally located hostels are easy enough to find and offer reasonably priced double rooms. Bed and breakfasts are a dependable and inexpensive, if rather simple, option. Hotels range from cheap, no-frills chains to boutique choices to luxury five-star historic hotels.

### Useful Websites

o **Lonely Planet** (www.lonelyplanet.com/london) Destination information, hotel bookings, traveller forum and more.

o **Visit London** (www.visitlondon.com) Wide range of accommodation options by area.

o **London Town** (www.londontown.com) Great deals and special offers.

## What to Bring

o **Rain jacket** The rumours about the weather are true.

o **Comfortable shoes** Cushion those endless strolls.

o **Small day-pack** For stowing that rain jacket when the sun does shine.

## Be Forewarned

o London is a fairly safe city, but employ common sense.

o **Cabs** After a night's clubbing, ensure you go for a black cab or a licensed minicab firm.

o **Areas to avoid** Avoid wandering alone at night in King's Cross, Dalston and Peckham, though sticking to the main roads offers a certain degree of safety.

o **Pickpocketing** Keep an eye on your handbag, especially in bars and nightclubs, and in crowded areas such as the Underground.

# The West End

This exciting and chaotic place is where your London adventure begins. This is London's shopping, eating and entertainment epicentre, made up of Soho, Chinatown and Covent Garden, stretching out in a rough rectangle between Oxford Circus, Piccadilly Circus, Aldwych and Holborn. You will find glitz, glamour and crowds of shoppers any day of the year, and this is the best place for an introduction to fast-paced London life.

One of the delights of the West End is its energy and there is no better way to enjoy it than by walking around and taking it all in. Atmospheric places for a breather include Covent Garden, Trafalgar Square and St James's Park.

The world-famous West End theatres dominate the main avenues, while in the back streets cocktail bars, sublime fashion stores and cutting-edge restaurants can be found almost anywhere you go, bar Westminster and Whitehall.

Piccadilly Circus (p64)

# West End Highlights

## Houses of Parliament (p58)

Not many visitors to London actually go inside but few countries allow such unrestricted access to their parliament. It's a unique experience to be able to watch Members of Parliament debate the latest laws, and the building itself is quite stunning. The sublime Houses of Parliament overlooking the Thames in their Gothic splendour with impressive Big Ben towering above is one of London's most unforgettable sights.

## British Museum (p54)

The British Museum is one of London's great wonders and holds one of the world's most impressive collections. It's truly a museum of the world and in the space of a day you can explore the history and culture of all the world's great civilisations. The museum is free, so you can line up a string of visits if you find yourself overwhelmed.

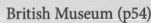
JUAN MOYANG/DREAMSTIME ©

## Covent Garden (p68)

Lovely (but packed) in fine weather, Covent Garden Piazza is great for fine architecture, street performers, shopping at Covent Garden Market, a glut of nearby fine restaurants, pubs and bars, and a host of important sights and entertainment venues, including the London Transport Museum (p68) and the Royal Opera House (p88).

## Westminster Abbey (p52)

Majestic Westminster Abbey has witnessed more historical events than most major cities. Indeed, this was where William the Conqueror was crowned in 1066 after the Battle of Hastings, and it has been the place of coronation of almost every monarch since, as well as being their final resting place and that of such luminaries as Chaucer, Dickens, and Laurence Olivier.

## Trafalgar Square & the National Gallery

Once encircled with snarling traffic and swarming with Hitchockian flocks of feral pigeons, Trafalgar Square (p68) today is quite a magnificent plaza, and is a great place to take in London and the views down Whitehall. Immediately north of the square is the standout National Gallery (p75) with its jaw-dropping collection of masterful art.

# West End Walk

*This walk starts from tourist-mecca Covent Garden, snakes through colourful Chinatown and bohemian Soho and ends at glorious Trafalgar Square. There are plenty of places to stop for a drink and soak up the heart of London.*

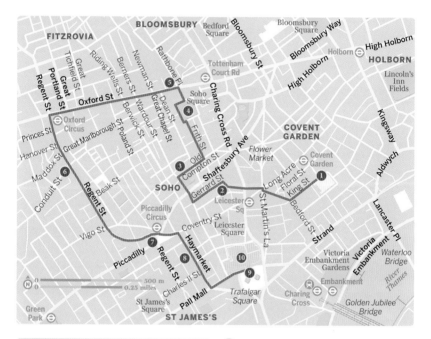

### ❶ Covent Garden Piazza

Touristy perhaps, but it's worth seeing this Inigo Jones **Piazza** (p68) and the street performers making a living in front of St Paul's Church, the modern day descendents of street performers who put on the first ever Punch and Judy show here in 1662.

### ❷ Chinatown

Avoid Leicester Square and pop down Lisle St and Gerrard St under the Oriental *pai-fang* (decorative gate) of **Chinatown** (p64). Breathe in the aromatic spices and stop for delicious Chinese eats at one of the many restaurants.

### ❸ Soho

Wander across Shaftesbury Ave, the main street of 'theatreland' and home to some of the West End's most prestigious theatres. Continue up Wardour St, turning right onto Old Compton St, London's gayest thoroughfare and the main street of **Soho** (p64).

### ④ Soho Square

Take Frith St, past Mozart's former home at No 20, and emerge into the open space of Soho Square, the perfectly formed park at the heart of the West End.

### ⑤ Oxford Street

Head into **Oxford St** (p88), past many of London's premier shops. At Oxford Circus, turn left into Regent St, the centrepiece of Nash's design for Regency London.

### ⑥ Regent Street

Wander down this regal shopping avenue, passing world-famous toyshop **Hamleys** (p90) and one of London's smartest department stores, **Liberty** (p90), both on the left as you walk down.

### ⑦ Piccadilly Circus

**Piccadilly Circus** (p64) is like New York's Times Square, full of flashing ads, tons of shops and tourists. Don't miss the famous statue incorrectly known as **Eros**.

### ⑧ Haymarket

Escape the chaos of Piccadilly Circus by plunging down grand Haymarket. On the way take note of terribly chic **Jermyn St**, noted for its gentlemen's clothing and accessories shops. From Haymarket turn left onto Pall Mall.

### ⑨ Trafalgar Square

Tourist magnet **Trafalgar Square** (p68) is a magnificent beauty of a square. Check out the views of Big Ben from its southern side, and don't miss the so-called **fourth plinth** (p69).

### ⑩ National Gallery

Take a few hours to admire the artwork at the **National Gallery** (p75). Then sit down for a well-deserved lunch or dinner in the stylish National Dining Rooms (p81), where you can enjoy British cuisine in its finest form.

## ★★★ The Best...

### PLACES TO EAT

**Providores & Tapa Room** Fusion food at its absolute best. (p81)

**Yauatcha** Top-drawer dim sum in a contemporary environment. (p79)

**Le Boudin Blanc** First-rate French flavours and an epic wine list. (p82)

**Mooli's** For succulent, flavour-packed and highly addictive Indian rotis. (p79)

### PLACES TO DRINK

**Experimental Cocktail Club** Inventive cocktail creations in marvellous surrounds. (p83)

**Purl** Subterranean cocktail bar with full marks for mood. (p87)

**Gordon's Wine Bar** Superbly atmospheric wine bar with historic charms. (p86)

### FREE SIGHTS

**British Museum** Supreme collection of international artefacts and an inspiring testament to human creativity. (p54)

**National Gallery** Tremendous gathering of largely pre-modern masters, entirely on the house. (p75)

**Houses of Parliament** When parliament is in session, it's free to watch UK democracy in action. (p58)

# Don't Miss
# Westminster Abbey

Westminster Abbey is such an important com-memoration site for both the British royalty and the nation's political and artistic idols that it's difficult to overstress its symbolic value or imagine its equivalent anywhere else in the world. With the exception of Edward V and Edward VIII, every English sovereign has been crowned here since William the Conqueror in 1066, and most of the monarchs from Henry III (died 1272) to George II (died 1760) were also buried here.

Map p78

www.westminster
abbey.org

Dean's Yard SW1

adult/child £16/6

⏰9.30am-4.30pm
Mon, Tue, Thu &
Fri, to 6pm Wed, to
2.30pm Sat

⊖Westminster or St
James's Park

# North Transept, Sanctuarium & Quire

The North Transept is often referred to as Statesmen's Aisle: politicians and eminent public figures are commemorated by large marble statues and plaques. At the heart of the Abbey is the **sanctuary** where coronations, royal weddings and funerals take place. The Quire, a sublime structure of gold, blue and red Victorian Gothic, dates back to the mid-19th century.

## Chapels

**Henry VII's Lady Chapel** is the most spectacular with its circular vaulting on the ceiling, colourful banners and dramatic oak stalls. Behind the altar is the elaborate sarcophagus of Henry VII and his queen.

Opposite the entrance to the Lady Chapel is the rather ordinary-looking **Coronation Chair**, upon which almost every monarch since the late 13th century is said to have been crowned.

## St Edward's Chapel

The most sacred spot in the Abbey lies behind the high altar; access is generally restricted to protect the 13th-century floor. St Edward was the founder of the Abbey and the original building was consecrated a few weeks before his death.

## Outer Buildings

The entrance to the Cloister is 13th century, while the cloister itself dates from the 14th. The octagonal **Chapter House** has one of Europe's best-preserved medieval tile floors and retains traces of religious murals. To the right of the entrance is what is claimed to be the oldest door in the UK – it's been there 950 years.

The adjacent **Pyx Chamber** is one of the few remaining relics of the original Abbey and contains the Abbey's treasures and liturgical objects.

## Poet's Corner

The south transept contains **Poets' Corner**, where many of England's finest writers are buried or commemorated.

## Local Knowledge

# Don't Miss

BY DAVID MOTT,
CANONS' VERGER,
WESTMINSTER ABBEY

**1 LADY CHAPEL & ST EDWARD'S CHAPEL**
My favourite part of Westminster Abbey church has to be the Lady Chapel with its absolutely exquisite architecture. Next for me in importance, however, is St Edward's Chapel for the significance of the Shrine of St Edward the Confessor and the great kings and queens buried around it.

**2 OUR LADY OF PEW**
Our Lady of Pew is a quite unique shrine – fully restored with much of its 14th-century paintwork still in place. As I am Warden of the Society of Our Lady of Pew, the shrine is of particular importance to me.

**3 ISLIP CHAPEL, ST FAITH'S CHAPEL & ST EDMUND'S CHAPEL**
Of other chapels, Islip Chapel is special to me for its sense of intimacy – a sensation rarely found in Westminster Abbey. St Faith's Chapel is the most prayerful and contemplative chapel in the abbey. Also of great significance is St Edmund's Chapel for its fine tombs and monuments, many of national importance.

**4 POET'S CORNER & ST BENEDICT'S CHAPEL**
Poet's Corner, with its great poets and writers, is naturally an important part of the abbey but there is also the sometimes forgotten chapel of St Benedict, where if you know where to look, you can still see where St Benedict's head was enshrined before the Reformation.

**5 CHAPTER HOUSE & THE PYX CHAPEL**
In the cloister, the wonderful Chapter House – with its floor tiles and wall paintings – is one of my favourite parts of the abbey. Finally, the Pyx Chapel, the oldest altar in the Abbey still in use, is a place where you can really connect with the earliest days of the Abbey's long history.

# ✓

## Don't Miss
# British Museum

One of London's most visited attractions, the British Museum draws an average of five million punters each year. It's an exhaustive and exhilarating stampede through world cultures, with galleries devoted to the ancient civilisations of Egypt, the Middle East, Rome, Greece, Britain and much more. It's huge, so make a few focused visits if you have time, and consider the choice of tours: there are 15 free 30- to 40-minute eyeOpener tours of individual galleries, excellent audioguides, and itineraries available on the museum's website.

Map p62

www.british museum.org

Great Russell St WC1

admission free; £3 donation suggested

🕘10am-5.30pm Sat-Thu, to 8.30pm Fri

🚇Tottenham Court Rd or Russell Sq

# Great Court

Covered with a spectacular glass-and-steel roof designed by Norman Foster in 2000, the Great Court is the largest covered public square in Europe. In its centre is the world-famous **Reading Room**, formerly the British Library, which has been frequented by all the big brains of history, from Mahatma Gandhi to Karl Marx.

# Ancient Egypt

The star of the show at the British Museum is the Ancient Egypt collection. It comprises sculptures, fine jewellery, papyrus texts, coffins and mummies, including the beautiful and intriguing **Mummy of Katebet** (Room 63). Perhaps the most prized item in the collection is the **Rosetta Stone** (Room 4), the key to deciphering Egyptian hieroglyphics.

# Ancient Greece

Another highlight of the museum is the **Parthenon Sculptures** (aka Parthenon Marbles; Room 18). The marble works are thought to show the great procession to the temple that took place during the Panathenaic Festival, on the birthday of Athena, one of the grandest events in the Greek world.

# Other Highlights

Kids will love the North American (Room 26) and Mexican (Room 27) galleries, with the 15th-century Aztec **Mosaic Mask of Tezcatlipoca** (or Skull of the Smoking Mirror), a human skull decorated with turquoise mosaic.

There are also superb collections on ancient Middle East civilisations, including rare artefacts from the **Royal Tombs of Ur** (Room 56) in modern-day Iraq and the exquisite gold figurines from the **Oxus Treasure** (Room 52), originating from the ancient Persian capital of Persepolis around 400 BC.

The 1820 **King's Library** is a stunning neoclassical space, and retraces how such disciplines as biology, archaeology, linguistics and geography emerged during the Enlightenment of the 18th century.

## Don't Miss

BY PAUL COLLINS, FORMER CURATOR IN THE MIDDLE EAST AT THE BRITISH MUSEUM

1 **ENLIGHTENMENT GALLERY (ROOM 1)**
This magnificent room contains an informative display that shows how collectors, antiquaries and travellers viewed and classified objects at the time the museum was founded (1753). It's an excellent introduction to the British Museum.

2 **ASSYRIAN LION HUNT FROM NINEVEH (ROOM 10)**
These are some of the greatest carvings from the ancient world. They originate from the city of Nineveh, in what is now modern-day Iraq. They've become especially important given the events of recent years in Iraq.

3 **CLOCKS & WATCHES GALLERY (ROOMS 38–9)**
These rooms contain a collection of mechanical devices for telling the time. My favourite clock is driven by a ball that rolls back and forward along a grooved plate that releases the mechanism. It's quite a strange experience to be surrounded by the ticking, striking and chiming of hundreds of clocks!

4 **EAST STAIRS**
An impressive collection of casts of Persian, Mayan and Egyptian reliefs line the stairs. These were made in the 19th and early 20th centuries, and are historically important as the original objects left at the sites have been damaged or have disappeared.

5 **JAPAN GALLERIES (ROOMS 92–4)**
Climb to the very top of the museum for a fascinating insight into the art, religion, and everyday life of the Japanese, ranging from Samurai warrior swords to Manga comic books.

☑

# Don't Miss
# Buckingham Palace

Built in 1705 as Buckingham House for the duke of the same name, this palace has been the Royal Family's London lodgings since 1837, when Queen Victoria moved in. St James's Palace was judged too old-fashioned and insufficiently impressive, although Buckingham underwent a number of modifications until it was deemed fit for purpose.

Map p78

www.royal
collection.org.uk

Buckingham Palace
Rd SW1

adult/child £18/10

⊘9.30am-6.30pm
late Jul-late Sep,
timed ticket with
admission every
15min

⊖St James's Park or
Green Park

## State Rooms

The tour starts in the Guard Room. It takes in the State Dining Room (all red damask and Regency furnishings), then moves on to the Blue Drawing Room (which has a gorgeous fluted ceiling by John Nash) and the White Drawing Room, where foreign ambassadors are received.

The Ballroom, where official receptions and state banquets are held, was a late addition to the palace, built between 1853 and 1855. The Throne Room is rather kitsch with its his-and-hers pink chairs initialled 'ER' and 'P', sitting smugly under a theatre arch.

## Picture Gallery & Gardens

The most interesting part of the tour (for all but royal sycophants) is the 76.5m-long Picture Gallery, featuring splendid works by such artists as Van Dyck, Rembrandt, Canaletto, Poussin, Canova and Vermeer.

Wandering the gardens is another highlight here – as well as admiring some of the 350 or so species of flowers and plants and listening to the many birds, you'll get beautiful views of the palace and a peek of the famous lake.

## Queen's Gallery

Over the last 500 years, the Royal Family has amassed paintings, sculpture, ceramics, furniture and jewellery. The splendid **Queen's Gallery** (www.royal collection.org.uk; southern wing, Buckingham Palace, Buckingham Palace Rd SW1; adult/child £9/4.50; ☉10am-5.30pm) showcases some of the palace's treasures on a rotating basis, through temporary exhibitions.

The gallery was originally designed as a conservatory by John Nash. A £20-million renovation for Elizabeth II's Golden Jubilee in 2002 enlarged the entrance and added a Greek Doric portico, a multimedia centre and three times as much display space. Entrance to the gallery is through Buckingham Gate. Combined tickets with the Royal Mews cost £16/9 per adult/child.

## Royal Mews

South of the palace, the **Royal Mews** (www.royalcollection.org.uk; Buckingham Palace Rd SW1; adult/child £8/5; ☉10am-5pm Apr-Oct, to 4pm Mon-Sat Nov & Dec) started life as a falconry but is now a working stable looking after the royals' immaculately groomed horses, along with the opulent vehicles the monarch uses for transport. Highlights for visitors include the enormous and opulent gold coach of 1762, which has been used for every coronation since that of George III; the 1910 Glass Coach used for royal weddings (Prince William and Catherine Middleton actually used the 1902 State Landau to make the best of the good weather); and a Rolls-Royce Phantom IV from the royal fleet.

### Changing of the Guard

At 11.30am daily from May to July, and on alternate days, weather permitting, from August to March, the old guard comes off duty to be replaced by the new guard on the forecourt of Buckingham Palace. The carefully choreographed marching and shouting of the guards in their bright red uniforms and bearskin hats lasts about half an hour and is very popular so arrive early if you want to get a good spot.

### Open to the Public

The palace was open to the public in the 1990s in a bid to revive popular support for the monarchy after tumultuous times. Commoners now get a peek of the State Rooms during August and September, when Her Majesty is holidaying in Scotland. The Queen's Gallery is open year-round, however, and the Royal Mews from April to December.

# Don't Miss
# Houses of Parliament

The House of Commons and House of Lords are housed in the sumptuous Palace of Westminster. The House of Commons is where Members of Parliament (MPs) meet to propose and discuss new legislation, and to grill the prime minister and other ministers.

Map p78

www.parliament.uk

St Margaret St SW1

admission free

🕑during parliamentary sessions

⊖Westminster

## Towers

The most famous feature of the Houses of Parliament is the Clock Tower, commonly known as **Big Ben**. Ben is the bell hanging inside and is named after Benjamin Hall, the commissioner of works when the tower was completed in 1858. Thirteen-tonne Ben has rung in the New Year since 1924.

## Westminster Hall

One of the most stunning features of the Palace of Westminster, seat of the English monarchy from the 11th to the early 16th centuries, is Westminster Hall. The building was originally built in 1099 and is today the oldest surviving part of the complex. The awe-inspiring roof was added between 1394 and 1401; it is the earliest known example of a hammerbeam roof and has been described as 'the greatest surviving achievement of medieval English carpentry'.

Westminster Hall was used for coronation banquets in medieval times, and also served as a courthouse until the 19th century. The trials of William Wallace (1305), Thomas More (1535), Guy Fawkes (1606) and Charles I (1649) all took place here. In the 20th century, monarchs and Winston Churchill lay in state here.

## House of Commons

The layout of the Commons Chamber is based on that of St Stephen's Chapel in the original Palace of Westminster. The current chamber, designed by Giles Gilbert Scott, replaced the earlier one destroyed by a 1941 bomb.

Although the Commons is a national assembly of 646 MPs, the chamber has seating for only 437. Government members sit to the right of the Speaker and Opposition members to the left. During debates, MPs wanting to speak stand up to catch the Speaker's eye.

## House of Lords

The **House of Lords** (⌚2.30-10pm Mon & Tue, 3-10pm Wed, 11am-7.30pm Thu, 10am to close of session Fri) is also open for visits,

via the amusingly named 'Strangers' Gallery'. The intricate Gothic interior led its poor architect, Pugin (1812–52), to an early death from overwork and nervous strain.

Most of the members of the House of Lords are life peers (appointed for their lifetime by the monarch); there is also a small number of hereditary peers and a group of 'crossbench' members (not affiliated to the main political parties).

## Tours

On Saturdays and when Parliament is in recess (July to September, and then holidays around Christmas, Easter and a couple of weeks in February and June), visitors can join a 75-minute **guided tour** ( 📞 bookings 0844 847 1672; www.parliament.uk; adult/child £15/6) of both chambers, Westminster Hall and other historic buildings. Tour schedules change with every recess, so check ahead. It's best to book.

### Debates

When Parliament is in session, visitors may attend debates. The best time is during Prime Minister's Question Time on Wednesday, but it's also the busiest. The debating style in the Commons is known for being quite combative but not all debates are flamboyant arguing duels; many are rather boring and long-winded. To find out what's being debated, check www.parliament.uk.

### Access & Security

Enter via St Stephen's Entrance. It's not unusual to have to wait up to two hours to access the chambers. Following a series of protest incidents in 2004, security was tightened, and a bulletproof screen now sits between members of the public and the debating chamber.

# Discover
# the West End

## 🔀 Getting There & Away

○ **Underground** Every tube line goes through the West End so wherever you're staying in London, you'll have no difficulty getting there. The tube is also good for getting from one end of the West End to the other (Russell Square to Green Park, or Baker St to Embankment).

○ **Walking** The West End is relatively compact so it'll be cheaper and generally more enjoyable to walk from one place to another than take public transport.

○ **Barclays Bikes** There are docking stations everywhere within the West End and cycling is your best bet for short journeys.

## ◎ Sights

### Westminster

**Westminster Abbey**      Church
See p52.

**Houses of Parliament**      Historic Building
See p58.

### Bloomsbury & Fitzrovia

**British Museum**      Museum
See p54.

**Squares of Bloomsbury**      Square
Map p62 The heart of Bloomsbury is **Russell Square**, laid out in 1800 by Humphrey Repton. It was dark and bushy until the striking facelift that pruned the trees, tidied up the plants and gave it a 10m-high fountain.

The centre of literary Bloomsbury was **Gordon Square** where, at various times, Bertrand Russell lived at No 57, Lytton Strachey at No 51 and Vanessa and Clive Bell, Maynard Keynes and the Woolf family at No 46.

Lovely **Bedford Square** is the only completely Georgian square still surviving in Bloomsbury.

**FREE** **New London Architecture**      Architecture
Map p62 (www.newlondonarchitecture.org; Bldg Centre, 26 Store St WC1; ⏱9.30am-6pm Mon-Fri, 10am-5pm Sat; ⊖Goodge St) An excellent excursion to see which way London's architectural development is going, this is a frequently changing exhibition that will capture the imagination and interest of anyone who loves London.

Burlington Arcade (p63)
JOHN KELLERMAN/ALAMY ©

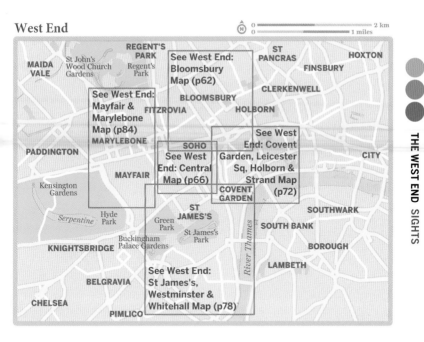

### Dickens House Museum
Historic Building

(www.dickensmuseum.com; 48 Doughty St WC1; adult/child £7/3; ⊙10am-5pm; ⊖Russell Sq) Charles Dickens, the great Victorian novelist, lived a nomadic life in the big city, moving around London so often that he left behind an unrivalled trail of blue plaques. This handsome four-storey house is his sole surviving residence before he upped and moved to Kent. At the time of writing, the museum was planning a substantial (and much-needed) refurbishment in time to commemorate the bicentenary of Dickens' birth in 2012.

# St James's

### Buckingham Palace
Palace

See p56.

### St James's Park
Park

Map p78 (www.royalparks.gov.uk; The Mall SW1; ⊙5am-dusk; ⊖St James's Park or Green Park) This is one of the smallest but most gorgeous of London's parks. It has brilliant views of the London Eye, Westminster, St James's Palace, Carlton Terrace and Horse Guards Parade, and the view of Buckingham Palace from the footbridge spanning St James's Park Lake is the best you'll find. The central lake is full of different types of ducks, geese, swans and general fowl, and its southern side's rocks serve as a rest stop for pelicans (fed at 2.30pm daily).

### Royal Academy of Arts
Gallery

Map p78 (www.royalacademy.org.uk; Burlington House, Piccadilly W1; ⊙10am-6pm, to 10pm Fri; ⊖Green Park) Britain's first art school was founded in 1768 but the organisation moved here only in the following century. The collection contains drawings, paintings, architectural designs, photographs and sculptures by past and present academicians such as John Constable, Sir Joshua Reynolds, Thomas Gainsborough, JMW Turner, David Hockney and Norman Foster. Highlights are displayed in the **John Madejski Fine Rooms**, which are accessible by **free guided tours** (1hr; ⊙1pm & 3pm Wed-Fri, 1pm Tue, 11.30am Sat). The displays change regularly.

The famous **Summer Exhibition** ( ⊙Jun–mid-Aug), which for nearly 250 years has showcased contemporary

# West End: Bloomsbury

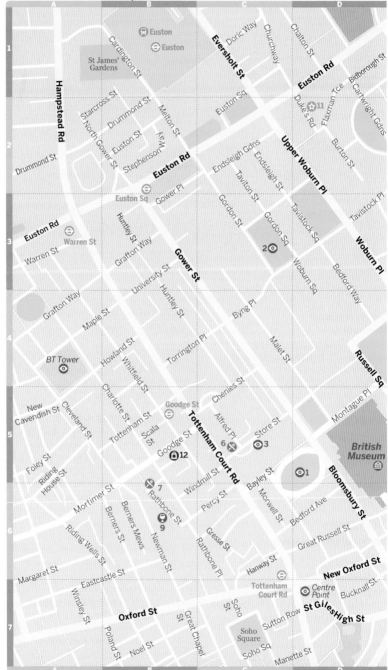

# West End: Bloomsbury

art for sale by established as well as unknown artists, is the Academy's biggest event of the year.

### Burlington Arcade    Historic Site

**Map p78 (51 Piccadilly W1; ⊖Green Park)** Flanking Burlington House (home of the Royal Academy of Arts) on its western side is the curious Burlington Arcade, built in 1819 and evocative of a bygone era. Today it is a shopping precinct for the very wealthy and is most famous for the Burlington Berties, uniformed guards who patrol the area keeping an eye out for punishable offences such as running, chewing gum or whatever else might lower the arcade's tone.

### St James's Piccadilly    Church

**Map p66 (197 Piccadilly W1; ⊙8am-7pm; ⊖Piccadilly Circus)** The only church Christopher Wren built from scratch and on a new site (most of the other London churches are replacements for ones razed in the Great Fire), this simple building is exceedingly easy on the eye and substitutes what some might call the pompous flourishes of Wren's most famous churches with a warm and elegant user-friendliness.

**FREE** **White Cube** Gallery

Map p78 (www.whitecube.com; 25-26 Mason's Yard SW1; ⏱10am-6pm Tue-Sat; ⊖Green Park or Piccadilly Circus) Housed in Mason's Yard, a traditional courtyard with brick houses and an old pub, the White Cube looks like an ice block – white, straight-lined and angular. The two contrasting styles work well together and the courtyard often serves as a garden for the gallery on popular opening nights.

**St James's Palace** Palace

Map p78 (Cleveland Row SW1; closed to the public; ⊖Green Park) The striking Tudor gatehouse of St James's Palace, the only surviving part of a building initiated by the palace-mad Henry VIII in 1530, is best approached from St James's St to the north of St James's Park. This was the official residence of kings and queens for more than three centuries.

**Guards Museum** Museum

Map p78 (www.theguardsmuseum.com; Wellington Barracks, Birdcage Walk SW1; adult/child £4/free; ⏱10am-4pm; ⊖St James's Park) If you found the crowds at the Changing of the Guards tiresome and didn't see much, be here at 10.50am any day from April to August to see the guards getting into formation before their march up to Buckingham Palace. Also, check out the history of the five regiments of foot guards and their role in military campaigns from Waterloo onwards inside this little museum.

**FREE** **Institute of Contemporary Arts** Arts Centre

Map p78 (ICA; www.ica.org.uk; Nash House, The Mall SW1; ⏱noon-11pm Wed, to 1am Thu-Sat, to 9pm Sun; ⊖Charing Cross or Piccadilly Circus; 📶) This was where Picasso and Henry Moore had their first UK shows, and ever since then the institute has sat comfortably on the cutting and controversial edge of the British arts world, with an excellent range of experimental/progressive/radical/obscure films, music and club nights, photography, art, theatre, lectures, multimedia works and book readings.

# Soho & Chinatown

Soho's reputation as the epicentre of nightlife and a proud gay neighbourhood is legendary and well deserved.

Immediately north of Leicester Square, but a world away in atmosphere, are Lisle and Gerrard Sts, the focal point for London's Chinese community. Although not as big as Chinatowns in many other cities – it's just two streets really – this is a lively quarter with fake oriental gates, Chinese street signs, red lanterns, many, many restaurants and great Asian supermarkets. To see it at its effervescent best, time your visit for Chinese New Year in late January/early February (p40).

At Soho's northern end, leafy **Soho Square** is the area's back garden. **Old Compton Street** is the epicentre of the gay village. That said, it is a street loved by all, gay or other, for its great bars, risqué shops and general good vibes.

**Piccadilly Circus** Street

Map p66 (⊖Piccadilly Circus) John Nash had originally designed Regent St and Piccadilly to be the two most elegant streets in town but, curbed by city planners, Nash couldn't realise his dream to the full. He would certainly be disappointed with what Piccadilly Circus has become: swamped with visitors, flanked by **flashing advertisement panels** and surrounded by shops flogging tourist tat.

At the centre of the circus is the famous aluminium statue, Anteros, twin brother of Eros, dedicated to the philanthropist and child-labour abolitionist Lord Shaftesbury. Down the years the angel has been mistaken for **Eros**, the God of Love, and the misnomer has stuck (you'll even see signs for 'Eros' from the Underground).

**Photographers' Gallery** Gallery

Map p66 (www.photonet.org.uk; 16-18 Ramillies St W1; admission free; ⊖Oxford Circus) This fantastic place was in the midst of a substantial refurbishment program at the time of writing and planned to reopen with a bang in early 2012, with three floors of exhibition space, a brand new cafe and a shop brimming with prints and photography books.

## ✓ Don't Miss
# Tate Britain

You'd think that Tate Britain might have suffered since its lavish, sexy sibling, Tate Modern (p124), took half its collection and all of the limelight upriver when it opened in 2000. But, on the contrary, the venerable Tate Britain, built in 1897, stretched out splendidly with its definitive collection of British art from the 16th to the late 20th centuries, while the Modern sister devoted its space to modern art.

The star of the show at Tate Britain is JMW Turner; after he died in 1851, his estate was settled by a decree declaring that whatever had been found in his studio – 300 oil paintings and about 30,000 sketches and drawings – would be bequeathed to the nation. The 'Turner Bequest', as it became known, forms the bulk of the Tate's Turner collection. You'll find such classics as *The Scarlet Sunset* and *Norham Castle, Sunrise*.

As well as Turner's art, there are seminal works by such artists as Constable, Gainsborough and Reynolds, but also more modern artists, such as Lucian Freud, Francis Bacon and Tracey Emin. Tate Britain also hosts the prestigious and often controversial Turner Prize for contemporary art from October to early December every year.

There are free one-hour **thematic tours** ( ⊙11am, noon, 2pm & 3pm Mon-Fri, noon & 3pm Sat & Sun), along with free 15-minute **Art in Focus talks** ( ⊙1.15pm Tue, 2.30pm Sat) on specific works. **Audioguides** (£3.50) are also available.

A good time to visit the gallery is on **Late at Tate** night, on the first Friday of the month, when the gallery stays open until 10pm.

### NEED TO KNOW

Map p78; www.tate.org.uk; Millbank SW1; admission free, prices vary for temporary exhibitions; ⊙10am-6pm; ⊖Pimlico

## West End: Central

THE WEST END

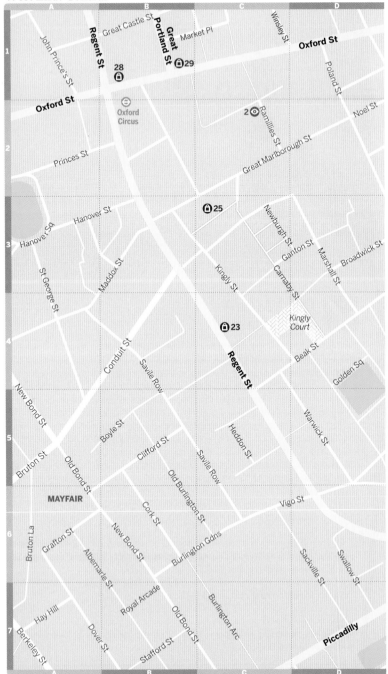

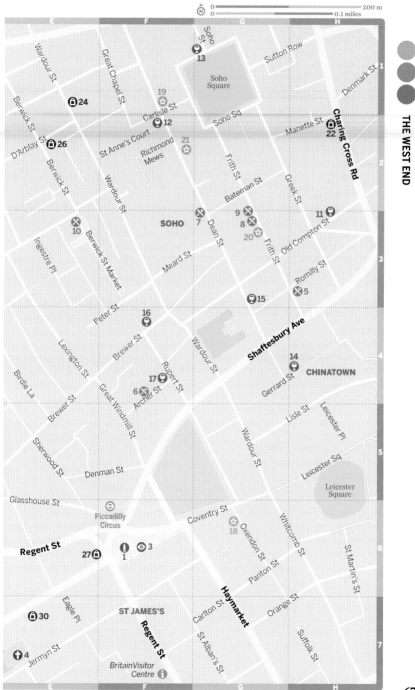

SOHO

CHINATOWN

ST JAMES'S

Soho Square

Leicester Square

Piccadilly Circus

Shaftesbury Ave

Regent St

Haymarket

Charing Cross Rd

BritainVisitor Centre

## West End: Central

### ◎ Sights
1 Eros Statue..............................................F6
2 Photographer's Gallery........................C2
3 Piccadilly Circus...................................F6
4 St James's Piccadilly............................E7

### ◈ Eating
5th View ......................................(see 30)
5 Bar Shu................................................H3
6 Bocca di Lupo.....................................F4
7 Dean Street Townhouse.....................G3
8 Koya.....................................................G3
9 Mooli's.................................................G3
10 Yauatcha..............................................E3

### ◉ Drinking & Nightlife
11 Academy...............................................H3
12 Candy Bar.............................................F2
Dean Street Townhouse.................(see 7)
13 Edge.....................................................G1
14 Experimental Cocktail Club.................H4

15 French House........................................G3
16 Madame Jo Jo's....................................F4
17 White Horse..........................................F4

### ◎ Entertainment
18 Comedy Store......................................G6
19 Pizza Express Jazz Club.......................F1
20 Ronnie Scott's.....................................G3
21 Soho Theatre.......................................F2

### ◉ Shopping
22 Foyle's..................................................H2
23 Hamleys...............................................C4
24 Joy........................................................E1
25 Liberty..................................................C3
26 Sister Ray.............................................E2
27 Sting.....................................................E6
28 TopShop & Topman.............................B1
29 Urban Outfitters..................................B1
30 Waterstone's........................................E7

## Covent Garden & Leicester Square

### Trafalgar Square
Square

Map p72 ( ⊖ Charing Cross or Leicester Sq) In many ways this is the centre of London, where rallies and marches take place, tens of thousands of revellers usher in the New Year and locals congregate for anything from communal open-air cinema to various political protests.

This square commemorates the victory of the British navy at the Battle of Trafalgar against the French and Spanish navies in 1805 during the Napoleonic wars. Standing in the centre of the square since 1843, the 52m-high Nelson's Column (upon which the admiral surveys his fleet of ships to the southwest) honours Admiral Lord Nelson, who led the fleet's victory over Napoleon. The column is flanked by four enormous bronze statues of lions, which were sculpted by Sir Edwin Landseer and cast with seized Spanish and French cannons. If you look southwest down Whitehall, you'll also get a glimpse of Big Ben down at the Houses of Parliament (p58).

### Covent Garden Piazza
Square

Map p72 ( ⊖ Covent Garden) London's first planned square is now the exclusive reserve of tourists who flock here to shop in the quaint old arcades, be entertained by buskers, pay through the nose for refreshments at outdoor cafes and bars, and watch street performers pretend to be statues. On its western flank is **St Paul's Church** (www.actorschurch.org; Bedford St WC2; ⊙8.30am-5.30pm Mon-Fri, 9am-1pm Sun). Check out the lovely courtyard at the back, perfect for a picnic.

### London Transport Museum
Museum

Map p72 (www.ltmuseum.co.uk; Covent Garden Piazza WC2; adult/child £14/free; ⊙10am-6pm Sat-Thu, 11am-6pm Fri; ⊖Covent Garden) This museum reopened in late 2007, after a £22-million refurbishment and redesign. You can now see the revitalised existing collection (consisting of buses from the horse age until today, plus taxis, trains and all other modes of transport) and new collections that feature other major cities' transport systems, fascinating insights on how the city developed as a result of better transport and tons of original advertising posters.

## National Portrait Gallery    Gallery

Map p72 (www.npg.org.uk; St Martin's Pl WC2; admission free, prices vary for temporary exhibitions; ⊙10am-6pm Sat-Wed, to 9pm Thu & Fri; ⊖Charing Cross or Leicester Sq) The National Portrait Gallery (NPG) is a wonderful combination of art and history. The gallery houses a primary collection of some 10,000 works, which are regularly rotated.

The NPG is organised chronologically (starting on the 2nd floor), and then by themes. One of the museum's highlights is the famous 'Chandos portrait' of Shakespeare; it is believed to be the only one to have been painted during the author's lifetime. Other highlights include a fascinating painting of Queen Elizabeth I displaying her might by standing over a map of England, and a touching sketch of novelist Jane Austen by her sister Cassandra.

The ground floor is dedicated to modern figures, using a variety of media (sculpture, photography, video etc). Among the most popular displays are the iconic Blur portraits by Julian Opie, and Sam Taylor-Wood's *David,* a video-portrait of David Beckham asleep after football training.

The gallery hosts brilliant temporary exhibitions and the excellent **audioguides** (£3) highlight 200 portraits and allow you to hear the voices of some of the people portrayed.

## St Martin-in-the-Fields    Church

Map p72 (www.stmartin-in-the-fields.org; Trafalgar Sq WC2; ⊙8am-6.30pm, evening concerts 7.30pm; ⊖Charing Cross) The 'royal parish church' is a delightful fusion of classical and baroque styles that was completed by James Gibbs (1682–1754) in 1726. The church is well known for its excellent classical music concerts, many by candlelight, and its links to the Chinese community (mass is held in English, Mandarin and Cantonese).

# Whitehall

## Churchill War Rooms    Museum

Map p78 (http://cwr.iwm.org.uk; Clive Steps, King Charles St SW1; adult/child £16/free; ⊙9.30am-6pm, last admission 5pm; ⊖Westminster) In 1938, with the prospect of war across Europe looming ever more seriously, the British government decided to look for a suitable site for a temporary emergency government shelter while plans for relocation to the suburbs were being finalised. The basement of what is now the treasury was selected and converted.

The bunker served as nerve centre of the war cabinet until the end of WWII in August 1945: here chiefs of staff slept, ate and plotted Hitler's downfall, blissfully believing they were protected from Luftwaffe bombs (turns out it would have crumpled had the area taken a hit).

The Cabinet War Rooms have been left much as they were when the lights were turned off on 15 August 1945 when Japan surrendered and everyone headed off for a well-earned drink. Many rooms have been preserved, including the room where the cabinet held more than 100 meetings, the Telegraph Room with a

# Fourth Plinth

Three of the four plinths located at Trafalgar Square's corners are occupied by notables: King George IV on horseback, and military men General Sir Charles Napier and Major General Sir Henry Havelock. One, originally intended for a statue of William IV, has largely remained vacant for the past 150 years. The Royal Society of Arts conceived the unimaginatively titled **Fourth Plinth Project** (www.london.gov.uk/fourthplinth) in 1999, deciding to use the empty space for works by contemporary artists. The Mayor's office has since taken over the Fourth Plinth Project, continuing with the contemporary-art theme.

hotline to Roosevelt, the cramped typing pool, the converted broom cupboard that was Churchill's office, and the all-important map room (which was the operational centre).

In the Chief of Staff's Conference Room, the walls are covered with huge, original maps that were discovered only in 2002.

The whizz-bang multimedia Churchill Museum was added during the 2003 refurbishment of the war rooms. There are more interactive displays than you'll know where to look, as well as some of Churchill's personal effects, from cigars to his formal Privy Council uniform, to his shockingly tasteless red velvet 'romper' outfit.

### No 10 Downing Street    Historic Building
Map p78 (www.number10.gov.uk; 10 Downing St SW1; ⊖Westminster or Charing Cross) This has been the official office of British leaders since 1732, when George II presented No 10 to Robert Walpole and, since refur-

bishment in 1902, it's also been the Prime Minister's official London residence. The street was cordoned off with a rather large iron gate during Margaret Thatcher's times so you won't see much.

### Horse Guards Parade    Historic Site
Map p78 ( ⊙Changing of the Guard 11am Mon-Sat, 10am Sun; ⊖Westminster or St James's Park) In a more accessible version of Buckingham Palace's Changing of the Guard, the mounted troopers of the Household Cavalry change guard here daily, at the official entrance to the royal palaces (opposite the Banqueting House). A lite-pomp version takes place at 4pm when the dismounted guards are changed. On the Queen's official birthday in June, the Trooping of the Colour is also staged here.

Fittingly, as the parade ground and its buildings were built in 1745 to house the Queen's so-called 'Life Guards', this will be the pitch for the beach volleyball during the London 2012 Olympics (see www.london2012.org).

**Left:** Horse Guards Parade; **Below:** Banqueting House
(LEFT) GAVIN GOUGH/LONELY PLANET IMAGES ©; (BELOW) MIKE BOOTH/ALAMY ©

## Banqueting House    Historic Building

Map p78 (www.hrp.org.uk; Whitehall SW1; adult/child £5/free; ◷10am-5pm Mon-Sat; ⊖Westminster or Charing Cross) This is the only surviving part of the Tudor Whitehall Palace, which once stretched most of the way down Whitehall and burned down in 1698. Designed as England's first purely Renaissance building by Inigo Jones after he returned from Italy, it looked like no other structure in the country at the time.

A bust outside commemorates 30 January 1649 when Charles I, accused of treason by Cromwell after the Civil War, was executed on a scaffold built against a 1st-floor window here. In a huge, virtually unfurnished hall on the 1st floor there are nine ceiling panels painted by Rubens in 1635.

# Holborn & the Strand

**Sir John Soane's Museum**   Museum
Map p72 (www.soane.org; 13 Lincoln's Inn Fields WC2; admission free; ◷10am-5pm Tue-Sat & 6-9pm 1st Tue of month; ⊖Holborn) This little museum is one of the most atmospheric and fascinating sights in London. The building is the beautiful, bewitching home of architect Sir John Soane (1753–1837), which he left brimming with surprising personal effects and curiosities, and the museum represents his exquisite and eccentric taste.

Soane was a country bricklayer's son, most famous for designing the Bank of England. In his work and life, he drew on ideas picked up while on an 18th-century grand tour of Italy.

The heritage-listed house is largely as it was when Sir John was carted out in a box, and is itself a main part of the attraction. It has a glass dome that brings light right down to the basement, a lantern room filled with statuary, rooms within rooms, and a picture gallery where paintings are stowed behind each other on folding wooden panes. This

# West End: Covent Garden, Leicester Sq, Holborn & Strand

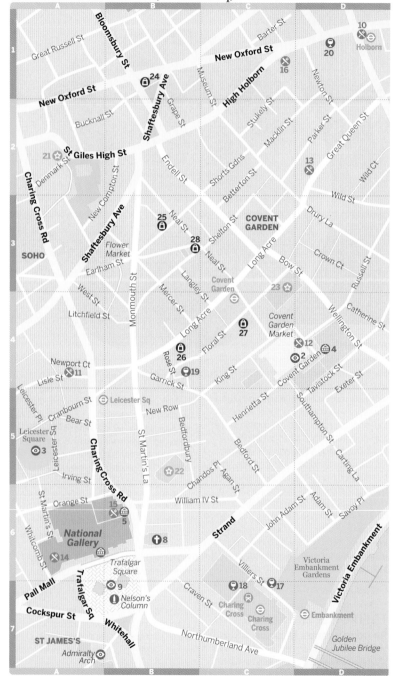

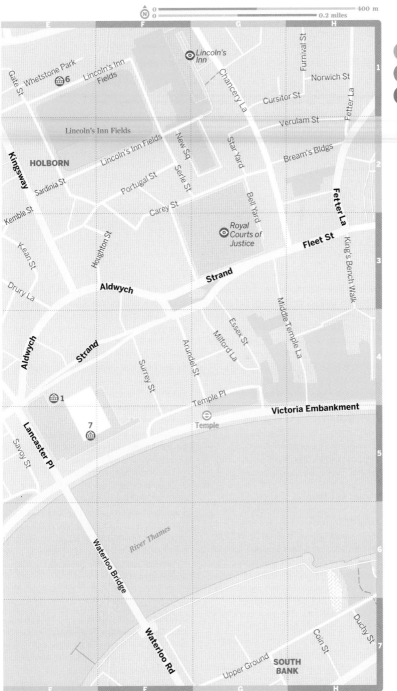

## West End: Covent Garden, Leicester Sq, Holborn & Strand

is where Soane's choice paintings are displayed, including *Riva degli Schiavoni, looking West* by Canaletto, drawings by Christopher Wren and Robert Adam, and the original *Rake's Progress,* William Hogarth's set of cartoon caricatures of late-18th-century London lowlife. You'll have to ask a guard to open the panes so that you can view all the paintings.

The first Tuesday evening of each month is the choice time to visit as the house is lit by candles and the atmosphere is even more magical (it is very popular and there are always long queues).

**Somerset House**   Historic Building
Map p72 (www.somerset-house.org.uk; The Strand WC2; admission free to courtyard & terrace; ⏰house 10am-6pm, Great Court 7.30am-11pm; ⊖Temple or Covent Garden) Passing beneath the arched entrance towards this splendid Palladian masterpiece, it's hard to believe that the magnificent courtyard in front of you, with its 55 dancing fountains, was a car park for tax collectors until a spectacular refurbishment in 2000. William Chambers designed the house in 1775 for royal societies and it now contains two fabulous galleries.

The **Courtauld Gallery** (www.courtauld.ac.uk; adult/child £6/free, 10am-2pm Mon free; ⏰10am-6pm) is located immediately to your right as you enter Somerset House from The Strand. Here, you can have an uncrowded stroll among masterpieces by Rubens, Botticelli, Cézanne, Degas, Renoir, Manet and Monet, to mention but a few. There are free, 15-minute **lunchtime talks** on specific works or themes from the collection at 1.15pm every Monday and Friday. The **Embankment Galleries** host regular photographic exhibitions.

The courtyard is transformed into a popular **ice rink** in winter and used for concerts and events in summer; the **Summer Screen** (when the Great Court turns into an outdoor cinema for 10 evenings in early August) is particularly popular. Behind the house, there's a sunny terrace and cafe overlooking the embankment.

# Marylebone

### Wallace Collection   Gallery
Map p84 (www.wallacecollection.org; Hertford House, Manchester Sq W1; admission free; ⏰10am-5pm; ⊖Bond St) Arguably London's finest small gallery, the Wallace Collection provides an enthralling

PETER D NOYCE/ALAMY ©

## ✓ Don't Miss
# National Gallery

With more than 2000 Western European paintings on display, this is one of the largest galleries in the world. There are seminal paintings from every important epoch in the history of art, including works by Leonardo da Vinci, Michelangelo, Titian, Van Gogh and Renoir.

The Sainsbury Wing on the gallery's western side houses paintings from 1260 to 1510. In these 16 rooms you will find plenty of fine religious paintings commissioned for private devotion as well more unusual masterpieces such as Boticelli's *Venus & Mars*.

The High Renaissance (1510–1600) is covered in the West Wing where Michelangelo, Titian, Correggio, El Greco and Bronzino hold court, while Rubens, Rembrandt and Caravaggio can be found in the North Wing (1600–1700). There are notably two self-portraits of Rembrandt and the beautiful *Rockeby Venus* by Velázquez.

The most crowded part of the gallery is likely to be the East Wing (1700–1900), with a great collection of 18th-century British landscape artists such as Gainsborough, Constable and Turner, and highbrow impressionist and postimpressionist masterpieces. Visitors will no doubt recognise Van Gogh's *Sunflowers* and Degas' *Dancers*.

The comprehensive **audioguides (£3.50)** are highly recommended, as are the free one-hour introductory guided tours that leave from the information desk in the Sainsbury Wing daily at 11.30am and 2.30pm.

## NEED TO KNOW

Map p72; www.nationalgallery.org.uk; Trafalgar Sq WC2; admission free; prices vary for temporary exhibitions; ⊙10am-6pm Sat-Thu, to 9pm Fri; ⊖Charing Cross or Leicester Sq

glimpse into 18th-century aristocratic life. The sumptuously restored Italianate mansion houses a treasure-trove of 17th- and 18th-century paintings, porcelain, artefacts and furniture collected by the same family and bequeathed to the nation by the widow of Sir Richard Wallace (1818–90) on condition it should always be on display in the centre of London.

Among the many highlights are paintings by Rembrandt, Delacroix, Titian, Rubens, Poussin, Velázquez and Gainsborough in the stunning **Great Gallery**. There's a spectacular array of medieval and Renaissance armour (including some to try on), stunning chandeliers and a sweeping staircase – deemed one of the best examples of French interior architecture in existence. The excellent audioguides (£4) can give you some insight into the plethora of objects and paintings.

Have lunch at the excellent glass-roofed restaurant and you'll have spent an outstanding day in London.

### Madame Tussauds     Museum

Map p84 (www.madame-tussauds.com; Marylebone Rd NW1; adult/child £29/25; ⊙9.30am-5.30pm Sep–mid-Jul, 9am-7pm mid-Jul–Aug;

⊖Baker St) Despite being kitsch and terribly overpriced, Madame Tussauds' (too-so) popularity doesn't seem to wane. The big attraction is getting a photo op with your dream celebrity: Kate Moss, Lady Gaga, David and Victoria Beckham, Hrithik Roshan of Bollywood fame, the Queen, Prince Charles and many more. If you're more into politics, then you could shake hands with Barack Obama or Tony Blair, or even London Mayor Boris Johnson with his signature mop haircut.

The whole place is shamelessly commercial, with shops and spending opportunities in every room (ranging from snacks to a Formula 1 simulator, a get-your-hand-in-wax workshop or a print shop where you can get your 'celebrity shots' printed on a mug or mouse mat).

### Sherlock Holmes Museum    Museum

Map p84 (www.sherlock-holmes.co.uk; 221b Baker St; adult/child £6/4; ⊙9.30am-6pm; ⊖Baker St) Though the museum gives its address as 221b Baker St, the actual fictional abode of Sherlock Holmes is the Abbey National building a bit further south. Fans of the Sherlock Holmes books will enjoy examining the three floors of

Sherlock Holmes Museum

reconstructed Victoriana, deerstalkers, burning candles and flickering grates, but may baulk at the dodgy waxworks of Professor Moriarty and 'the Man with the Twisted Lip'.

# Eating

Many of the city's most eclectic, fashionable and, quite simply, best restaurants are dotted around the West End. As with most things in London, it pays to be in the know: while there's a huge concentration of mediocre places to eat along the main tourist drags, the best eating experiences are frequently tucked away on backstreets and are not at all obvious.

## Westminster

### Vincent Rooms    Modern European £
Map p78 ( 7802 8391; www.thevincentrooms. com; Westminster Kingsway College, Vincent Sq SW1; mains £6-10.50; lunch noon-2pm Mon-Fri, dinner selected evenings only; Victoria) Here you're essentially offering yourself up as a guinea pig for the student chefs at Westminster Kingsway College, where celebrity chef Jamie Oliver was trained. Service is nervously eager to please, the atmosphere in both the Brasserie and the Escoffier Room is smarter than expected, and the food (including excellent vegie options) ranges from wonderful to exquisite – at prices that puts other culinary stars to shame.

### Cinnamon Club    Indian £££
Map p78 ( 7222 2555; www.cinnamonclub.com; Old Westminster Library, 30 Great Smith St SW1; mains £14-32; closed Sun; St James's Park) Domed skylights, high ceilings, parquet flooring and a book-lined mezzanine all convey an atmosphere reminiscent of a colonial club. The food is sumptuous: a mix of traditional Indian with a modern European twist. The club also does breakfast, with options ranging from European-style eggs to Indian *uttapams* (stuffed, crispy rice pancakes).

# Bloomsbury & Fitzrovia

### Abeno    Japanese ££
Map p62 (www.abeno.co.uk; 47 Museum St WC1; mains £7.50-18; lunch & dinner; Tottenham Court Rd) This understated Japanese restaurant specialises in *okonomiyaki*, a savoury pancake that hails from Osaka. The pancakes consist of cabbage, egg and flour, and are combined with the ingredients of your choice (there are more than two-dozen varieties, including anything from sliced meats and vegetables to egg, noodles and cheese). The pancakes are cooked on a hotplate at your table.

### Hummus Bros    Middle Eastern £
Map p62 (www.hbros.co.uk; Victoria House, 37-63 Southampton Row WC1; mains £2.50-6; 11am-9pm Mon-Fri; Holborn) The deal at this very popular outlet is a bowl of filling hummus with your choice of topping (beef, chicken, tabouleh etc) eaten with warm pita bread. It's very filling and you can eat in or take away.

### Busaba Eathai    Thai £
Map p62 (www.busaba.com; 22 Store St WC1; mains £7-9; lunch & dinner; Goodge St) The Store St premises of this hugely popular mini-chain is slightly less hectic than some of the other West End branches, but it retains all the signature features that have made it a roaring success: uberstyled Asian interior, large communal wooden tables, and heavenly cheap and tasty Thai food. This isn't the restaurant to come to for a long and intimate dinner, but it's a superb option if you are looking for an excellent and speedy meal.

### Fino    Spanish ££
Map p62 (www.finorestaurant.com; 33 Charlotte St W1; tapas £4-17; lunch Mon-Fri, dinner Mon-Sat; Goodge St or Tottenham Court Rd) Critically acclaimed (and it's easy to see why), Fino is the perfect example of great Spanish cuisine in a London that is unfortunately all too dominated by dreary and uninventive tapas bars. Enter from Rathbone St.

# West End: St James's, Westminster & Whitehall

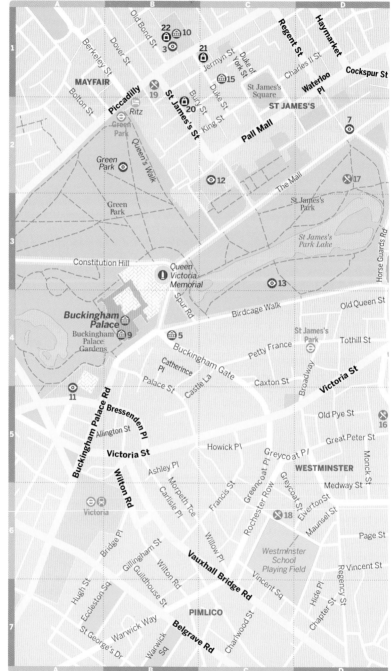

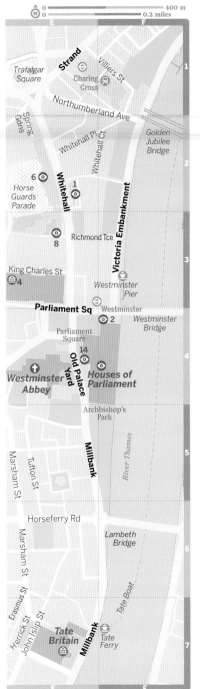

# St James's

### Inn the Park
British ££

Map p78 ( ☎7451 9999; www.innthepark.com; St James's Park SW1; mains £13.50-18.50; ☺8am-11pm; ⊖Trafalgar Sq) This stunning wooden cafe and restaurant in St James's Park (p61) is run by Irish wonderchef Oliver Peyton and offers cakes and tea as well as excellent British food with a monthly changing menu. The terrace, which overlooks one of the park's fountains with views of Whitehall's grand buildings, is wonderful on spring and summer days. If you're up for a special dining experience, come here for dinner when the park is quiet and slightly illuminated.

# Soho & Chinatown

### Yauatcha
Chinese ££

Map p66 (www.yauatcha.com; 15 Broadwick St W1; dim sum £4-16; ☺lunch & dinner; ⊖Oxford Circus) This most glamorous of dim sum restaurants (housed in the award-winning Ingeni building) is divided into two parts: the upstairs dining room offers a delightful blue-bathed oasis of calm from the chaos of Berwick Street Market, while downstairs has a smarter, more atmospheric feel with constellations of 'star' lights.

### Mooli's
Indian £

Map p66 (www.moolis.com; 50 Frith St W1; roti wrap £5; ☺noon-10pm Mon-Wed, to 11.30pm Thu-Sat, closed Sun; ⊖Tottenham Court Rd or Leicester Sq) Started by a duo of Indian friends who'd had enough of the City life, Mooli's is a breath of fresh air in the quick-bite world (not least because it was partly funded through late-night poker sessions). A cheerful little eatery, it serves fresh, homemade rotis (Indian soft bread) with delicious filling (meat as well as paneer and chickpeas, all prepared with their own sauce and seasoning).

### Bocca di Lupo
Italian ££

Map p66 ( ☎7734 2223; www.boccadilupo.com; 12 Archer St W1; mains £8.50-17.50; ☺lunch & dinner Mon-Sat, lunch Sun; ⊖Piccadilly Circus) Hidden on a dark Soho backstreet, Bocca radiates elegant sophistication. The menu

## West End: St James's, Westminster & Whitehall

has dishes from across Italy (the menu tells you which region they're from) and every main can be served as small or large portions. It's often full so make sure you book.

### Koya                                    Noodles £
Map p66 (www.koya.co.uk; 49 Frith St W1; mains £7-14; ☉lunch & dinner Mon-Sat; ⊖Tottenham Court Rd or Leicester Sq) Arrive early or late if you don't want to queue at this excellent Japanese eatery. Londoners come here for their fill of authentic Udon noodles (hot or cold, served in broth or with a cold sauce), the efficient service and very reasonable prices.

### 5th View                        International ££
Map p66 (www.5thview.co.uk; 5th fl, Waterstone's Piccadilly, 203-206 Piccadilly W1; mains £9-15; ☉9am-9pm Mon-Sat, to 5pm Sun; ⊖Piccadilly Circus) The views of Westminster from the top of Waterstone's on Piccadilly are really quite dreamy. Add a relaxed, sophisticated dining room and some lovely food, and you have a gem of a place.

### Bar Shu                            Chinese ££
Map p66 (www.bar-shu.co.uk; 28 Frith St W1; mains £8-20; ☉lunch & dinner; ⊖Leicester Sq) The story goes that a visiting businessman from Chengdu, capital of Szechuan Province in China, found London's Chinese food offerings so inauthentic that

he decided to open up his own restaurant with five chefs from home. The result is authentic Szechuan cuisine, with dishes redolent of smoked chillies and the all-important ubiquitous peppercorn. Service is a little brusque but the food is delicious and the portions are huge.

## Covent Garden & Leicester Square

### Ben's Cookies                      Bakery £
Map p72 (www.benscookies.com; 13Aa The Piazza, Covent Garden WC2; cookie £1.50; ☉10am-8pm Mon-Sat, 11am-7pm Sun; ⊖Covent Garden) The cookies at Ben's are, quite possibly, the best in the history of cookie-making. There are 18 different kinds to choose from, from triple chocolate to peanut butter, oatmeal and raisin to chocolate and orange, all wonderfully gooey and often warm (they're baked fresh on the premises throughout the day).

### Great Queen Street              British ££
Map p72 (☎7242 0622; 32 Great Queen St WC2; mains £9-18; ☉lunch & dinner Mon-Sat, lunch Sun; ⊖Covent Garden or Holborn) One of Covent Garden's best places to eat, Great Queen Street is sister to the **Anchor & Hope** (p135) in Waterloo. The menu is seasonal (and changes daily), with an emphasis on quality, hearty dishes and good ingredients – there are always

delicious stews, roasts and simple fish dishes. The staff are knowledgeable about what they serve, the wine list is good and booking is, as you may have guessed, essential.

### Baozi Inn
Chinese £

Map p72 (25 Newport Ct WC2; mains £6-7; ⊙closed Sun; ⊖Leicester Sq) The smaller sister of **Bar Shu** (p80) has its own personality and a unique (and cheap) menu. Decorated in a vintage style that plays at kitsch communist pop (complete with old Chinese communist songs tinkling out of the speakers), Baozi Inn serves quality Beijing- and Chengdu-style street food, such as dan dan noodles with spicy pork and Baozi buns (steamed buns with stuffing) handmade daily.

## Holborn & the Strand

### Asadal
Korean ££

Map p72 (www.asadal.co.uk; 227 High Holborn WC1; mains £7-18; ⊙closed lunch Sun; ⊖Holborn) If you fancy Korean but want a bit more style thrown into the act, head for this spacious basement restaurant next to the Holborn tube station. The *kimchi* (pickled Chinese cabbage with chillies) is

searing, the barbecues (£7 to £11.50) are done on your table and the *bibimbab* – rice served in a sizzling pot topped with thinly sliced beef, preserved vegetables and chilli-laced soybean paste – are the best in town.

### Shanghai Blues
Chinese £££

Map p72 (☑7404 1668; www.shanghaiblues. co.uk; 193-197 High Holborn WC1; mains £15-52; ⊖Holborn) What was once the St Giles Library now houses one of London's most stylish Chinese restaurants. The dark and atmospheric interior – think black and blue tables and chairs punctuated by bright red screens – recalls imperial China with a modern twist. On Friday and Saturday nights, you can also enjoy live jazz.

## Marylebone

### Providores & Tapa Room
Fusion £££

Map p84 (☑7935 6175; www.theprovidores. co.uk; 109 Marylebone High St W1; mains £18-26; ⊙lunch & dinner; ⊖Baker St or Bond St) This place is split over two levels: tempting tapas (£2.80 to £15) on the ground floor (no bookings); and outstanding fusion

# Museum Restaurants

**National Dining Rooms** (Map p72; www.peytonandbyrne.co.uk; Sainsbury Wing, National Gallery, Trafalgar Sq WC2; mains £15; ⊙10am-5.30pm Sat-Thu, to 8.30pm Fri; ⊖Charing Cross) Chef Oliver Peyton's restaurant at the National Gallery styles itself as 'proudly and resolutely British', and what a great idea. The menu features an extensive and wonderful selection of British cheeses for a light lunch. For something more filling, go for the county menu, a monthly changing menu honouring regional specialities from across the British Isles. The all-day bakery also churns out fresh cakes and pastries for mid-morning and afternoon treats.

**Portrait** (Map p72; ☑7312 2490; www.npg.org.uk/live/portrest.asp; 3rd fl, National Portrait Gallery, St Martin's Pl WC2; mains £14-29; ⊙lunch 11.45am-3pm daily, dinner Thu-Sat 5.30pm-8.15pm; ⊖Charing Cross) This stunningly located restaurant above the excellent National Portrait Gallery (p69) – with views over Trafalgar Sq and Westminster – is a great place to relax after a morning or afternoon at the gallery; the brunch (weekend only) and afternoon tea (daily) come highly recommended. Unfortunately, Portrait is restricted in its opening times by the gallery, so dinner is rather early by London standards. Booking is advisable.

HELENA SMITH/LONELY PLANET IMAGES ©

cuisine in the elegant and understated dining room above. There is also a fantastic brunch on Saturdays and Sundays.

## Locanda Locatelli
Italian £££

Map p84 (🕿7935 9088; www.locandalocatelli.com; 8 Seymour St W1; mains £14-33; ⏱lunch & dinner; ⊖Marble Arch) This dark but quietly glamorous restaurant in an otherwise unremarkable Marble Arch hotel is one of London's hottest tables, and you're likely to see some famous faces being greeted by celebrity chef Giorgio Locatelli at some point during your meal. Booking is essential.

## Mayfair

### Le Boudin Blanc
French £££

Map p84 (🕿7499 3292; www.boudinblanc.co.uk; 5 Trebeck St W1; mains £18-27; ⏱lunch & dinner; ⊖Green Park) This has to be (one of?) the best French restaurants in the capital: the meat is cooked to perfection, the sauces mouth-wateringly good and the portions huge. The *frites* (French fries) are the best you'll find this side of the pond. And there is, of course, a whopping 500 wines to choose from. No wonder it's always full.

## Gordon Ramsay at Claridge's
British £££

Map p84 (🕿7499 0099; www.gordonramsay.com; 55 Brook St W1; 3-course set lunch/dinner £30/80; ⏱lunch & dinner; ⊖Bond St) This match made in heaven – London's most celebrated chef in arguably its grandest hotel – will make you weak at the knees. A meal in the gorgeous art deco dining room is a special occasion indeed; the Ramsay flavours will have you reeling, from the Thai-spiced lobster ravioli with lemongrass and coconut to the chorizo-studded John Dory with Jersey Royals and asparagus and morel velouté, all the way to the cheese trolley, whether you choose from the French or British selections.

## Momo
Moroccan £££

(🕿7434 4040; www.momoresto.com; 25 Heddon St W1; mains £18-25, 2-/3-course set lunches £15/19; ⏱closed Sun lunch; ⊖Piccadilly Circus) This wonderfully atmospheric Moroccan restaurant is stuffed with cushions and lamps, and staffed by all-dancing, tambourine-playing waiters. There's outside seating in this quiet backstreet in the warmer months.

# Drinking & Nightlife

Over the last decade or so, the East End has trumped Soho and the West End as the coolest place in town. However, the West End is still a wonderful place for a night out – Friday and Saturday nights are buzzing with excitement and decadence, particularly the areas around Soho, Leicester Square and Covent Garden, where you'll find people, booze and rickshaws in the streets till the early hours.

## Bloomsbury & Fitzrovia

### Newman Arms
Pub

Map p62 (www.newmanarms.co.uk; 23 Rathbone St W1; ⊖ Goodge St or Tottenham Court Rd) A lovely local that is also one of the few family-run pubs in central London, Newman Arms is a one-tiny-room affair with a 150-year history of providing great beer to thirsty locals. George Orwell and Dylan Thomas were regulars in their day, and Michael Powell's *Peeping Tom* was filmed here in 1960. There's also an excellent pie room upstairs.

### Queen's Larder
Pub

Map p62 (www.queenslarder.co.uk; 1 Queen Sq WC1; ⊖ Russell Sq) In a lovely square southeast of Russell Square, this pub is so called because Queen Charlotte, wife of 'Mad' King George III, rented part of the pub's cellar to store special foods for him while he was being treated nearby. It's a tiny but wonderfully cosy pub; there are benches outside for fair-weather fans and a good dining room upstairs.

## Soho & Chinatown

### Experimental Cocktail Club
Cocktail Bar

Map p66 (www.experimentalcocktailclublondon.com; 3a Gerrard St W1; ⊙ 6pm-3am Mon-Sat, 5pm-midnight Sun; ⊖ Leicester Sq or Piccadilly Circus) Once a late-night premises of a less reputable kind, the Experimental is now

---

# London's Best Afternoon Teas

The concept of afternoon tea (generally served between 3pm and 5pm) can be misleading to the non-initiated: of course, there will be a cup of tea (or coffee), but it's really all about the cakes! Cream tea includes scones with thick clotted cream and jam; afternoon tea is basically a meal, with finger sandwiches, pastries and scones, artfully presented on a tiered tray. The following are some of the best in town. Top-end hotels such as the Ritz and Claridges also offer afternoon tea but you will have to book six weeks in advance to guarantee a reservation.

**Dean Street Townhouse** (Map p66; www.deanstreettownhouse.com; 69-71 Dean St W1; tea £16; ⊙ daily; 🛜; ⊖ Tottenham Court Rd) Afternoon tea in the parlour of the Dean Street Townhouse hardly gets better; it's old world cosy, with its upholstered furniture and roaring fireplace, and the pastries are divine.

**Bea's of Bloomsbury** (www.beasofbloomsbury.com; 44 Theobalds Rd WC1; tea £15; ⊙ daily; ⊖ Holborn or Chancery Lane) Bea's made its name with signature cupcakes so it was only natural for them to offer a full afternoon tea, too. The cafe is tiny but original with its mix of open kitchen and boutique decor.

**Wolseley** (Map p78; 📞 7499 6996; www.thewolseley.com; 160 Piccadilly W1; cream/afternoon tea £9/21; ⊙ daily; ⊖ Green Park) This erstwhile Bentley car showroom has been transformed into an opulent Viennese-style brasserie, with golden chandeliers and stunning black-and-white tiled floors.

# West End: Mayfair & Marylebone

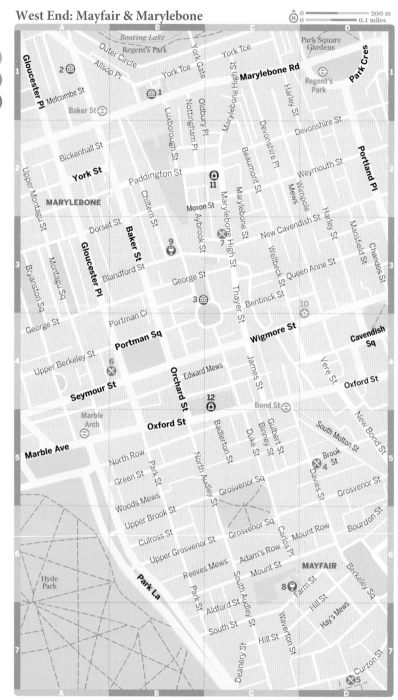

## West End: Mayfair & Marylebone

THE WEST END DRINKING & NIGHTLIFE

a sensational cocktail bar. The interior, with its soft lighting, mirrors, bare brick wall and elegant furnishings matches the sophistication of the cocktails: rare and original spirits (purple *shiso*-infused Ketel One Vodka, bird's-eye-chilli-infused Ocho Blanco Tequila etc), vintage martinis, Billecart and Krug Champagne and homemade fruit syrups. There is a £5 cover charge after 11pm.

### Academy                  Cocktail Bar
Map p66 (www.labbaruk.com; 12 Old Compton St W1; ⏰4pm-midnight Mon-Sat, to 10.30pm Sun; ⊖Leicester Sq or Tottenham Court Rd) A long-standing favourite in Soho, the Academy has some of the best cocktails in town. The menu is the size of a small book but, fear not, if you can't be bothered to read through it, just tell the bartender what you feel like (gin and exotic fruit, why, no problem Madam!) and he'll mix you something divine.

### White Horse                  Pub
Map p66 (45 Rupert St W1; ⊖Piccadilly Circus or Leicester Sq) A lovely pub in a very busy part of Soho, the White Horse ticks all our boxes: friendly staff, cheap drinks (it's part of the Sam Smith brewery) and a great traditional interior with etched glass and wood panels. The upstairs area is particularly cosy and generally quieter than downstairs.

### French House                  Bar
Map p66 (www.frenchhousesoho.com; 49 Dean St W1; ⊖Leicester Sq or Piccadilly Circus) French House is Soho's legendary boho

boozer with a history to match: this was the meeting place of the Free French Forces during WWII, and de Gaulle is said to have drunk here often, while Dylan Thomas, Peter O'Toole and Francis Bacon all frequently ended up on the wooden floors.

### Edge                  Gay
Map p66 (www.edgesoho.co.uk; 11 Soho Sq W1; ⏰to 1am Mon-Sat; ⊖Tottenham Court Rd) Overlooking Soho Square in all its four-storey glory, the Edge is London's largest gay bar and heaves every night of the week: there are dancers, waiters in bunny (or other) outfits, good music and a generally super friendly vibe. There's a heavy straight presence, as it's so close to Oxford Street.

### Candy Bar                  Lesbian
Map p66 (www.candybarsoho.com; 4 Carlise St W1; ⏰to midnight Sun-Thu, to 2am Fri & Sat; ⊖Tottenham Court Rd) This brilliant bar has been the centre of London's small but fun lesbian scene for years and is showing no signs of waning. Busy most nights of the week, this is very much a girls' space (one male guest per two women are allowed, though) and this should definitely be your first port of call on the London lesbian scene.

### Madame Jo Jo's                  Club
Map p66 (www.madamejojos.com; 8 Brewer St W1; ⊖Leicester Sq or Piccadilly Circus) The renowned subterranean, crimson cabaret bar and all its sleazy fun comes into its own with Kitsch Cabaret on

Saturday and Burlesque Idol on Fridays. Keb Darge's Lost & Found night on Saturday is legendary, attracting a cool crew of breakdancers, jazz dancers and people just out to have a good time. It's Tranny Schak Up (drag queen night) on Wednesdays.

## Covent Garden & Leicester Square

### Lamb & Flag                                    Pub
Map p72 (33 Rose St WC2; ⊖Covent Garden or Leicester Sq) Pocket-sized but packed with charm and history, the Lamb & Flag is still going strong after more than 350 years. Rain or shine, you'll have to elbow your way to the bar through the merry crowd drinking outside.

### Sports Cafe                                    Bar
(www.thesportscafe.com; 80 Haymarket SW1; ☺Mon-Sat noon-3am, to 10.30pm Sun; 🛜; ⊖Piccadilly Circus) For those keen to watch the latest ice hockey, American football, baseball or even soccer fixtures, the Sports Cafe is the place to be. It's a huge place, with four bars over two floors, giant screens everywhere and sports posters and memorabilia on the walls.

### Heaven                                         Gay
Map p72 (www.heavennightclub-london.com; Villiers St WC2; ☺11pm-6am Mon, 11pm-4am Thu & Fri, 10pm-5am Sat; ⊖Embankment or Charing Cross) This long-standing and perennially popular gay club, under the arches beneath Charing Cross station, has always been host to good club nights.

## Holborn & The Strand

### Gordon's Wine Bar                         Wine Bar
Map p72 (www.gordonswinebar.com; 47 Villiers St WC2; ⊖Embankment or Charing Cross) Gordon's is somewhat a victim of its popularity; it is relentlessly busy and unless you arrive before the office crowd does (generally around 6pm), you can forget getting a table. It's cavernous and dark, and the French and New World wines are heady and reasonably priced.

### Princess Louise · Pub

Map p72 (208 High Holborn WC1; ⊖Holborn) This late-19th-century Victorian pub is spectacular with its riot of fine tiles, etched mirrors, plasterwork and stunning horseshoe bar. Beers are Sam Smith's only but at just over £2 a pint, it's no wonder many spend the whole evening here.

## Marylebone

### Purl · Cocktail Bar

Map p84 ( ☎7935 0835; www.purl-london.com; 50-54 Blandford St W1; ⊖Baker St) This 'purveyor of fine matches and alcoholic libations', a fabulous underground drinking den with vintage furniture, serves intriguing cocktails ('What's Your Poison?' or 'Mr Hyde's No 2'). Booking is recommended.

## Mayfair

### Punch Bowl · Pub

Map p84 (www.punchbowllondon.com; 41 Farm St W1; ⊖Bond St) Partly owned by film director Guy Ritchie (*Lock, Stock & Two Smoking Barrels; Snatch*), the Punch Bowl attracts a young and happening crowd sipping cask ales, fine wines and whisky rather than run-of-the-mill pints. The pub retains many of its original 18th-century features (wood panels, cornicing etc), although the dining room at the back definitely has a more modern feel to it.

## ⭐ Entertainment

### 12 Bar · Live Music

Map p72 (www.12barclub.com; Denmark St WC2; admission £7; ⊙7pm-3am Mon-Sat, to 12.30am Sun; ⊖Leicester Sq) Small, intimate, with a rough and ready feel, 12 Bar is one of our favourite live music venues, with anything from solo acts to bands performing nightly. The emphasis is on songwriting and the music is very much indie rock, with anything from folk and jazzy influences to full-on punk and metal sounds.

## Royal Opera House · Opera

Map p72 (www.roh.org.uk; Bow St WC2; ⊖Covent Garden) The £210-million redevelopment for the millennium gave classic opera a fantastic setting, and coming here for a night is a sumptuous prospect. Although the program has been fluffed up by modern influences, the main attractions here are still the classical ballet and opera – all are wonderful productions and feature world-class performers.

Midweek matinees are usually much cheaper than evening performances and restricted-view seats cost as little as £7. There are same-day tickets (one per customer available to the first 67 people in the queue) from 10am for £8 to £40. Half-price stand-by tickets are only occasionally available.

## Comedy Store · Comedy

Map p66 (www.thecomedystore.co.uk; Haymarket House, 1a Oxendon St SW1; ⊖Piccadilly Circus) This was one of the first (and is still one of the best) comedy clubs in London. Although it's a bit like conveyor-belt comedy, it gets some of the biggest names. Tickets are generally around £20.

## Pizza Express Jazz Club · Jazz

Map p66 (www.pizzaexpresslive.com; 10 Dean St W1; ⊖Tottenham Court Rd) Believe it or not, this is one of the most consistently popular and good jazz venues in London. It's a bit of a strange arrangement, having a small basement venue beneath the main chain restaurant, but it seems to work well. Admission is £15 to £20.

## Ronnie Scott's · Jazz

Map p66 (www.ronniescotts.co.uk; 47 Frith St W1; ⊖Leicester Sq) Ronnie Scott originally opened his jazz club on Gerrard St in 1959 under a Chinese gambling den. The club moved to its current location six years later and became widely known as Britain's best jazz club. Gigs are nightly and usually last until 2am. Expect to pay between £18 and £40.

## Soho Theatre · Theatre

Map p66 (www.sohotheatre.com; 21 Dean St W1; ⊖Tottenham Court Rd) Soho Theatre has developed a superb reputation for showcasing new writing talent and quality comedy. It's also hosted some top-notch stand-up or sketch-based comedians; US acts (such as Louis CK and Kirsten Schaal) frequently come here to perform. Tickets cost around £10 to £20.

## Place · Dance

Map p62 (www.theplace.org.uk; 17 Duke's Rd WC1; ⊖Euston Sq) One of the most exciting modern dance venues, the Place was the birthplace of modern British dance. It concentrates on challenging, contemporary and experimental choreography. Tickets cost from £5 to £15.

## Wigmore Hall · Classical Music

Map p84 (www.wigmore-hall.org.uk; 36 Wigmore St W1; ⊖Bond St) This is one of the best concert venues in town, not only because of its fantastic acoustics, beautiful art nouveau hall and great variety of concerts and recitals, but also because of the sheer standard of the performances.

## London Coliseum · Opera

Map p72 (www.eno.org; Coliseum, St Martin's Lane WC2; ⊖Leicester Sq or Charing Cross) The Coliseum is home to the English National Opera (ENO), celebrated for making opera modern and relevant; all operas here are sung in English. The English National Ballet also does regular performances at the Coliseum.

# 🔒 Shopping

The West End's shopping seldom needs introducing. Oxford St is heaven or hell, depending on what you're after; it's all about chains, from Marks & Spencer to H&M, TopShop to Gap. Covent Garden is also beset with high-street outlets but they tend to be smaller and counterbalanced by independent boutiques, vintage in particular. As well as fashion, the West End is big on music. There are some great independent record shops, especially in Soho.

ADINA TOVY AMSEL/LONELY PLANET IMAGES ©

# Westminster & St James's

### Penhaligon's — Accessories

Map p78 (www.penhaligons.com; 16-17 Burlington Arcade W1; ⊖Piccadilly or Green Park) Most people's perfume buying experience nowadays is limited to picking up their favourite scent at the airport duty-free. Penhaligon's is the antidote to such an anonymous and soulless process: here, attendants will ask you about your favourite smells, take you on a little exploratory tour of their signature range and help you discover new scents. All products are made in Devon, England.

### Fortnum & Mason — Food

Map p78 (www.fortnumandmason.co.uk; 181 Piccadilly W1; ⊖Piccadilly Circus) London's oldest grocery store celebrated its 300th birthday in 2007 by not yielding to modern times (its staff are still dressed in old-fashioned tailcoats) and keeping its glam food hall supplied with its famed food hampers, cut marmalade, speciality teas and so on.

### DR Harris — Beauty

Map p78 (www.drharris.co.uk; 29 St James's St SW1; ⊙closed Sun; ⊖Green Park) Operating as chemist and perfumer since 1790 and the Prince of Wales's royal pharmacist, come here for your moustache wax and pick up a bottle of DR Harris Crystal Eye Drops to combat the red eyes after a late night.

# Bloomsbury & Fitzrovia

### Bang Bang Exchange — Vintage

Map p62 (www.myspace.com/bangbangexchange; 21 Goodge St W1; ⊖Goodge St) Got some designer pieces you're tired of? Bang Bang exchanges, buys and sells vintage pieces, proving the saying 'One girl's faded Prada dress is another girl's top new wardrobe piece'.

### James Smith & Sons — Accessories

Map p72 (www.james-smith.co.uk; 53 New Oxford St WC1; ⊙closed Sun; ⊖Tottenham Court Rd) 'Outside every silver lining is a big black cloud', claim the cheerful owners of this quintessential English shop. Nobody makes and stocks such elegant umbrellas, walking sticks and canes as this traditional place and, thanks to bad English weather, they'll hopefully do great business for years to come.

# Soho & Chinatown

### Joy
Fashion

Map p66 (www.joythestore.com; 162-170 Wardour St W1; ⊖ Oxford Circus or Tottenham Court Rd) Joy is an artistic blend of high street and vintage: there are excellent clothes, from silk dresses for women, fabulous shirts for men and timeless T-shirts for both, to funky gadgets such as a floating radio duck and dollar- and euro-shaped ice-cube trays. Conventional shoppers abstain!

### TopShop & Topman
Fashion

Map p66 (www.topshop.co.uk; 36-38 Great Castle St W1; ⊖ Oxford Circus) TopShop is the 'It'-store when it comes to high-street shopping. Encapsulating London's supreme skill at bringing catwalk fashion to the youth market affordably and quickly, it constantly innovates by working with young designers and celebrities.

### Urban Outfitters
Fashion

Map p66 (www.urbanoutfitters.co.uk; 200 Oxford St W1; ⊖ Oxford Circus) Probably the trendiest of all chains, this cool American store serves both men and women and has the best young designer T-shirts, an excellent designer area (stocking Paul & Joe Sister, Vivienne Westwood's Red Label, Hussain Chalayan and See by Chloé, among others), 'renewed' secondhand pieces, saucy underwear, silly homewares and quirky gadgets.

### Hamleys
Toys

Map p66 (www.hamleys.com; 188-196 Regent St W1; ⊖ Oxford Circus) Reportedly the largest toy store in the world and certainly the most famous, Hamleys is a layer cake of playthings. Computer games are in the basement and the latest playground trends are at ground level. But that's just the start.

### Liberty
Department Store

Map p66 (www.liberty.co.uk; Great Marlborough St W1; ⊖ Oxford Circus) An irresistible blend of contemporary styles in an old-fashioned mock-Tudor atmosphere, Liberty has a huge cosmetics department and an accessories floor, along with a breathtaking lingerie section, all at very inflated prices.

### Sister Ray
Music

Map p66 (www.sisterray.co.uk; 34-35 Berwick St W1; ⊖ Oxford Circus or Tottenham Court Rd) If you were a fan of the late, great John Peel on the BBC/BBC World Service, this specialist in innovative, experimental and indie music is just right for you.

# Covent Garden & Leicester Square

### Urban Outfitters
Fashion

Map p72; (www.urbanoutfitters.co.uk; 42-56 Earlham St WC2; ⊖ Covent Garden) Another great outlet of this ubertrendy chain.

Liberty

# Bookworm Paradise: the West End's Best Bookshops

**Daunt Books** (Map p84; www.dauntbooks.co.uk; 83-84 Marylebone High St W1; ⊖Baker St) An original Edwardian bookshop, with oak panels and gorgeous skylights, Daunt is one of London's loveliest travel bookshops.

**Foyle's** (Map p66; www.foyles.co.uk; 113-119 Charing Cross Rd WC2; ⊖Tottenham Court Rd) This is London's most legendary bookshop, where you can bet on finding even the most obscure of titles.

**Stanford's** (Map p72; www.stanfords.co.uk; 12-14 Long Acre WC2; ⊖Leicester Sq or Covent Garden) As a 150-year-old seller of maps, guides and literature, the grand-daddy of travel bookshops is a destination in its own right.

**Waterstone's** (Map p66; www.waterstones.com; 203-206 Piccadilly W1; ⊖Piccadilly Circus) The chain's megastore is the largest bookshop in Europe, boasting knowledgeable staff and regular author readings and signings. The store spreads across four floors, and there is a cafe in the basement and a fabulous rooftop bar-restaurant, **5th View** (p80).

## Neal's Yard Dairy                    Food
Map p72 (www.nealsyarddairy.co.uk; 17 Shorts Gardens WC2; ⊙closed Sun; ⊖Covent Garden) A fabulous, smelly cheese house that would be at home in rural England, this place is proof that the British can do just as well as the French when it comes to big rolls of ripe cheese. There are more than 70 varieties that the shopkeepers will let you taste, including independent farmhouse brands.

## Ted Baker                          Fashion
Map p72 (www.tedbaker.com; 9-10 Floral St WC2; ⊖Covent Garden) The one-time Glaswegian tailoring shop has grown into a superb brand of clothing with elegant men- and womenswear.

# Mayfair
## Sting                              Fashion
Map p66 (www.thesting.nl; 1 Piccadilly Circus W1; ⊙10am-10pm Mon-Sat, noon-6pm Sun; ⊖Piccadilly Circus) The new kid on the fashion block, the Sting is a 'network of brands': most of the clothes it stocks are European labels that are little known in the UK. Spread over three floors, you'll find anything from casual sweatpants and fluoro T-shirts to elegant dresses, frilly tops and handsome shirts.

## Selfridges                    Department Store
Map p84 (www.selfridges.com; 400 Oxford St W1; ⊖Bond St) Selfridges loves innovation – it's famed for its inventive window displays by international artists, gala shows and, above all, its amazing range of products.

# The City

**The City's ancient, hallowed streets are among London's most fascinating.** The Square Mile occupies pretty much exactly the same patch of land around which the Romans first flung up a defensive wall almost two millennia ago, and probably contains more history within it than the rest of London combined.

The tiny backstreets and ancient churches are today juxtaposed with skyscrapers, office blocks and headline-making financial institutions. Very few people live here and so, while Monday to Friday it is very animated, the frantic industry and hum stops at the weekend, when you can hear a pin drop (most places shut tight till Monday). Things also go quiet on weeknights after 9pm, as workers head outwards and home.

Don't miss the standout sights, including St Paul's Cathedral, the Gherkin, the Monument and London's ultimate sight – the Tower of London. All of the big-hitting sights are open at least one weekend day.

Tower Bridge (p104)

# City Highlights

## Tower of London (p98)

Of cardinal importance to London as a historic town and a magnificent counterpoint to the modern architecture rising above the City, the Tower of London is crucial to an understanding of this ancient metropolis. The tower's most famous residents are the marvellously attired Yeoman Warders ('beefeaters') and the ravens whose wings are clipped to prevent them from flying the coop.

## 30 St Mary Axe (p108)

London has never strived for absolute altitude in its towers, instead aiming for modest height achieved with innovation and imagination. As much an icon of London as St Paul's Cathedral or Big Ben, the Norman Foster–designed 'Gherkin' sums up the city's fusion of style and originality. It's sadly inaccessible to visitors, but it makes for some excellent photos.

## Tower Bridge (p104)

This London icon is a masterpiece of Victorian engineering and a sight you're unlikely to miss if you spend any time around the City of London. Some of the best views of Tower Bridge can be had from the embankment in front of the Tower of London. If you can, try to catch the bridge when it rises dramatically to allow large boats through.

## Historic City Pubs (p115)

Whetting your whistle in a London pub is essential to catch Londoners in their element, and where better than a pub with lashings of history? Some of London's most venerable pubs are found in the City, including the hoary Ye Olde Cheshire Cheese (p116) – where a pub has stood since the 16th century, although this one was rebuilt soon after the Great Fire – and the adorably distinctive Black Friar (p115).

## St Paul's Cathedral (p102)

This astonishing church is known to all, but a visit to its hallowed ground must be made to fully appreciate its sublime architecture. The key experience is the climb up into the dome, rewarded with some truly majestic all-around views of London, but the rest of the cathedral is equally rewarding, on all levels. Try to tie in your visit with a meal at the cathedral's restaurant, atmospherically located in the crypt.

# City Walk

*Beginning at Chancery Lane tube station, this saunter through the ancient heart of the City can take under two hours or fill an entire day, depending on how long you spend at each sight. You'll end up at iconic Tower Bridge.*

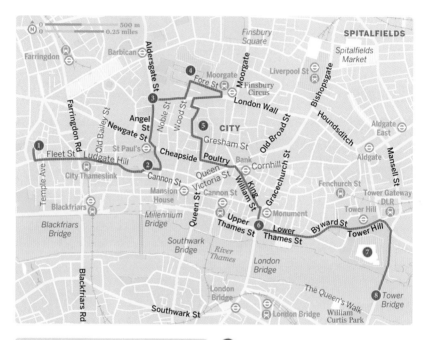

## WALK FACTS

- **Start** Chancery Lane tube station
- **Finish** Tower Bridge
- **Distance** 3 miles
- **Duration** Two hours

## 1 Dr Johnson's House

Find your way to this miraculously well-preserved **early-18th-century mansion** (p112) in the heart of the City and explore the story of Dr Johnson's amazing life, perhaps even dropping by his local, **Ye Olde Cheshire Cheese** (p116) on Fleet St.

## 2 St Paul's Cathedral

Wren's beautiful domed masterpiece, this **cathedral** (p102) somehow eluded Luftwaffe bombs during the Blitz and is one of the London skyline's best-loved features. Join the crowds to see the dazzling interior, intriguing crypt, whispering gallery and breathtaking views over the capital from the cupola.

## 3 Museum of London

This wonderful **museum** (p105) may not look like much from the outside, but it's one of the city's best, totally devoted to documenting the multifaceted history of the capital through its many stages of development from Saxon village to three-time Olympic city.

### ④ Barbican

Built on the site of an old Roman watchtower (hence its name), the modern **Barbican** (p111) is the City's fabulous arts centre and Brutalist masterpiece – check out the **greenhouse**, the **lakes** and Shakespeare's parish Church, **St Giles' Cripplegate**.

### ⑤ Guildhall

Once the very heart of the City, the seat of power and influence, the **Guildhall** (p110) is today home to the Corporation of London. See the excellent **Guildhall Art Gallery** (p110) and go back in time two millennia to see the remains of London's **Roman Amphitheatre** (p110).

### ⑥ Monument

This historic **column** (p105) commemorates the Great Fire of London, and – while not for those suffering vertigo – is a superb way to see the City up close. Despite the number of high-rises all around, the Monument still feels high altitude, giving you an idea of how massive it would have looked in the 17th century.

### ⑦ Tower of London

The sheer amount of history within the huge stone walls of the **Tower of London** (p98) is hard to fathom. The **White Tower**, the **Crown Jewels**, the **Yeoman Warders** and **Traitor's Gate** are all fascinating, and the Tower of London deserves at least a half-day's visit at the end of the walk.

### ⑧ Tower Bridge

A symbol of London since the day it was built, **Tower Bridge** (p104) is a must-see. A walk across it (and a visit to the interesting exhibition, from which the views are spectacular) is crucial to appreciate old Father Thames at its widest and most spectacular.

### ✦ The Best...

#### PLACES TO EAT

**Sweeting's** The place for seafood in the City, with real pedigree. (p114)

**Café Below** Great spot with oodles of atmosphere in the crypt of St Mary-le-Bow. (p114)

**Restaurant at St Paul's** Fine Modern British fare in a classic setting. (p114)

**City Càphê** Winning Vietnamese flavours; eat in or take out. (p114)

#### PLACES TO DRINK

**Vertigo 42** Plump for a day with clear skies and settle down for the bravura performance of sunset. (p115)

**Black Friar** Fine pub with distinctive, much-loved interior and bags of character. (p115)

**Volupté** Burlesque, vaudeville, cabaret, live tunes and more. (p116)

#### CHURCHES

**St Bartholomew-the-Great** Authentic Norman remains and an age-old sense of tranquillity. (p112)

**St Stephen Walbrook** Seventeenth-century Wren masterpiece in the City. (p109)

**All Hallows-by-the-Tower** Church with a Saxon crypt and intriguing fragments from the Roman era. (p107)

St Stephen Walbrook
TIM GARTSIDE LONDON/ALAMY ©

Don't Miss

# Tower of London

The absolute heart of London, with a history as bleak and bloody as it is fascinating, the Tower of London should be very near the top of anyone's list of London's sights. Begun during the reign of William the Conqueror (1066–87), the Tower is in fact a castle, and has served over the years as a palace, observatory, storehouse and mint. But it is, of course, most famous for its grizzly past as a prison and site of execution.

Map p106

www.hrp.org.uk

Tower Hill EC3

adult/child £19.80/10.45

9am-5.30pm Tue-Sat, 10am-5.30pm Sun & Mon, closes 4.30pm daily Nov-Feb

Tower Hill

# Chapel Royal of St Peter ad Vincula

The culmination of your tour will leave you at the Chapel Royal of St Peter ad Vincula (St Peter in Chains), a rare example of ecclesiastical Tudor architecture and the burial place of those beheaded on the scaffold outside, most notably Anne Boleyn, Catherine Howard and Lady Jane Grey.

# Tower Green Scaffold Site

Those 'lucky' enough to meet their fate here (rather than suffering the embarrassment of execution on Tower Hill) include the alleged adulterers Anne Boleyn and Catherine Howard; the latter's lady-in-waiting, Jane Rochford; Margaret Pole, countess of Salisbury, descended from the House of York; 16-year-old Lady Jane Grey, who fell foul of Henry VIII's daughter Mary I by being her rival for the throne; William, Lord Hastings; and Robert Devereux, Earl of Essex, once a favourite of Elizabeth I.

# Crown Jewels

To the east of the chapel and north of the White Tower is the building that visitors most want to see: **Waterloo Barracks**, the home of the Crown Jewels. A travelator takes you past the dozen or so crowns that are the centrepiece, including the £27.5-million Imperial State Crown, set with diamonds (2868 of them, to be exact), sapphires, emeralds, rubies and pearls, and the platinum crown of the late Queen Mother, Elizabeth, which is famously set with the 105-carat Koh-i-Noor (Mountain of Light) diamond.

# St John's Chapel

This chapel, dating from 1080, with its vaulted ceiling, rounded archways and 12 stone pillars, is actually one of the finest examples of Romanesque architecture in the country.

## 1 A TOWER TOUR

To understand the Tower and its history, a guided tour with one of the Yeomen Warders is essential. Few people appreciate that the Tower is actually our home as well as our place of work; all the Warders live inside the outer walls. The Tower is rather like a miniature village – visitors are often rather surprised to see our washing hanging out beside the castle walls!

## 2 CROWN JEWELS

Visitors often think the Crown Jewels are the Queen's personal jewellery collection. They're not, of course; the Crown Jewels are actually the ceremonial regalia used during the Coronation. The highlights are the Sceptre and the Imperial State Crown, which contains the celebrated diamond known as the Star of Africa. People are often surprised to hear that the Crown Jewels aren't insured (as they could never be replaced).

## 3 WHITE TOWER

The White Tower is the original royal palace of the Tower of London, but it hasn't been used as a royal residence since 1603. It's the most iconic building in the complex – inside you can see exhibits from the Royal Armouries collection, including a suit of armour belonging to Henry VIII.

## 4 RAVENS

A Tower legend states that if its resident ravens ever left, the monarchy would topple – a royal decree states that we must keep a minimum of six ravens at any time. We currently have seven ravens, looked after by the Ravenmaster and his three assistants.

## 5 CEREMONY OF THE KEYS

We hold three daily ceremonies: the 9am Official Opening, the Ceremony of the Word at 3pm (when the day's password is issued), and the 10pm Ceremony of the Keys, when the gates are locked after the castle has closed; visitors may attend the latter, but must apply to the Tower in writing.

# Tackling the Tower of London

Although it's usually less busy in the late afternoon, don't leave your assault on the Tower until too late in the day. You could easily spend hours here and not see it all. Start by getting your bearings with the hour-long Yeoman Warder (Beefeater) tours; they are included in the cost of admission, entertaining and the only way to access the **Chapel Royal of St Peter ad Vincula** ❶, which is where they finish up.

When you leave the chapel, the **Tower Green scaffold site** ❷ is directly in front. The building immediately to your left is Waterloo Barracks, where the **Crown Jewels** ❸ are housed. These are the absolute highlight of a Tower visit, so keep an eye on the entrance and pick a time to visit when it looks relatively quiet. Once inside, take things at your own pace. Slow-moving travelators shunt you past the dozen or so crowns that are the treasury's centrepiece, but feel free to double-back for a second or even third pass – particularly if you ended up on the rear travelator the first time around. Allow plenty of time for the **White Tower** ❹, the core of the whole complex, starting with the exhibition of royal armour. As you continue onto the 2nd floor, keep an eye out for **St John's Chapel** ❺. The famous **ravens** ❻ can be seen in the courtyard around the White Tower. Head next through the towers that formed the **Medieval Palace** ❼, then take the **East Wall Walk** ❽ to get a feel for the castle's mighty battlements. Spend the rest of your time poking around the many, many other fascinating nooks and crannies of the Tower complex.

MIKE BOOTH/ALAMY

### Chapel Royal of St Peter ad Vincula
This chapel serves as the resting place for the royals and other members of the aristocracy who were executed on the small green out front. Several notable identities are buried under the chapel's altar.

### Tower Green scaffold site
Seven people, including three queens (Anne Boleyn, Catherine Howard and Jane Grey), lost their heads here during Tudor times, saving the monarch the embarrassment of public executions on Tower Hill. The site now features a sculpture by Brian Catling.

**Beauchamp Tower**

**Main Entrance**

**Bell Tower**

### White Tower
Much of the White Tower is taken up with this exhibition of 500 years of royal armour. Look for the virtually cuboid suit made to match Henry VIII's bloated body, complete with an oversized armoured pouch to protect his, ahem, crown jewels.

PAWEL LIBERA IMAGES/ALAMY

## St John's Chapel
Kept as plain and unadorned as it would have been in Norman times, the White Tower's 2nd-floor chapel is the oldest surviving church in London, dating from 1080.

## Crown Jewels
When they're not being worn for affairs of state, Her Majesty's bling is kept here. Among the 23,578 gems, look out for the 530-carat Cullinan diamond at the top of the Royal Sceptre, the largest part of what was (until 1985) the largest diamond ever found.

**Bowyer Tower**

**Martin Tower**

**Bloody Tower**

**New Armouries**

**Traitors' Gate**

**Wakefield Tower**

**Salt Tower**

## Medieval Palace
This part of the Tower complex was commenced around 1220 and was home to England's medieval monarchs. Look for the recreations of the bedchamber of Edward I (1272–1307) in St Thomas's Tower and the throne room on the upper floor of the Wakefield Tower.

## Ravens
This stretch of green is where the Tower's famous ravens are kept, fed on raw meat and blood-soaked bird biscuits. According to legend, if the birds were to leave the Tower, the kingdom would fall.

## East Wall Walk
Follow the inner ramparts, starting from the 13th-century Salt Tower, passing through the Broad Arrow and Constable Towers, and ending at the Martin Tower, where the Crown Jewels were once stored.

TOM HANLEY/ALAMY

ENIGMA/ALAMY

# ✓ Don't Miss
# St Paul's Cathedral

Towering over Ludgate Hill, in a superb position that has been a place of worship for over 1400 years, St Paul's Cathedral is one of London's most majestic and recognisable buildings. For Londoners the vast dome, which still manages to dominate the skyline despite the far higher skyscrapers of the Square Mile, is a symbol of resilience and pride, standing tall for over 300 years.

Map p106

www.stpauls.co.uk

St Paul's
Churchyard EC4

adult/child
£14.50/5.50

⊘8.30am-4.30pm
Mon-Sat, last
admission 4pm

# Dome

Consisting of three domes, one inside the other, the dome made the cathedral Wren's tour de force. It's a three-stage journey to the top: through a door on the western side of the southern transept and some 30m above, you reach the interior walkway around the dome's base. This is the **Whispering Gallery**. Climbing even more steps you reach the **Stone Gallery**, an exterior viewing platform rather obscured by pillars. The iron steps to the **Golden Gallery** are steeper and narrower than below but are really worth the effort. From here, 85m above London, you can enjoy superb 360-degree views.

# Interior

Just beneath the dome is a compass and **epitaph** written for Wren by his son: *Lector, si monumentum requiris, circumspice (Reader, if you seek his monument, look around you)*. In the northern aisle you'll find the grandiose **Duke of Wellington Memorial** (1875). In the north transept chapel is Holman Hunt's celebrated painting, *The Light of the World*, which depicts Christ knocking at an overgrown door that can only be opened from the inside. Beyond, in the cathedral's heart, are the particularly spectacular **quire** (or chancel) – its ceilings and arches dazzling with green, blue, red and gold mosaics – and the **high altar.**

# Crypt

On the eastern side of both the north and south transepts are stairs leading down to the crypt and **OBE Chapel**, where services are held for members of the Order of the British Empire. The crypt has memorials to some 300 military demigods, including Florence Nightingale and Lord Kitchener.

**Wren's tomb** is also in the crypt, and architect Edwin Lutyens, painter Joshua Reynolds and poet William Blake are remembered here too. The **Oculus,** opened in 2010 in the former treasury, projects four short films onto its walls (you'll need to have picked up the iPod audiotour to hear the sound).

## Don't Miss

BY MARK MCVAY, ST PAUL'S CATHEDRAL DIRECTOR OF VISITOR SERVICES, MARKETING & PUBLIC RELATIONS

### 1 ARCHITECTURE

St Paul's was designed by Sir Christopher Wren and is one of the first examples of the English Baroque style of architecture, crowned with a magnificent dome, the third largest in Europe. The exterior and interior are ornately carved with the most wonderful swags of fruit and flowers and cherubs.

### 2 INTERIOR

The magnificent interior is flooded with light and is decorated with statues commemorating famous British people; the dome is painted with scenes from the life of St Paul while the quire is decorated in mosaics with scenes from the creation. Through all this richness there is a wonderful sense of spirituality as the cathedral is first and foremost a working church.

### 3 UPPER GALLERIES

There are three galleries about the cathedral floor – the first is a climb of 257 steps to the Whispering Gallery, where if you talk into the wall it can be heard on the other side. It also has a view down to the cathedral floor. The second is the Stone Gallery (another 119 steps) and the third is the Golden Gallery (another 152 steps) at the top of the dome where you get wonderful views over London.

### 4 CRYPT

The Crypt is the burial space in the cathedral where many important people are interred. The two large tombs in the central space in the crypt are for Admiral Lord Nelson and the Duke of Wellington – two of the greatest 19th-century military men who fought against Napoleon.

# Discover the City

## 🔀 Getting There & Away

○ **Underground** A veritable tangle of tube lines crosses over in the City and you're never too far away from one of them. Handiest are St Paul's (Central Line) and Bank (Central, Northern, DLR and Waterloo & City), but Blackfriars (Circle and District), Barbican (Circle, Metropolitan and Hammersmith & City) and Tower Hill (Circle & District) are all useful for the further-flung sights.

○ **Bus** For a west-to-east sweep from Oxford Circus through St Paul's, Bank and Liverpool St, hop on the 8; and from Piccadilly Circus via Fleet St and the Tower, the 15. The 11 sets off from Liverpool St and passes Bank and Mansion House on its way to Chelsea. The 26 follows the same route through the City but branches off for Waterloo.

Trinity Square Gardens and the Tower of London (p98)
NOBLEIMAGES/ALAMY ©

## ⊙ Sights

**Tower of London**  Historical Building
See p98.

**St Paul's Cathedral**  Church
See p102.

**Tower Bridge**  Bridge
Map p106 (Bridge lift times ☎ 7940 3984 or check web; www.towerbridge.org.uk; Tower Bridge Rd SE1; adult/child £8/3.40; ⊙10am-6.30pm Apr-Oct, 9.30am-6pm Nov-Mar, last admission 1hr before closing; ⊖ Tower Hill) Perhaps second only to Big Ben as London's most recognisable symbol, Tower Bridge doesn't disappoint up close. Built in 1894 as a much-needed crossing point in the east, it was equipped with a then revolutionary bascule (see-saw) mechanism that could clear the way for oncoming ships in three minutes. Although London's days as a thriving port are long over, the bridge still does its stuff, lifting around 1000 times a year and as often as 10 times a day in summer.

Housed within is the **Tower Bridge Exhibition,** which explains the nuts and bolts of it all. If you're not technically minded, it's still fascinating to get inside the bridge and look along the Thames from its two walkways. A lift takes you to the top of the structure, 42m above the river, from where you can walk along the east- and west-facing walkways, lined with information boards. There are a couple of stops on the way down before you exit and continue on to the Engine Rooms, which provide the real mechanical detail, and also house a few interactive exhibits and a couple of short films.

Citizens

DOUG MCKINLAY/LONELY PLANET IMAGES ©

## Museum of London    Museum

Map p106 (www.museumoflondon.org.uk;
London Wall EC2; admission free; ⊙10am-6pm;
⊖Barbican or St Paul's) One of the capital's
best museums, this is a fascinating walk
through the various incarnations of the
city from Anglo-Saxon village to 21st-
century metropolis. The first gallery,
London Before London, brings to life the
ancient settlements that pre-dated the
capital and is followed by the Roman era,
full of interesting displays and models.
The rest of the floor takes you through the
Saxon, medieval, Tudor and Stuart periods, culminating in the Great Fire of 1666.
From here head down to the modern galleries, opened in 2010, where, in Expanding City, you'll find exquisite fashion and
jewellery, the graffitied walls of a prison
cell (1750) and the *Rhinebeck Panorama*,
a detailed watercolour of London in the
early 1800s. After a quick spin through
the Pleasure Gardens, you emerge onto a
glorious re-creation of a Victorian street.
Highlights of the galleries leading up to the
present day include a 1908 taxi cab, an art
deco lift from Selfridges and an interactive
water pump that makes clear the perils of
the once insanitary water system. There's
also a great shop and two cafes.

## Monument    Landmark

Map p106 (www.themonument.info; Monument St EC3; adult/child £3/1.50; ⊙9.30am-
5.30pm, last admission 5pm; ⊖Monument) Sir
Christopher Wren and Dr Robert Hooke's
huge 1677 column, known simply as the
Monument, is a memorial to the Great
Fire of London of 1666, whose impact on
London's history cannot be overstated.
Tens of thousands of Londoners were
left homeless and much of the city was
destroyed.

An immense Doric column made of
Portland stone, it is 4.5m wide, and 60.6m
tall – the exact distance it stands from
the bakery in Pudding Lane where the fire
reputedly started – and is topped with a
gilded bronze urn of flames that some call
a big gold pincushion. Although a midget
by today's standards, the Monument
would have been gigantic, and towered
over London, when first built.

Climbing up the column's 311 steps,
which wind round an impressive circular
staircase, rewards you with some of the
best 360-degree views over London (due
to its centrality as much as to its height).
And after your descent, you'll also be
the proud owner of a certificate that
commemorates your achievement.

THE CITY SIGHTS

The City

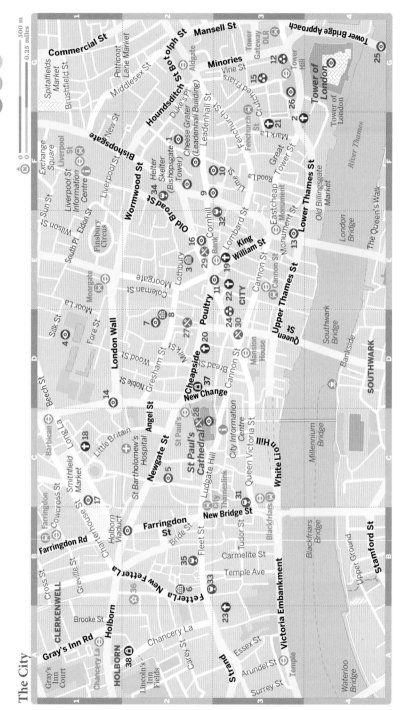

# The City

## ◉ Top Sights

## ◉ Sights

## ◎ Eating

## ◎ Drinking & Nightlife

## ◎ Entertainment

## ◎ Shopping

### FREE All Hallows-by-the-Tower
Church

Map p106 (www.ahbtt.org.uk; Byward St EC3; ☉8am-6pm Mon-Fri, 10am-5pm Sat & Sun; ⊖Tower Hill) A church by the name All Hallows (meaning 'All Saints') has stood on this site since AD 675, and the best bit of the building today is undoubtedly its atmospheric Saxon undercroft (crypt). There you'll find a pavement of reused Roman tiles and walls of the 7th-century Saxon church, as well as coins and bits of local history. Above ground it's a pleasant enough church, rebuilt after WWII. There's a copper spire (added in 1957 to make the church stand out more), a pulpit from a Wren church in Cannon St that was destroyed in WWII and a beautiful 17th-century font cover by the master woodcarver Grinling Gibbons. From April to September, free 20-minute church tours leave at 2pm each day.

### Trinity Square Gardens
Gardens

Map p106 (⊖Tower Hill) Trinity Square Gardens, just to the west of Tower Hill tube station, was once the site of the Tower Hill scaffold where many met their fate, the last in 1747. Now it's a much more peaceful place and home to Edwin Lutyens' memorial to the marines and merchant sailors who lost their lives during WWI. Just outside Tower Hill tube station, a giant bronze **sundial** depicts the history of London from AD 43 to 1982, and on a grassy area next to the tube's main exit there's a stretch of the **medieval wall** built on Roman foundations, with a modern statue of Emperor Trajan (r AD 98–117) in front of it. At the other end of the tunnel, to the right, is a postern (gate) dating from the 13th century. See more of the **roman wall** around the corner from the tube station, in the forecourt of the **Grange Hotel** (8-14 Cooper's Row), where there's also an information board.

WIBOWO RUSLI/LONELY PLANET IMAGES ©

### St Olave · Church

Map p106 (www.sanctuaryinthecity.net; 8 Hart St EC3; ⏰9am-5pm Mon-Fri, closed Aug; ⊖Tower Hill) Tucked at the end of quiet Seething Lane, St Olave's was built in the mid-15th century, and restored in the 1950s. Most famous of those who worshipped at the church is Samuel Pepys, who is buried here with his wife Elizabeth.

### 30 St Mary Axe (Gherkin) · Building

Map p106 (www.30stmaryaxe.co.uk; 30 St Mary Axe EC3; ⊖Aldgate or Bank) Known to one and all as 'the Gherkin' (for obvious reasons when you see its incredible shape), 30 St Mary Axe – as it is officially and far more prosaically named – remains London's most distinctive skyscraper, dominating the city despite actually being slightly smaller than the neighbouring NatWest Tower.

Built in 2002–03 to a multi-award-winning design by Norman Foster, this is London's first ecofriendly skyscraper: Foster laid out the offices so they spiral around internal 'sky gardens'. The windows can be opened and the gardens are used to reprocess stale air, so air-conditioning is kept to a minimum. You'll

have to take our word for it, though, as there's unfortunately no access to the public.

### Lloyd's of London · Building

Map p106 (www.lloyds.com; 1 Lime St EC3; ⊖Aldgate or Bank) While the world's leading insurance brokers are inside underwriting everything from cosmonauts' lives to film stars' legs, people outside still stop to gawp at the stainless-steel external ducting and staircases of the Lloyd's of London building. The work of Richard Rogers, one of the architects of the Pompidou Centre in Paris, its brave-new-world postmodernism strikes a particular contrast with the olde-worlde Leadenhall Market next door. While you can watch people whizzing up and down the outside of the building in its all-glass lifts, sadly you can't experience it yourself.

### Leadenhall Market · Market

Map p106 (www.leadenhallmarket.co.uk; Whittington Ave EC3; ⏰public areas 24hr, shop hours vary; ⊖Bank) Like stepping into a small slice of Victorian London, a visit to this covered mall off Gracechurch St is a minor time-travelling experience. There's been a market on this site since the Roman era, but the surviving architecture is all cobblestones and late-19th-century ironwork; even modern restaurants and chain stores decorate their facades in period style here. The market appears as Diagon Alley in *Harry Potter and the Philosopher's Stone*.

### FREE Bank of England Museum
*Museum*

Map p106 (www.bankofengland.co.uk; Bartholomew Lane EC2; ⏰10am-5pm Mon-Fri; ⊖Bank) Sir John Soane built the original structure, although unfortunately most of his splendid bank was demolished in the early 20th century and replaced with a more utilitarian model. The centrepiece of the museum – which explores the evolution of money and the history of this venerable institution, and is not *nearly* as dull as it sounds – is a reconstruction of Soane's original stock office, complete with original mahogany counters.

### Royal Exchange
*Historic Building*

Map p106 (www.theroyalexchange.com; cnr Threadneedle St & Cornhill EC3; ⏰10am-11pm Mon-Fri; ⊖Bank) Founded by Thomas Gresham, this imposing, colonnaded building was the third built on a site originally chosen in 1564 by Gresham. It hasn't functioned as a financial institution since the 1980s and now houses a posh shopping centre and a cafe (Royal Exchange Grand Café & Bar; p115) and restaurant (Sauterelle; p115).

### Mansion House
*Historic Building*

Map p106 (www.cityoflondon.gov.uk; guided tour adult/concession £6/4; ⏰tour 2pm Tue; ⊖Bank) Between King William St and Walbrook stands the grand, porticoed Mansion House, the official residence of the Lord Mayor of London, which was built in the mid-18th century by George Dance the Elder. It's not open to the public except on the weekly tour, which leaves from the porch entrance on Walbrook, with a maximum of 40 participants; tickets are sold on a first-come-first-served basis. Inside there are magnificent interiors, an impressive art collection and a stunning banqueting hall.

### St Stephen Walbrook
*Church*

Map p106 (www.ststephenwalbrook.net; 39 Walbrook EC4; ⏰10am-4pm Mon-Fri; ⊖Bank) Along Walbrook, past the City of London Magistrates Court, is St Stephen Walbrook, built in 1672. Widely considered to be the finest of Wren's City churches and a forerunner to St Paul's Cathedral, this light and airy building is indisputably impressive.

### St Mary Woolnoth
*Church*

Map p106 (⏰9.30am-4.30pm Mon-Fri; ⊖Bank) In the angle between Lombard and King William Sts, Nicholas Hawksmoor's St Mary Woolnoth is recognisable by its distinctive twin towers. Completed in 1727, it is the architect's only City church and its interior Corinthian columns are a foretaste of his Christ Church in Spitalfields.

## Temple of Mithras

A short way along Queen Victoria St, on the left, you'll find the remains of the 3rd-century AD **Temple of Mithras** (Map p106; Queen Victoria St; ⊖Bank). This potentially fascinating site was uncovered in the 1950s during the construction of Bucklersbury House, an office block on Walbrook St. The entire site was moved to its current location shortly afterwards for display. There's not a lot to see but if you're interested in this Persian god, artefacts found in the temple are on display at the Museum of London (p105). At the time of writing, the creation of Walbrook Square, an office and retail development, was underway, within which the remains are set to be displayed on their original site.

**FREE** **St Mary-le-Bow** Church

Map p106 (www.stmarylebow.co.uk; Cheapside EC2; ☺7.30am-6pm Mon-Wed, to 6.30pm Thu, to 4pm Fri; ⊖Bank or St Paul's) Another of Wren's great churches, St Mary-le-Bow was built in 1673. It's famous as the church with the bells that dictate who is – and who isn't – a cockney; it's said that a true cockney has to have been born within earshot of Bow Bells, although before the advent of motor traffic this would have been a far greater area than it is today.

**FREE** **Guildhall** Historic Building

Map p106 (www.cityoflondon.gov.uk; Gresham St EC2; ☺9am-5pm unless closed for events, closed Sun Oct-Apr; ⊖Bank or St Paul's) Bang in the centre of the Square Mile, the Guildhall has been the City's seat of government for nearly 800 years. The present building dates from the early 15th century, making it the only secular stone structure to have survived the Great Fire of 1666, although it was severely damaged both then and during the Blitz of 1940.

Check in at reception to visit the impressive **Great Hall** (ring ahead as it often closes for formal functions), where you can see the banners and shields of London's 12 guilds (principal livery companies), which used to wield absolute power throughout the city. Among the monuments to look out for are statues of Winston Churchill, Admiral Nelson, the Duke of Wellington and the two prime ministers Pitt the Elder and Younger.

**FREE** **Guildhall Art Gallery & Roman London Amphitheatre** Gallery

Map p106 (www.guildhall-art-gallery.org.uk; Guildhall Yard EC2; charge for temporary exhibits; ☺10am-5pm Mon-Sat, noon-4pm Sun; ⊖Bank) The gallery of the City of London provides a fascinating look at the politics of the Square Mile over the past few centuries, with a great collection of paintings of London in the 18th and 19th centuries, as well as the vast frieze entitled *The*

**Left:** Guildhall;
**Below:** Tim Crawley's bust of Sir Christopher Wren, Guildhall Art Gallery

*Defeat of the Floating Batteries* (1791), depicting the British victory at the Siege of Gibraltar in 1782.

The real highlight of the museum is deep in the darkened basement, where the archaeological remains of Roman London's amphitheatre (coliseum) lie. While only a few remnants of the stone walls lining the eastern entrance still stand, they're imaginatively fleshed out with a black-and-fluorescent-green *trompe l'oeil* of the missing seating, and computer-meshed outlines of spectators and gladiators. Markings on the square outside the Guildhall indicate the original extent of the amphitheatre, allowing people to visualise its scale.

## Barbican
Historic Building

Map p106 (www.barbican.org.uk; Silk St EC2; ⊙arts centre 9am-11pm Mon-Sat, noon-11pm Sun; 🛜; ⊖Barbican or Moorgate) Londoners remain fairly divided about the architectural legacy of this vast housing and cultural complex in the heart of the City. While the Barbican is named after a Roman fortification that may once have stood here protecting ancient Londinium, what you see today is very much a product of the 1960s and '70s. Yet, although it has topped several polls as London's ugliest building, many Londoners see something very beautiful about its cohesion and ambition – incorporating Shakespeare's local church, **St Giles Cripplegate**, into its brave-new-world design and embellishing its public areas with lakes and ponds. Guided **architectural tours** (£8; ⊙Wed, Thu, Sat & Sun, check web for times) are fascinating and the best way to make sense of the purpose and beauty of the estate.

The Barbican is still London's pre-eminent cultural centre (see p116), boasting the Barbican Hall, two theatres, a cinema, and two well-regarded art galleries, the **Barbican Gallery** (⊙11am-8pm Fri-Tue, to 6pm Wed, to 10pm Thu), and the

**Curve** (🕐11am-8pm Fri-Wed, to 10pm Thu). It also has three restaurants, including the highly recommended canteen-style **Barbican Foodhall** (🕐9am-8.30pm Mon-Sat, 11am-8pm Sun), offering a tempting array of freshly made sandwiches, cakes and pastries, daily changing hot meals and plenty of seating inside and on its lakeside terrace.

### St Bartholomew-the-Great   Church

Map p106 (www.greatstbarts.com; West Smithfield EC1; adult/concession £4/3.50; 🕐8.30am-5pm Mon-Fri, 10.30am-4pm Sat & 8.30am-8pm Sun; ⊖Farringdon or Barbican) This spectacular Norman church dates from 1123. It was originally a part of the monastery of Augustinian Canons, but became the parish church of Smithfield in 1539 when King Henry VIII dissolved the monasteries. The cloisters house a lovely little **cafe** (🕐10am-4pm Mon-Fri, 9.30am-1.30pm & 5.15-6.30pm Sun).

### Smithfield Market   Market

Map p106 (www.smithfieldmarket.com; West Smithfield EC1; 🕐3am-noon Mon-Fri; ⊖Far-ringdon) Smithfield is central London's last surviving meat market. Built on the site of the notorious St Bartholomew's fair, where witches were traditionally burned at the stake, this is where Scottish independence leader William Wallace was executed in 1305 (there's a large plaque on the wall of St Bart's Hospital south of the market), as well as the place where the leader of the Peasants' Revolt, Wat Tyler, met his end in 1381. Described in terms of pure horror by Dickens in *Oliver Twist*, this was once the armpit of London, where animal excrement and entrails created a sea of filth. Today it's a very smart annexe of Clerkenwell and full of bars and restaurants, while the market itself is a wonderful building. Visit before 7am to see it in full swing.

### FREE Central Criminal Court (Old Bailey)   Historic Building

Map p106 (www.cityoflondon.gov.uk; cnr Newgate & Old Bailey Sts; 🕐approx 10am-1pm & 2-4pm Mon-Fri; ⊖St Paul's) Just as fact is often better than fiction, taking in a trial at the 'Old Bailey' leaves watching a TV courtroom drama for dust.

Choose from 18 courts, of which the oldest – courts one to four – usually have the most interesting cases. As cameras, video equipment, mobile phones, large bags and food and drink are all forbidden inside, and there are no cloakrooms or lockers, it's important not to take these with you. Take a cardigan or something to cushion the hard seats, though, and if you're interested in a high-profile trial, get there early.

### Dr Johnson's House   Museum

Map p106 (www.drjohnsonshouse.org; 17 Gough Sq EC4; adult/child £4.50/1.50; 🕐11am-5.30pm Mon-Sat

Central Criminal Court (Old Bailey)
ERIC NATHAN/ALAMY ©

# Baffled by the Barbican

Navigating your way around the Barbican can be a source of utter frustration. Built on a bomb site, the architects Chamberlin, Powell and Bon created an estate where the main focus was to look inward, rather than to what was a desolate city beyond its parameters. A structure (sometimes likened to a fortress) built for 4000 inhabitants, the complex was also designed to raise citizens above road level and allow them to move around with ease. Despite this, once inside, the Barbican is notoriously confusing. There are stairs from Barbican tube station that take you up onto the highwalks, from where a yellow line guides you to the arts complex, but if you're just heading straight there, most people opt to walk through the Beech St road tunnel to the recently added Silk St entrance, making the experience a little more straightforward.

May-Sep, to 5pm Mon-Sat Oct-Apr; ⊖Chancery Lane or Blackfriars) This wonderful house, built in 1700, is a rare surviving example of a Georgian city mansion. All around it today huge office blocks loom, and tiny Gough Square can be quite hard to find. The house has been preserved, as it was the home of the great Georgian wit Samuel Johnson, the author of the first serious dictionary of the English language and the man who proclaimed 'When a man is tired of London, he is tired of life'.

The museum doesn't exactly crackle with Dr Johnson's immortal wit, yet it's still an atmospheric and worthy place to visit, with its antique furniture and artefacts from Johnson's life.

### Temple Church — Church
Map p106 (www.templechurch.com; Temple EC4; admission £3; ☺approx 2-4pm Wed-Sun, call or check website; ⊖Temple or Chancery Lane) This magnificent church lies within the walls of the Temple, built by the legendary Knights Templar, an order of crusading monks founded in the 12th century to protect pilgrims travelling to and from Jerusalem. Today the sprawling oasis of fine buildings and pleasant traffic-free green space is home to two Inns of Court (housing the chambers of lawyers practising in the City) and the Middle and the Lesser Temple.

The Temple Church has a distinctive design: the Round (consecrated in 1185 and designed to recall the Church of the Holy Sepulchre in Jerusalem) adjoins the Chancel (built in 1240), which is the heart of the modern church. Both parts were severely damaged by a bomb in 1941 and have been lovingly reconstructed. Its most obvious points of interest are the life-size stone effigies of nine knights that lie on the floor of the Round. In recent years the church has become a must-see for readers of *The Da Vinci Code* because a key scene was set here.

Check opening times in advance as they change frequently. During the week the easiest access to the church is via Inner Temple Lane, off Fleet St. At weekends you'll need to enter from Victoria Embankment.

# 🍴 Eating

**The financial heart of London unsurprisingly caters for a well-heeled crowd and it can be a tough place to find a meal at the weekend, if not on a weekday evening. But neighbouring districts such as Shoreditch, Spitalfields and Clerkenwell offer a good selection of eating options if you get really stuck. During the week, Leadenhall Market stalls offer a delicious array of food, from steaming noodles to mountains of sweet treats (11am to 4pm).**

113

HEMIS/ALAMY ©

### Sweeting's
Seafood ££

Map p106 (www.sweetingsrestaurant.com; 39 Queen Victoria St EC4; mains £13.50-32; ◷lunch Mon-Fri; ⊖Mansion House) Sweeting's is a City institution, having been around since 1830. It hasn't changed much, with its small sit-down dining area, mosaic floor and narrow counters, behind which stand waiters in white aprons. Dishes include sustainably sourced fish of all kinds (grilled, fried or poached), potted shrimps, eels and Sweeting's famous fish pie (£13.50).

### Café Below
Cafe £

Map p106 (www.cafebelow.co.uk; St Mary-le-Bow church, Cheapside EC2; mains £8-12; ◷7.30am-9pm Mon-Fri; ⚲; ⊖Mansion House) This atmospheric cafe and restaurant is in the crypt of one of London's most famous old churches. From breakfast to dinner, the menus here are good value and offer tasty dishes such as fish cakes and steak sandwiches at lunch and fillet of sea bream or courgette filo pie in the evening. The menu includes a better-than-average choice for vegetarians, too.

### Restaurant at St Paul's
Modern British ££

Map p106 (www.restaurantatstpauls.co.uk; St Paul's Cathedral, St Paul's Churchyard EC4; 2/3 courses £21.50/25.95; ◷noon-3pm; ☎; ⊖St Paul's) The quality of the dishes at this restaurant, set in the crypt of St Paul's, does a fair job of living up to the grandeur above. The short and simple menu offers two- or three-course lunches, including such dishes as potted lemon and thyme chicken and pork loin chop with a rarebit glaze. It also does a good-value daily express lunch (£15, including a glass of wine) and afternoon tea (served until 4.30pm Monday to Saturday).

### City Càphê
Vietnamese £

Map p106 (www.citycaphe.com; 17 Ironmonger Lane EC2; dishes £3.85-6.40; ◷11.30am-3pm Mon-Fri; ⊖Bank) Down a quiet little lane off Cheapside, this small cafe attracts queues of City workers for its excellent and good-value Vietnamese street food to eat in or take away. Choose from *pho* (noodle soup), salads or summer rolls, or go for the classic (and very reasonable) *banh mi* (baguettes), which are simply delicious.

### Sauterelle
Modern French £££

Map p106 (☎7618 2483; www.sauterelle-restaurant.co.uk; cnr Threadneedle St & Cornhill EC3; mains £18-31; ☺Mon-Fri; ⊖Bank) Up on the mezzanine level of the ornate Royal Exchange, Sauterelle ('grasshopper' in French) offers distinct yet subtly flavoured fine dining, where beautifully cooked and presented dishes are accompanied by a comprehensive and well-chosen wine list. The setting is particularly romantic, with views to the covered courtyard below. Set menus (two/three courses £20/23.50) are good value.

### Royal Exchange Grand Café & Bar
Modern European ££

Map p106 (www.danddlondon.com; cnr Threadneedle St & Cornhill EC3; mains £12-16.50; ☺8am-11pm Mon-Fri; ⊖Bank) This cafe is located in the middle of the covered courtyard of the beautiful Royal Exchange building. The menu here runs the gamut from breakfast, salads and sandwiches to oysters (from £11 a half-dozen) and duck confit (£13).

and champagne and cocktails start at £14, and there's also a limited food menu. Reservations are essential and security is thorough.

### Black Friar
Pub

Map p106 (174 Queen Victoria St EC4; ⊖Blackfriars) It may look like Friar Tuck just stepped out of this 'olde pubbe' just north of Blackfriars station, but the interior is actually an Arts and Crafts makeover dating back to 1905. Built on the site of a Dominican monastery, the theme is appealingly celebrated throughout the pub. Unusually for this part of town, it opens at the weekend.

### Counting House
Pub

Map p106 (50 Cornhill EC3; ☺Mon-Fri; 📶; ⊖Bank or Monument) They say that old banks – with their counters and basement vaults – make perfect homes for pubs, and this award winner certainly looks and feels comfortable in the former headquarters of NatWest with its domed skylight and beautifully appointed main bar.

## ☻ Drinking & Nightlife

### Vertigo 42
Bar

Map p106 (☎7877 7842; www.vertigo42.co.uk; Tower 42, 25 Old Broad St EC2; ☺noon-4.30pm & 5-11pm Mon-Fri, from 5pm Sat; ⊖Liverpool St or Bank) On the 42nd floor of a 183m-high tower, this circular bar has expansive views over the city; they can stretch for miles on a clear day, and are particularly stunning at sunset. The classic drinks list is, as you might expect, pricier than average – wine by the glass starts at £9.20

Counting House
ALEX SEGRE/ALAMY ©

### El Vino
Wine Bar

Map p106 (www.elvino.co.uk; 47 Fleet St EC4; ⏰8.30am-10pm Mon-Fri; 🚇Blackfriars or Temple) A venerable institution that plays host to barristers, solicitors and other legal types from the Royal Courts of Justice across the way, this wine bar (one of five in a small chain) has one of the better wine lists in the City and prices at the attached shops are reasonable.

### Ye Olde Cheshire Cheese
Pub

Map p106 (Wine Office Ct, 145 Fleet St EC4; ⏰Mon-Sat; 🚇Blackfriars) The entrance to this historic pub is via a narrow alley off Fleet St. Over its long history locals have included Dr Johnson, Thackeray and Dickens.

# ⭐ Entertainment

### Barbican
Concert Venue

Map p106 (📞7638 8891; www.barbican.org.uk; Silk St EC2; 🚇Moorgate or Barbican) Urging Londoners to 'do something different', the extensive program of events on offer at the Barbican always provides something new and adventurous. It's home to the wonderful London Symphony Orchestra, and the centre's associate orchestra, the lesser-known BBC Symphony Orchestra, also plays regularly, as do scores of leading international musicians. On the contemporary scene, it hosts all manner of high-quality musicians, focusing in particular on jazz, folk, world and soul artists. Dance is another strong point and its multidisciplinary festival, **Barbican International Theatre Events** (bite; www. barbican.org.uk/theatre/about-bite), showcases some great performances, as well as the work of exciting overseas drama companies alongside local fringe-theatre troupes. It's also a dream to watch a film here, with an interesting line-up and brilliant sloping seating that ensures a full-screen view wherever you sit.

### Volupté
Cabaret

Map p106 (www.volupte-lounge.com; 7-9 Norwich St EC4; ⏰from 11.30am Tue-Fri, from 7.30pm Sat; 🛜; 🚇Chancery Lane) A gorgeous little cabaret venue just behind Fleet St, Volupté offers a real variety of burlesque, vaudeville, comedy and live music. The monthly Black Cotton Club is a hark-back to the 1920s in terms of dress code and

Barbican

DAVIDMARTYN/DREAMSTIME ©

## Lonely Planet's Top Tip

Designed by Jean Nouvel, **One New Change** (Map p106; www.onenewchange .com; Cheapside EC2; ⊖St Paul's), a recently opened shopping centre, houses mainly run-of-the-mill, high-street brands, but if you take the lift to its 6th floor, a great open viewing platform, you will be rewarded with up-close views of the dome of St Paul's Cathedral and panoramic ones out over London.

music choice. At the weekend sit down to Tea & Tassels or an Afternoon Tease, a rather more alternative take on the classic afternoon tea, with live music, cabaret or burlesque performances.

# 🔒 Shopping

### Silver Vaults                         Silverware

Map p106 (www.thesilvervaults.com; 53-64 Chancery Lane WC2; ⊙9am-5.30pm Mon-Fri, to 1pm Sat; ⊖Chancery Lane) The shops in these incredibly secure subterranean vaults make up the world's largest collection of silver. Each one specialises in a particular type of silverware, from cutlery sets to picture frames and lots of jewellery.

# The South Bank

**The South Bank is today one of London's must-see neighbourhoods.** A roll call of riverside sights lines this section of the Thames, commencing with the London Eye, running past the cultural enclave of the Southbank Centre and on to the Tate Modern, the Millennium Bridge and Shakespeare's Globe. It continues: waterside pubs, busy boutique shopping quarters, a cathedral, one of London's most-visited food markets and a handful of fun diversions for kids and irrepressible kidults. A stunning panorama unfolds on the far side of the Thames, as head-swivelling architecture rises up on either bank.

The drawcard sights stretch out in a manageable waterside melange, so doing it on foot is the best way. If you follow the Silver Jubilee Walkway and the South Bank section of the Thames Path along the southern riverbank – one of the most pleasant strolls in town – you can catch it all.

London Eye (p128)

# South Bank Highlights

## Tate Modern (p124)

London's world-class modern and contemporary art museum remains a firm favourite with visitors as much for its superb Pritzker Prize–winning conversion of the former Bankside Power Station as for its contents. But while the conversion and the views are incomparable, there's little chance they'll outshine the magnificent collection of international art.

## Eating & Drinking by the River

For some of London's tastiest and most photogenic views, you can't go wrong booking a table at one of the South Bank's swish riverside restaurants. Both Skylon (p135) and the Oxo Tower Restaurant & Brasserie (p135) pair excellent food with superb vistas, but if it's just a beer on your list, raise a glass to the views of St Paul's from the Anchor Bankside (p137; pictured left).

MARKA/ALAMY ©

## London Eye (p128)

Despite being erected as a temporary structure, rather like Paris' Eiffel Tower, the London Eye is now an integral part of the London skyline and the city would be almost unthinkable without it. But don't miss taking a 'flight' – the views are spectacular and the entire experience is a highlight of many people's visit. Book online to avoid the lines or fast-track your way on.

## Shakespeare's Globe (p138)

Shakespeare's Globe, a meticulous reproduction of the theatre where the Bard worked and put on many of his plays for the first time, allows you to experience Elizabethan drama exactly as people four centuries ago would have done, including having to stand under roofless skies if you buy the cheapest tickets. Just pray it doesn't rain... Costume worn in the first Shakespeare production at the Globe

## Borough Market (p129)

If you hear the way that some Londoners talk about Borough Market, you'd imagine it was a holy shrine or a sacred place of pilgrimage. And for foodies and incorrigible gastronomes, it's just that. Come and peruse the freshest produce in the city from Thursday to Saturday and keep an eye out for free samples.

# South Bank Walk

*This relaxed riverside walk will take you past some of London's best views, standout cultural establishments and architectural highlights. It can be done in under an hour, though it's much better not to rush this one.*

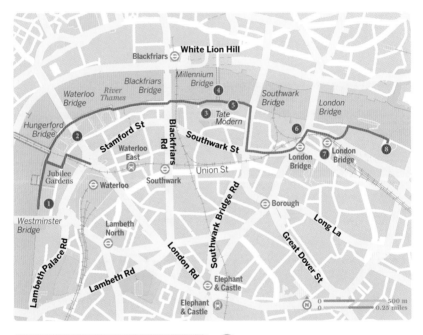

## WALK FACTS

- **Start** Waterloo Station
- **Finish** City Hall
- **Distance** 1.5 miles
- **Duration** One to two hours

### 1 County Hall

Across Westminster Bridge from the splendid Houses of Parliament, this grand building was once the seat of London's local government and affords glorious views of the river. It now houses a film museum, the Sea Life London Aquarium (p128) and some hotels.

### 2 BFI Southbank

The flashy headquarters of the **BFI South-bank** (p138) is a mecca for celluloid buffs and film historians alike. It screens thousands of films in four theatres each year, with archived films available for viewing in the Mediatheque.

### 3 Tate Modern

London's most popular attraction, the cutting-edge **Tate Modern** (p124) is housed in the inventively converted Bankside Power Station overlooking Millennium Bridge and the river. One of London's best treats, its incredible permanent collection of modern art is free to visit. Don't miss the excellent installations in the main Turbine Hall.

### 4 Millennium Bridge

Carrying up to 10,000 pedestrians each day, this **pedestrian bridge** (p129) staples together the north and south banks of the Thames. A slender 'blade of light' designed by Sir Norman Foster, it's everything contemporary architecture should be: modern, beautiful and useful.

### 5 Shakespeare's Globe

Firmly entrenched as a London must, the **Globe** (p138) is a superb recreation of the theatre where Shakespeare worked and saw many of his plays first performed. It is definitely worth stopping to see and even if you don't see a play, you can hop on a tour.

### 6 Southwark Cathedral

This fantastic **house of worship** (p132) is well worth a visit, especially for its historical associations and medieval remnants. A monument to Shakespeare, whose great works were originally written for the Bankside playhouses nearby, takes pride of place. **Borough Market** (p129) is just around the corner.

### 7 The Shard

Rising up above you at London Bridge is the splinterlike **Shard**, designed by Italian architect Renzo Piano. The tallest building in the European Union and a stunning addition to London's architectural landscape, it will house a five-star hotel, restaurants and London's highest public viewing gallery.

### 8 City Hall

Nicknamed 'the egg' (or, more cheekily, 'the glass gonad') and 'The Leaning Tower of Pizzas', this bulbous building has also been likened to Darth Vader's helmet. An interior spiral ramp ascends above the assembly chamber to the building's roof, fitted with energy-saving solar panels. Beyond is the gorgeous form of Tower Bridge, taking you to the City.

 **The Best...**

#### PLACES TO EAT

**Anchor & Hope** Much-loved gastropub famed for its full-on, flavoursome British dishes. (p135)

**Laughing Gravy** Tremendous British menu and relaxing setting. (p135)

**Skylon** Fifties styling, stunning Thames vistas, fine modern international menu. (p135)

**Magdalen** Stylish and delightful restaurant with excellent cooking and attentive staff. (p136)

#### PLACES TO DRINK

**Rake** Slightly larger than a pigeon hole, with an exemplary range of ales. (p137)

**George Inn** Historic coaching inn, bursting at the seams with age-old charm. (p137)

#### ATTRACTIONS

**Tate Modern** A feast of wonderfully housed modern and contemporary art. (p124)

**London Eye** The perfect perspective on town if the sun's out. (p128)

**Borough Market** A total banquet and a bustling cornucopia of gastronomic delights. (p129)

**Shakespeare's Globe** Nowhere is the authentic open-air Elizabethan effect better. (p138)

City Hall, designed by Norman Foster
JANE SWEENEY/LONELY PLANET IMAGES ©

# Don't Miss
## Tate Modern

The public's love affair with this phenomenally successful modern art gallery shows no sign of cooling a decade after it opened. In fact, so enraptured are art goers with the Tate Modern that over 50 million visitors flocked to the former power station in its first 10 years. The world's most popular art gallery is naturally one of the most-visited sights in London and is set to expand even further in 2012 by converting two of the power station's huge subterranean oil tanks into display space.

Map p130

☎ 7887 8000

www.tate.org.uk/modern

Bankside SE1

admission free

🕙10am-6pm Sun-Thu, to 10pm Fri & Sat

⊖Southwark or London Bridge

# Turbine Hall

First to greet you as you pour down the ramp off Holland St (the main entrance), the cavernous 3300-sq-metre Turbine Hall originally housed the power station's humungous turbines. Today the Turbine Hall has been transformed into a commanding space for large-scale, temporary exhibitions.

# Unilever Series

Some art critics swipe at the populism of this annual commission, designed for display in Turbine Hall, but others insist this makes art and sculpture more accessible. Past works have included Carsten Höller's funfair-like slides *Test Site;* Doris Salcedo's enormous fissure in the floor *Shibboleth* and Chinese artist Ai Weiwei's thoughtful and compelling *Sunflower Seeds* – a huge carpet of hand-painted ceramic seeds.

# Permanent Collection

Tate Modern's permanent collection (on Levels 3 and 5) is arranged by both theme and chronology. More than 60,000 works are on constant rotation, and the curators have at their disposal paintings by Georges Braque, Henri Matisse, Piet Mondrian, Andy Warhol, Mark Rothko, Jackson Pollock, Auguste Rodin and others.

# Surrealism

On Level 3 Poetry and Dream submerges the viewer in the fantastic mindscapes of Yves Tanguy, Max Ernst, Paul Delvaux and other artists either directly connected with surrealism or influenced by the movement.

# Special Exhibitions

Special exhibitions (which are held on Level 4 and carry an admission charge) constantly feed fresh ideas into the Tate Modern. Past exhibitions have included retrospectives on Edward Hopper, Frida Kahlo, August Strindberg, local 'bad boys' Gilbert & George and Joan Miró. Some exhibitions are also held on Level 2.

# States of Flux

Found on Level 5 and focussing on early-20th-century avant-garde movements, including cubism, futurism and vorticism, States of Flux opens with a dramatic pairing of Umberto Boccioni's *Unique Forms of Continuity in Space* and Roy Lichtenstein's pop icon *Whaam!*. Groundbreaking works from Georges Braque, Picasso and other cubists lie beyond.

American Pop Art is also explored, with vibrant and colourful works from Roy Lichtenstein, Andy Warhol and others commenting on the culture of postwar consumerism.

# Energy & Process

The main focus of this gallery on Level 5 is Arte Povera, a radical art movement closely associated with Italian artists in the late 1960s. A hallmark of the style was the employment of a diverse range of materials in the creation of sculpture, attempting to involve the intrinsic energy of those materials in the art work, while moving away from more traditional substances.

## Architecture

The conversion of the empty Bankside Power Station – all 4.2 million bricks of it – to art gallery in 2000 was a design triumph. Leaving the building's single central 99m-high chimney, adding a two-storey glass box onto the roof and employing the cavernous Turbine Hall as a dramatic entrance space were three strokes of genius. Visitors will have to wait until 2016 for the opening of the Tate Modern's funky 11-storey geometric extension, also designed by Herzog & de Meuron.

# A Tour Down the River Thames

London's history has always been determined by the Thames. The city was founded as a Roman port nearly 2000 years ago and over the centuries since then many of the capital's landmarks have lined the river's banks. A boat trip is a great way to experience the attractions.

There are piers dotted along both banks at regular intervals where you can hop on and hop off the regular services to visit places of interest. The best place to board is Westminster Pier, from where boats head

downstream, taking you from the City of Westminster, the seat of government, to the original City of London, now the financial district and dominated by a growing band of skyscrapers. Across the river, the once shabby and neglected South Bank now bristles with as many top attractions as its northern counterpart.

In our illustration we've concentrated on the top highlights you'll enjoy at a fish's-eye view as you sail along. These are, from west

MARK DAFFEY / LPI ©

### St Paul's Cathedral

Though there's been a church here since AD 604, the current building rose from the ashes of the 1666 Great Fire and is architect Christopher Wren's masterpiece. Famous for surviving the Blitz intact and for the wedding of Charles and Diana, it's looking as good as new after a major clean-up for its 300th anniversary.

**Blackfriars**

### Somerset House

This grand neoclassical palace was once one of many aristocratic houses lining the Thames. The huge arches at river level gave direct access to the Thames until the Embankment was built in the 1860s.

**③ ⊖ Temple**

**Charing Cross**

**Blackfriars Pier**

**Blackfriars Bridge**

**Savoy Pier**

**Waterloo Bridge**

**Victoria Embankment Gardens**

**National Theatre**

**Embankment**

**OXO Tower**

**Southbank Centre**

### London Eye

Built in 2000 and originally temporary, the Eye instantly became a much-loved landmark. The 30-minute spin takes you 135m above the city from where the views are unsurprisingly amazing.

**②**

**Waterloo Millennium Pier**

**Westminster Pier**

### Houses of Parliament

Rebuilt in neo-Gothic style after the old palace burned down in 1834, the most famous part of the British parliament is the clocktower. Generally known as Big Ben, it's named after Benjamin Hall who oversaw its construction.

**⊖ Westminster**

**①**

**Westminster Bridge**

RICHARD I'ANSON / LONELY PLANET IMAGES ©

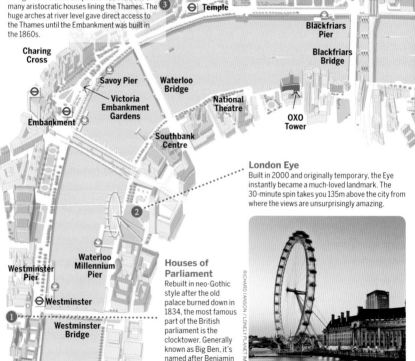

to east, the Houses of **Parliament** ❶,
the **London Eye** ❷, **Somerset House** ❸,
**St Paul's Cathedral** ❹, **Tate Modern** ❺,
**Shakespeare's Globe** ❻, the **Tower of
London** ❼ and **Tower Bridge** ❽.

Apart from covering this central section
of the river, boats can also be taken upstream
as far as Kew Gardens and Hampton Court
Palace, and downstream to Greenwich and
the Thames Barrier.

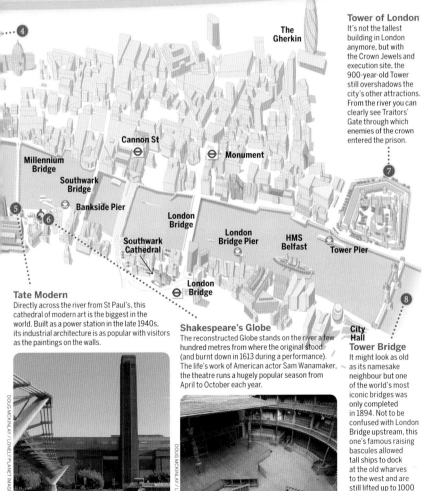

**Tower of London**
It's not the tallest
building in London
anymore, but with
the Crown Jewels and
execution site, the
900-year-old Tower
still overshadows the
city's other attractions.
From the river you can
clearly see Traitors'
Gate through which
enemies of the crown
entered the prison.

The
Gherkin

❹

Cannon St

Monument

Millennium
Bridge

Southwark
Bridge

Bankside Pier

❺
❻

London
Bridge

London
Bridge Pier

HMS
Belfast

Tower Pier

❼

Southwark
Cathedral

London
Bridge

❽

**Tate Modern**
Directly across the river from St Paul's, this
cathedral of modern art is the biggest in the
world. Built as a power station in the late 1940s,
its industrial architecture is as popular with visitors
as the paintings on the walls.

**Shakespeare's Globe**
The reconstructed Globe stands on the river a few
hundred metres from where the original stood
(and burnt down in 1613 during a performance).
The life's work of American actor Sam Wanamaker,
the theatre runs a hugely popular season from
April to October each year.

**City
Hall**

**Tower Bridge**
It might look as old
as its namesake
neighbour but one
of the world's most
iconic bridges was
only completed
in 1894. Not to be
confused with London
Bridge upstream, this
one's famous raising
bascules allowed
tall ships to dock
at the old wharves
to the west and are
still lifted up to 1000
times a year.

DOUG MCKINLAY / LONELY PLANET IMAGES ©

DOUG MCKINLAY / LPI ©

# Discover the
# South Bank

## Getting There & Away

○ **Underground** The South Bank is lashed into the tube system by stations at Waterloo, Southwark, London Bridge and Bermondsey, all on the Jubilee Line; the Northern Line runs through London Bridge and Waterloo (the Bakerloo line runs through the latter).

○ **On Foot** Cross to South Bank from the City over Tower Bridge, or from the West End across Westminster Bridge or any other vehicle and pedestrian bridges.

○ **Bicycle** Jump on a Barclays bike (p283).

○ **Bus** The Riverside RV1 runs around the South Bank and Bankside, linking all the main sights (running between Covent Garden and Tower Gateway).

Rose Theatre
CHRIS PEARSALL/ALAMY ©

## ◉ Sights

### Waterloo

**London Eye** — Viewpoint

Map p130 (☎ 0870 500 0600; www.londoneye.com; Jubilee Gardens SE1; adult/child £19/10; ⊙10am-8.30pm Sep-Mar, to 9pm Apr-Jun, to 9.30pm Jul & Aug; ⊖Waterloo) A ride – or 'flight', as it is called here – in one of the wheel's 32 glass-enclosed eye pods holding up to 28 people draws 3.5 million visitors annually. At peak times (July, August and school holidays) it may seem like they are all in the queue with you; save money and shorten queues by buying tickets online, or cough up an extra £10 to showcase your fast-track swagger. Alternatively, visit before 11am or after 3pm to avoid peak density. It takes a gracefully slow 30 minutes and, weather permitting, you can see 25 miles in every direction from the top of the western hemisphere's tallest Ferris wheel.

**County Hall** — Historic Building

Map p130 (Riverside Bldg, Westminster Bridge Rd SE1; 🛜; ⊖Westminster or Waterloo) Begun in 1909 but not completed until 1922, this grand building with its curved, colonnaded facade contains a vast aquarium and a museum devoted to the local film industry.

The excellent **Sea Life London Aquarium** (☎0871 663 1678; www.sealife.co.uk; adult/child £17/12.50; ⊙10am-6pm Mon-Thu, to 7pm Fri-Sun; 🛜) is one of the largest in Europe. There are over 40 sharks, a colony of gentoo penguins and other Antarctic creatures, ever-popular clownfish and a rewarding rainforests section.

# Detour:
## Imperial War Museum

Fronted by a pair of intimidating 15in naval guns, this riveting **museum (Map p130; www.iwm.org.uk; Lambeth Rd SE1; admission free; ⊙10am-6pm; ⊖Lambeth North)** is housed in what was once Bethlehem Royal Hospital, also known as Bedlam. Although the museum's focus is on military action involving British or Commonwealth troops during the 20th century, it rolls out the carpet to war in the wider sense.

In the Trench Experience on the lower ground floor you walk through the grim reality of life on the Somme front line in WWI; the Blitz Experience has you cowering inside a mock bomb shelter during a WWII air raid before emerging through ravaged East End streets.

### Southbank Centre — Arts Centre

Map p130 (☑0871 663 2500; www.southbankcentre.co.uk; Belvedere Rd SE1; admission free, tickets for performances & exhibition; ⊖Waterloo) The flagship venue of the Southbank Centre and its oldest standing building, the **Royal Festival Hall** with its gently curved facade of glass and Portland stone is more humane than its 1970s brutalist neighbours.

Just north, the austere **Queen Elizabeth Hall** is a brutalist icon, the second-largest concert venue in the centre, hosting chamber orchestras, quartets, choirs, dance performances and sometimes opera. It also contains the smaller **Purcell Room**, while underneath its elevated floor is a long-term, graffiti-decorated skateboarders' hang-out.

The opinion-dividing 1968 **Hayward Gallery** (☑0871 663 2509; www.southbankcentre.co.uk; admission £7-9; ⊙10am-6pm Sat-Wed, to 8pm Thu & Fri) is one of London's premier exhibition spaces for major international art shows.

## Bankside & Southwark

### Tate Modern — Gallery

See p124.

### Millennium Bridge — Bridge

Map p130 The elegant Millennium Bridge connects the south bank of the Thames, in front of Tate Modern, with the north bank, at the steps of Peter's Hill below St Paul's Cathedral. The low-slung frame designed by Sir Norman Foster and Anthony Caro looks spectacular, particularly lit up at night with fibre optics, and the view of St Paul's from the South Bank is one of London's iconic images.

### Rose Theatre — Theatre

Map p130 (☑7902 1400; www.rosetheatre.org.uk; 56 Park St SE1; adult/child £7.50/4.50; ⊙1-5pm Mon-Sat, noon-5pm Sun late Apr–mid-Oct; ⏚; ⊖London Bridge) The Rose, for which Christopher Marlowe and Ben Jonson wrote their greatest plays and in which Shakespeare learned his craft, is unique: its original 16th-century foundations were discovered in 1989 beneath an office building and given a protective concrete cover. Administered by the nearby Globe Theatre, the Rose is open to the public only when matinees are being performed at the Globe and can only be visited as part of a group.

## Borough & Bermondsey

### Borough Market — Market

Map p130 (☑7407 1002; www.boroughmarket.org.uk; cnr Southwark & Stoney Sts SE1; ⊙11am-5pm Thu, noon-6pm Fri, 8am-5pm Sat; ⊖London Bridge) Located here in some form or another since the 13th century, 'London's Larder' has enjoyed an astonishing renaissance in the past decade. Always overflowing with food lovers, inveterate gastronomes, wide-eyed newcomers, guidebook-toting visitors

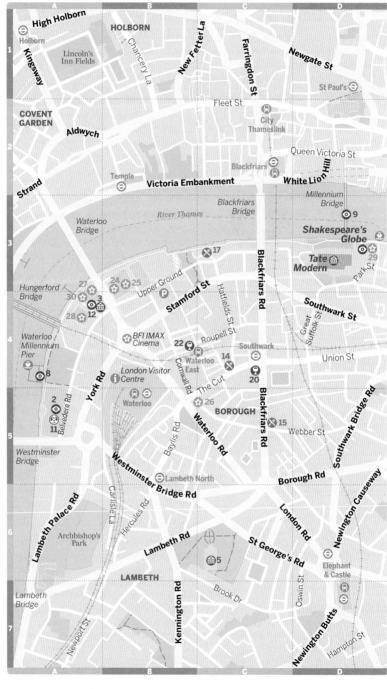

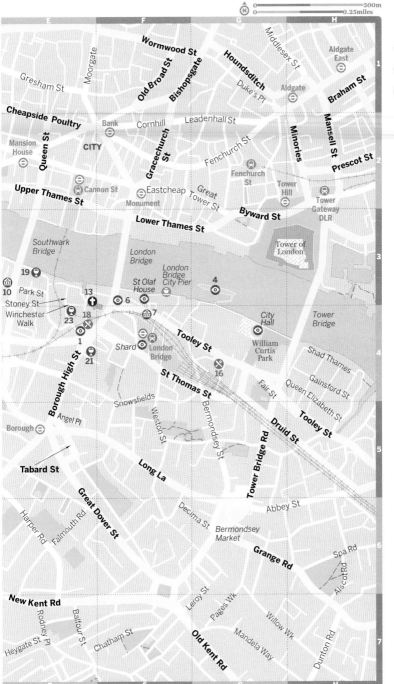

0 500m
0 0.25miles

Wormwood St

Houndsditch

Gresham St

Moorgate

Old Broad St

Bishopsgate

Duke's Pl

Middlesex St

Aldgate
East

Aldgate

Braham St

Cheapside  Poultry

Cornhill

Leadenhall St

Bank

Mansion
House

Queen St

CITY

Gracechurch St

Fenchurch St

Minories

Mansell St

Prescot St

Upper Thames St

Cannon St

Eastcheap
Monument

Great
Tower St

Fenchurch
St

Byward St

Tower
Hill

Tower
Gateway
DLR

Lower Thames St

Southwark
Bridge

London
Bridge

St Olaf
House

London
Bridge
City Pier

4

Tower of
London

10

19

Park St

13

6

Stoney St
Winchester
Walk

23

18

7

City
Hall

Tower
Bridge

1

Shard

London
Bridge

Tooley St

William
Curtis
Park

Shad Thames

21

St Thomas St

16

Fair St

Queen Elizabeth St

Gainsford St

Tooley St

Snowsfields

Weston St

Bermondsey St

Tower Bridge Rd

Druid St

Borough High St

Angel Pl

Borough

Tabard St

Long La

Abbey St

Great Dover St

Harper Rd

Falmouth Rd

Decima St

Bermondsey
Market

Grange Rd

Spa Rd

Alscot Rd

New Kent Rd

Heygate St Pl

Rodney St

Balfour St

Chatham St

Leroy St

Pages Wk

Old Kent Rd

Mandela Way

Willow Wk

Dunton Rd

THE SOUTH BANK

131

# The South Bank

## ◎ Top Sights

Shakespeare's Globe ..............................D3
Tate Modern..............................................D3

## ◎ Sights

1 Borough Market.....................................E4
2 County Hall............................................A5
3 Hayward Gallery....................................A4
4 HMS Belfast...........................................G3
5 Imperial War Museum...........................C6
6 London Bridge Experience & London
   Tombs..................................................F3
7 London Dungeon ...................................F4
8 London Eye............................................A4
9 Millennium Bridge.................................D3
   National Theatre.............................(see 25)
   Queen Elizabeth Hall.....................(see 27)
10 Rose Theatre.........................................E3
   Royal Festival Hall.........................(see 28)
11 Sea Life London Aquarium ...................A5
12 Southbank Centre ................................A4
13 Southwark Cathedral............................E3

## ⊗ Eating

14 Anchor & Hope......................................C4
15 Laughing Gravy......................................C5
16 Magdalen...............................................G4
17 Oxo Tower Restaurant & Brasserie......C3
18 Roast......................................................E4
   Skylon .............................................(see 28)

## ⊖ Drinking & Nightlife

19 Anchor Bankside ..................................E3
20 Baltic.....................................................C4
21 George Inn.............................................E4
22 King's Arms............................................B4
23 Rake.......................................................E4

## ✪ Entertainment

24 BFI Southbank......................................B3
25 National Theatre...................................B3
26 Old Vic...................................................C5
   Purcell Room...................................(see 27)
27 Queen Elizabeth Hall............................A3
28 Royal Festival Hall ...............................A4
29 Shakespeare's Globe............................D3
30 Southbank Centre.................................A4

and all types in between, this fantastic market has become firmly established as a sight in its own right.

Along with a section devoted to quality fresh fruit, exotic vegetables and organic meat, there's a fine-foods retail market, with the likes of home-grown honey and homemade bread plus loads of free samples. Throughout, takeaway stalls supply sizzling gourmet sausages, chorizo sandwiches and quality burgers in spades, filling the air with meaty aromas. The market simply heaves on Saturday (get here early for the best pickings).

### London Bridge Experience & London Tombs                          Museum

Map p130 ( ☎ 0800 043 4666; www.london bridgeexperience.com; 2-4 Tooley St SE1; adult/ child £23/17; ☉ 10am-5pm Mon-Fri, 10am-6pm Sat & Sun; ⊖ London Bridge) Winner of the 'Screamie' award (a prize for scary and haunted attractions in the UK) three years on the trot, this attraction marries history with hysteria. It's essentially for kids, so the roll call includes 'the Keeper of the Heads', who preserved (mummi-

fied) the severed heads of the executed for display on the bridge. Things ratchet up as you descend into a series of tombs and plague pits dating as far back as the 14th century, where darkness, rodents (animatronics) and claustrophobia meet zombies-from-nowhere (actors).

### Southwark Cathedral                          Church

Map p130; ( ☎ 7367 6700; www.southwark.angli can.org/cathedral; Montague Close SE1; admission free, requested donation £4; ☉ 8am-6pm Mon-Fri, from 9am Sat & Sun; ⊖ London Bridge) The earliest surviving parts of this relatively small cathedral are the retrochoir at the eastern end, which contains four chapels and was part of the 13th-century Priory of St Mary Overie; some ancient arcading by the southwest door; 12th-century wall cores in the north transept; and an arch that dates back to the original Norman church. But most of the cathedral is Victorian.

Enter via the southwest door and immediately to the left is a length of arcading dating back to the 13th century; nearby is a selection of intriguing medieval roof bosses from the 15th century.

DOUG MCKINLAY/LONELY PLANET IMAGES ©

## ✓ Don't Miss
# Shakespeare's Globe

Unlike other venues for Shakespearean plays, the new Globe was designed to resemble the original as closely as possible, painstakingly constructed with 600 oak pegs (nary a nail or a screw in the house), specially fired Tudor bricks and thatching reeds from Norfolk that pigeons supposedly don't like. It even means having the arena open to the fickle London skies and roar of passing aircraft, leaving the 700 'groundlings' to stand in London's notorious downpours.

Despite the worldwide popularity of Shakespeare over the centuries, the Globe was almost a distant memory when American actor (and, later, film director) Sam Wanamaker came searching for it in 1949. Undeterred by the fact that the theatre's foundations had vanished beneath a row of heritage-listed Georgian houses, Wanamaker set up the Globe Playhouse Trust in 1970 and began fundraising for a memorial theatre.

Shakespeare's Globe consists of the reconstructed Globe Theatre and, beneath it, an exhibition hall, entry to which includes a tour (departing every 15 to 30 minutes) of the theatre, except when matinees are being staged in season. Then the tour shifts to the nearby Rose Theatre (p129) and costs less.

### NEED TO KNOW
Map p130; ☎7902 1400, bookings 7401 9919; www.shakespeares-globe.org; 21 New Globe Walk SE1; exhibition incl guided tour of theatre adult/child £11.50/7; ⊙exhibition 9am-12.30pm & 1-5pm Mon-Sat, 9-11.30am & noon-5pm Sun late Apr–mid-Oct, 9am-5pm mid-Oct–late Apr; ⊖St Paul's or London Bridge

Cross into the choir to admire the 16th-century Great Screen separating the choir from the retrochoir.

In the south aisle of the nave have a look at the green alabaster monument to William Shakespeare.

Do hunt down the exceedingly fine Elizabethan sideboard in the north transept.

## HMS Belfast     Ship

Map p130 ( 7940 6300; www.iwm.org.uk; Morgan's Lane, Tooley St SE1; adult/child £13.50/free; 10am-6pm Mar-Oct, to 5pm Nov-Feb; ; London Bridge) White ensign flapping on the Thames breeze, HMS *Belfast* is a magnet for naval-gazing kids of all ages. A short walk west of testicular City Hall, this large, light cruiser – launched in 1938 – served in WWII, helping to sink the German battleship *Scharnhorst,* shelling the Normandy coast on D-Day and later participating in the Korean War. Her six-inch guns could bombard a target 14 land miles distant.

## London Dungeon     Museum

Map p130 ( 7403 7221, bookings 0871 423 2240; www.thedungeons.com; 28-34 Tooley St SE1; adult/child £23/17; usually 10am-5pm; London Bridge) Starting with a stagger through a mirror maze (the Labyrinth of Lost Souls) and followed by a peep at the Great Plague, trip through torture and waltz through bedlam to head for a close shave with Sweeney Todd, the demon barber of Fleet St, and an encounter with Jack the Ripper.

The best bits are the vaudevillian delights of being sentenced by a mad, bewigged judge on trumped-up charges, the fairground-ride boat to Traitor's Gate and the Extremis Drop Ride to Doom that has you 'plummeting' to your death by hanging from the gallows. A new attraction, Vengeance, is a spookily entertaining '5D laser ride' on which you are menaced by reawakened spirits that you fight off with lasers.

Buy tickets more cheaply online for this camped-up 90-minute gore-fest to avoid the mammoth queues. Hours vary according to season, so check the website.

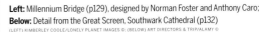

**Left:** Millennium Bridge (p129), designed by Norman Foster and Anthony Caro;
**Below:** Detail from the Great Screen, Southwark Cathedral (p132)

(LEFT) KIMBERLEY COOLE/LONELY PLANET IMAGES ©; (BELOW) ART DIRECTORS & TRIP/ALAMY ©

#  Eating

## Waterloo

### Skylon
Modern European **££**

Map p130 (📞7654 7800; www.skylonrestaurant
.co.uk; 3rd fl, Royal Festival Hall, Southbank
Centre, Belvedere Rd SE1; grillroom mains £12.50-
19.50, restaurant 2-/3-course meals £40/45;
🕐grillroom noon-11pm, restaurant lunch daily,
dinner to 10.30pm Mon-Sat; ⊖Waterloo) Named
after the defunct 1950s tower, this excellent restaurant atop the refurbished Royal
Festival Hall is divided into a grillroom and
fine-dining area by a large bar (open 11am
to 1am). The decor is cutting-edge 1950s:
muted colours and period chairs (trendy
then, trendier now) and floor-to-ceiling
windows have magnificent views of the
Thames and the City. Dress smart casual.

### Oxo Tower Restaurant &
**Brasserie** Modern European **£££**

Map p130 (📞7803 3888; www.harveynichols.com;
8th fl, Barge House St SE1; restaurant dinner mains
£19.50-32.50, 3-course set lunch £35, brasserie
2-/3-course set lunch £22.50/26.50; 🕐lunch &
dinner ⊖Waterloo) The iconic Oxo Tower's
conversion, with this restaurant on the 8th
floor, helped spur much of the local dining
renaissance. In the stunning glassed-in terrace you have a front-row seat for the best
view in London; you pay for this handsome-
ly in the brasserie and stratospherically in
the restaurant. Strong wine list.

### Anchor & Hope
Gastropub **££**

Map p130 (36 The Cut SE1; mains £11.50-22;
🕐lunch Tue-Sun, dinner Mon-Sat; ⊖Southwark
or Waterloo) The hope is that you'll get a
table without waiting hours because you
can't book at this quintessential gastropub, except for Sunday lunch at 2pm. The
anchor is gutsy, British food.

## Borough & Bermondsey

### Laughing Gravy
British **££**

Map p130 (📞7998 1707; www.thelaughinggravy.
co.uk; 154 Blackfriars Rd SE1; mains £8.50-17.50;

135

JULIO ETCHART/ALAMY ©

⏱11am-late Mon-Fri, 5.30pm-late Sat, noon-6pm Sun; ⊖Southwark) Recently steered in a lucratively fresh direction by new owners, this is a true gem, with a sure-fire menu that's a combination of locally sourced food (cider-marinated lamb rump, pan-fried red mullet) and culinary talent from chef Michael Facey, with splendid roasts on Sunday. Few complain, many return for a second sitting.

### Magdalen
Modern British ££

Map p130 (www.magdalenrestaurant.co.uk; 152 Tooley St SE1; mains £13.50-21, 2-/3-course set lunch £15.50/18.50; ⏱closed lunch Sat & all day Sun; ⊖London Bridge) You can't go wrong with this stylish dining room (with a couple of tables optimistically positioned outside). The Modern British fare adds its own appetising spin to familiar dishes (grilled calves' kidneys, creamed onion and sage, smoked haddock choucroute). The welcome is warm and the service excellent; a true diamond in the rough.

### Roast
Modern British ££

Map p130 (www.roast-restaurant.com; 1st fl, Floral Hall, Borough Market, Stoney St SE1; mains £14-25; ⏱closed dinner Sun; ⊖London Bridge) The focal point at this unique restaurant

and bar perched directly above Borough Market is the glassed-in kitchen with an open spit, where ribs of beef, suckling pigs, birds and game are roasted. Also open for good breakfasts (Monday to Saturday); trading days at Borough Market (Thursday to Saturday) are the restaurant's busiest.

## ⊖ Drinking & Nightlife

The South Bank is a strange combination of good, down-to-earth boozers, which just happen to have been here for hundreds of years, and modern bars – all neon and alcopops – patronised by a younger, trendier crowd.

## Waterloo

### Baltic
Bar

Map p130 (www.balticrestaurant.co.uk; 74 Blackfriars Rd SE1; ⏱noon-midnight Mon-Sat, to 10.30pm Sun; ⊖Southwark) This very stylish bar at the front of an Eastern European restaurant specialises – not surprisingly – in vodkas; some 50-plus, including bar-infused concoctions, along with cocktails. The bright and airy, high-ceilinged dining room, with a glass roof and lovely amber wall, is just behind, should you need some blotter.

### King's Arms · Pub
Map p130 (25 Roupell St SE1; ⊖Waterloo or Southwark) Relaxed and charming when not crowded, this award-winning neighbourhood boozer at the corner of a terraced Waterloo backstreet was a funeral parlour in a previous life, so show some respect. The large traditional bar area, serving up a good selection of ales and bitters, gives way to a fantastically odd conservatory bedecked with junk-store eclectica of local interest and serving decent Thai food.

## Bankside & Southwark
### Anchor Bankside · Pub
Map p130 (34 Park St SE1; ⊖London Bridge) Firmly anchored in many guidebooks (including this one) – but with good reason – this riverside boozer dates back to the early 17th century (subsequently rebuilt after the Great Fire and again in the 19th century). Trips to the terrace are rewarded with superb views across the Thames but brace for a constant deluge of drinkers. Dictionary writer Samuel Johnson, whose brewer friend owned the joint, drank here, as did diarist Samuel Pepys.

## Borough & Bermondsey
### George Inn · Pub
Map p130 (Talbot Yard, 77 Borough High St SE1; ⊖Borough) This magnificent old boozer is London's last surviving galleried coaching inn, dating from 1676 and mentioned in Dickens' *Little Dorrit*. No wonder it falls under the protection of the National Trust.

It is on the site of the Tabard Inn (thus the Talbot Yard address), where the pilgrims in Chaucer's *Canterbury Tales* gathered before setting out (well lubricated, we suspect) on the road to Canterbury, Kent.

### Rake · Pub
Map p130 (14 Winchester Walk SE1; ⊗noon-11pm Mon-Fri, from 10am Sat; ⊖London Bridge) A place of superlatives – it's the only pub actually in Borough Market and the smallest boozer in London – the Rake tucks a strong line-up of bitters and real ales (with one-third pint measures) into its pea-sized premises.

## ✪ Entertainment

The South Bank's National Theatre is a must for thoughtful and innovative drama. Into the South Bank's creative milieu will pirouette the Rambert Dance Company, leaping to new premises here in 2013.

## National Theatre · Theatre

Map p130 ( 7452 3000; www.nationaltheatre.org.uk; South Bank SE1; tickets £10-41; Waterloo) England's flagship theatre showcases a mix of classic and contemporary plays performed by excellent casts in three theatres (Olivier, Lyttelton and Cottesloe). Outstanding artistic director Nicholas Hytner has overseen some recent landmark productions and slashed ticket prices.

## Southbank Centre · Concert Venue

Map p130 ( 0871 663 2500; www.southbankcentre.co.uk; Belvedere Rd SE1; tickets £8-45; Waterloo) The overhauled **Royal Festival Hall** ( 7960 4242; tickets £6-60) is London's premier concert venue and seats 3000 in a now-acoustic amphitheatre. It's one of the best places for catching world-music artists and hosts the fantastic Meltdown festival. The sound is fantastic, the programming impeccable and there are frequent free gigs in the wonderfully expansive foyer.

There are more eclectic gigs at the smaller **Queen Elizabeth Hall** and **Purcell Room**.

## Shakespeare's Globe · Theatre

Map p130 ( information 7902 1400, bookings 7401 9919; www.shakespeares-globe.org; 21 New Globe Walk SE1; adult £15-37.50, concession £12-34.50, standing £5; St Paul's or London Bridge) This authentic Shakespearean theatre (p133) is a wooden O without a roof over the central stage area, and although there are covered wooden bench seats in tiers around the stage, many people (there's room for 700) do as 17th-century 'groundlings' did, standing in front of the stage, shouting and heckling. Because the building is quite open to the elements, you may have to wrap up. No umbrellas are allowed, but cheap raincoats are on sale.

The theatre season runs from late April to mid-October and includes works by Shakespeare and his contemporaries such as Christopher Marlowe. Cheapest tickets at Shakespeare's Globe are all-weather standing tickets.

## BFI Southbank · Cinema

Map p130 ( information 7928 3535, bookings 7928 3232; www.bfi.org.uk; Belvedere Rd SE1; Waterloo) Tucked almost out of sight

National Theatre, designed by Denys Lasdun

# Globe History

The original Globe – known as the 'Wooden O' after its circular shape and roofless centre – was erected in 1599. Rival to the Rose Theatre, all was well but did not end well when the Globe burned to the ground within two hours during a performance of a play about Henry VIII in 1613 (a stage cannon ignited the thatched roof). A tiled replacement was speedily rebuilt only to be closed in 1642 by Puritans, who saw the theatre (p133) as the devil's workshop, and it was dismantled two years later.

under the arches of Waterloo Bridge is the British Film Institute, containing four cinemas that screen thousands of films each year, a gallery devoted to the moving image and the **Mediatheque** ( ☎ 7928 3535; admission free; ☺ noon-8pm Tue-Sun), where you watch film and TV highlights from the BFI National Archive.

### Old Vic                                    Theatre
Map p130 ( ☎ 0844 871 7628; www.oldvicthea tre.com; Waterloo Rd SE1; ⊖ Waterloo) Never has there been a London theatre with a more famous artistic director. American actor Kevin Spacey took the theatrical helm in 2003, looking after this glorious theatre's program. Spacey keeps going from strength to strength, with such recent pickings as Brian Friel's *Dancing at Lughnasa* with singer Andrea Corr (who knew?) and *Richard III,* directed by ex-Donmar Warehouse honcho Sam Mendes and starring the Oscar-winning Spacey in the lead role.

# Kensington & Hyde Park

**The area from Hyde Park to Chelsea is high-class territory.** But it's not all about multimillion-pound properties, Chinese tycoons and exclusive shopping. The area serves up some of the capital's highlight attractions, particularly museums, and its communities are among the most cosmopolitan (albeit in the well-heeled sense). The restaurants, meanwhile, are to die for.

Thanks to Prince Albert and the 1851 Great Exhibition, South Kensington is first and foremost museumland, with three of London's most magnificent practically cheek-by-jowl: the Natural History Museum, the Science Museum and the Victoria & Albert Museum.

Splendid Hyde Park and Kensington Gardens – one delightfully big sprawling mass of green – buffers more sedate Knightsbridge and Kensington from the energy, bright lights and havoc of the West End. Exclusive hotels and expensive shopping tend to keep this area the preserve of the wealthy, but literally everyone and their best friend seems to be in Harrods.

Harrods (p160)

# Kensington & Hyde Park Highlights

### Victoria & Albert Museum (p146)

The extraordinary Victoria & Albert Museum is a true classic, and riveting for anyone interested in art or design. Within its vast Cromwell Rd premises the museum contains a staggering 145 galleries embracing everything from ancient Chinese ceramics to the Sony Walkman. The collection is, without question, the best of its kind in the world (and it has no admission fee).

### Shopping Around Knightsbridge & Chelsea

You need to put aside some time for quality shopping in Knightsbridge and Chelsea. Start with two of Britain's most famous department stores – the glitzy but incomparable Harrods (p160) and the rather chic Harvey Nichols (p161) – before waltzing down Sloane St or Brompton Rd for fashion must-haves in luxurious boutiques.

Harrods

## Science Museum (p148)

This fantastic collection is not just here for bad weather days, even though some kids make an instant beeline for the ground floor shop's voice warpers, bouncy globes and alien babies, and pretty much stay put. There's an astonishing range of exhibits, from Stephenson's steam engine, the *Rocket* (1829), to another rocket (the Nazi V-2), early computers (including the hefty Pegasus from 1959) and much more.

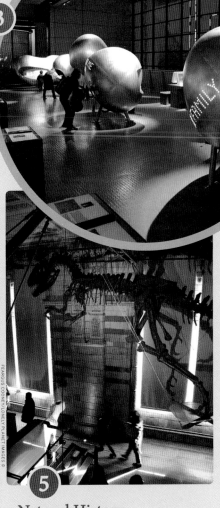

## Albert Memorial (p155)

London boasts some stupendous relics from its Victorian heyday, but perhaps none is as extravagant or ostentatious as this highly ornate Kensington monument. Capturing the ambitious zeal of the Victorian age and the imperial authority of the 19th-century monarchy, the memorial defines a bygone age. Hop on a tour to examine the allegorical detail in its bombastic stonework.

## Natural History Museum (p153)

This is a must for anyone with an interest in the natural world, or those with kids in tow. From its roaring T-Rex to the restful Wildlife Garden, the museum is an enthusiastic celebration of the natural world. The museum itself is a stunning piece of architecture, while the Central Hall with its astonishing diplodocus skeleton will simply blow you away. Furthermore, it's entirely free.

# Hyde Park & Kensington Walk

*Embark on this leisurely two-mile walk around central London's enormous green lung from Hyde Park Corner tube station. The walk takes in all of the main park and gardens, and ends up in Notting Hill.*

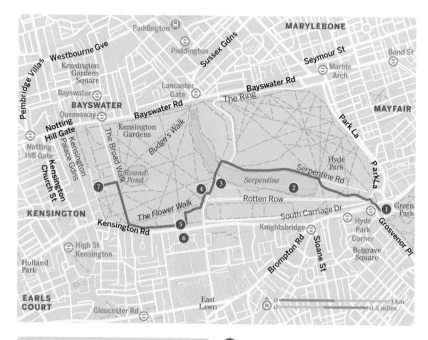

## WALK FACTS

- **Start** Wellington Arch
- **Finish** Kensington Palace
- **Distance** 2.5 miles
- **Duration** 1½ hours

## ❶ Hyde Park Corner

Amid a swirl of traffic, climb monumental **Wellington Arch** (p149) for superb views. In the same small square of grass, you will find the rather tasteful wall of eucalypt-green granite of the **Australian War Memorial** and the **New Zealand War Memorial**. To your north stands magnificent **Apsley House** (p149).

## ❷ The Serpentine

This lake will host the Olympic triathlon and marathon swimming events in 2012. Keep to the northern side and consider renting a paddle boat from the **Serpentine boathouse** (📞 7262 1330; adult/child per 30min £8/4, per 1hr £10/5). The **Serpentine solar shuttle boat** (adult/child £2.50/1.50; ⏱ every 30min noon-5pm) uses solar power to shunt you from the boathouse to the Diana, Princess of Wales Memorial Fountain.

## ❸ Diana, Princess of Wales Memorial Fountain

This Cornish granite memorial fountain sits on a perfectly manicured lawn. Water flows from the highest point in both directions, into a small pool at the bottom. Bathing is forbidden, although you are allowed to dip your feet. To rest your feet, take a break at the **Lido Café**.

### 4 Serpentine Gallery

This former teahouse is now one of the city's best contemporary **art galleries** (p154) and houses interesting exhibitions and summer pavilions designed by the world's leading architects.

### 5 Albert Memorial

Gilded and spectacular, the **Albert Memorial** (p155) is an astonishing chunk of Victoriana, completed when the British Empire spanned the globe. Commissioned by Queen Victoria in honour of her late husband, the extravagant and convoluted memorial was restored at vast expense at the end of the last millennium.

### 6 Royal Albert Hall

Opposite the Albert Memorial, this famous **concert hall** (p155) is a further monument to Queen Victoria's beloved husband. It has seen more big names and significant performances in its time than most others, including the choral version of Blake's *Jerusalem,* held to celebrate the granting of the vote to women in 1928.

### 7 Kensington Palace

Princess Diana's former home and a long-standing and recently restored **royal residence** (p154). Stop off and take a look at the permanent and temporary exhibitions, and the stunning interiors, before surrendering to one of Kensington Gardens' many stretches of grass.

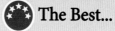 **The Best...**

## PLACES TO EAT

**Zuma** Decidedly stylish Japanese dining experience in Knightsbridge. (p157)

**Gordon Ramsay** A glorious culinary experience, garnering three Michelin stars for over a decade. (p158)

**Dinner by Heston Blumenthal** Winning celebration of British cuisine with both traditional and modern accents. (p158)

**Launceston Place** Fantastic looks, outstanding food. (p157)

## PLACES TO DRINK

**Galvin at Windows** Come here for twilight views, seen through a raised cocktail. (p159)

**606 Club** Snap your fingers to some of the finest jazz sounds in London. (p160)

## MUSEUMS

**Victoria & Albert Museum** Unique array of decorative arts and design in an awe-inspiring setting. (p146)

**Natural History Museum** A major hit with kids and adults alike in a beautiful building. (p153)

**Science Museum** Inventions, gadgets, eye-opening facts and figures plus an amazing shop. (p148)

Kensington Palace
GREG BALFOUR EVANS/ALAMY ©

# Don't Miss
# Victoria & Albert Museum

The Museum of Manufactures, as the V&A was known when it opened in 1852, specialises in decorative art and design, with some two million objects reaching back as far as 3000 years, from Britain and around the globe. It was part of Prince Albert's legacy to the nation in the aftermath of the successful Great Exhibition of 1851, and its original aims – which still hold today – were the 'improvement of public taste in design' and 'applications of fine art to objects of utility'. Free 45-minute guided tours leave the main reception area every hour from 10.30am to 3.30pm.

Map p150

📞 7942 2000

www.vam.ac.uk

Cromwell Rd SW7

admission free

🕐 10am-5.45pm Sat-Thu, to 10pm Fri

🚇 South Kensington

# Level 1

The TT Tsui China collection (rooms 44 and 47e) displays lovely pieces, including an art deco–style woman's jacket (1925–35) and exquisite Tang dynasty sancai porcelain. More than 400 objects from the Islamic Middle East are within the Islamic Middle East Gallery (room 42), including ceramics, textiles, carpets, glass and woodwork from the 8th-century caliphate up to the years before WWI.

The highly celebrated Raphael cartoons belong in room 48a while the photography collection (room 38a) is one of the nation's best, with over 500,000 images collected since 1852.

# Level 2

The British Galleries, featuring every aspect of British design from 1500 to 1900, are divided between levels 2 (1500–1760) and 4 (1760–1900). They include Henry VIII's writing box (room 58e) and the so-called Great Bed of Ware (room 57) from the late 16th century, big enough to sleep five!

# Level 3

The Jewellery Gallery (rooms 91–93) in Materials and Techniques is outstanding, including pieces of exquisite intricacy, from early Egyptian, Greek and Roman jewellery to dazzling tiaras and contemporary designs. The 20th Century Gallery (rooms 74–76) embraces design classics from a Le Corbusier chaise longue to a Sony Walkman.

# Level 4

The Architecture Gallery (rooms 127 to 128a) vividly describes architectural styles via models and videos, while the brightly illuminated Contemporary Glass Gallery (room 131) is quite spectacular.

Local Knowledge

# Don't Miss

BY LUCY TRENCH, AUTHOR OF *THE VICTORIA & ALBERT MUSEUM*

## 1 THE CAST COURTS

Question: in what single space can you see Trajan's *Column,* Michelangelo's *David* and a medieval Norwegian doorway enlaced with writhing monsters? Answer: the V&A's Cast Courts. This extraordinary collection of over 300 plaster casts is one of the wonders of the V&A, an exhilarating spectacle that has inspired and baffled visitors since it first opened in 1873.

## 2 THE ARDABIL CARPET

The Ardabil carpet, woven in Iran in 1539–40, is a masterpiece of weaving and design. It lies at the centre of the V&A's Islamic gallery. To see the carpet in its full glory you must wait for the 10 minutes every half-hour when the light level rises, bringing the subtle colours and intricate design into full view.

## 3 THE ASCENSION RELIEF

The V&A has an outstanding collection of Renaissance sculpture. One of its greatest treasures is the Ascension relief, made by Donatello around 1428–30; its surface is carved with a miraculously light touch.

## 4 TIPU'S TIGER

Of the two million objects in the V&A, Tipu's Tiger is the best loved and most weird. Made in India in about 1793–4, it is an automaton, housing an organ inside a wooden tiger. The tiger crouches over the rigid body of an English officer, sinking his fangs into the man's cravat.

## 5 CHINESE TEAPOT

The V&A was founded in the 1850s to educate designers, manufacturers and the public in the principles of good design. An object that epitomises this lofty aim is the white porcelain teapot made in Dehua in China in the late 17th century. A slightly squashed globe of pure white porcelain, with a perfect circle as a handle, it anticipates modernism by more than two centuries.

# Discover Kensington & Hyde Park

## Getting There & Away

○ **Underground** Kensington and Hyde Park are excellently connected to the rest of London via stations at South Kensington, Sloane Sq, Victoria, Knightsbridge and Hyde Park Corner. The main lines are Circle, District, Piccadilly and Victoria.

○ **Bus** Handy routes include 74 from South Kensington to Knightsbridge and Hyde Park Corner, 52 from Victoria to High St Kensington, and bus 360 from South Kensington to Sloane Sq and Pimlico, and 11 from Fulham Broadway to the King's Rd, Sloane Sq and Victoria.

○ **Bicycle** Barclays Cycle Hire (p283) is a very handy scheme for pedal powering your way in, out and around the neighbourhood.

## ◉ Sights

### Knightsbridge, Kensington & Hyde Park

**Victoria & Albert Museum**　Museum
See p146.

**Science Museum**　Museum
Map p150 (☎0870 870 4868; www.science museum.org.uk; Exhibition Rd SW7; admission free; ☺10am-6pm; ⊖South Kensington) With seven floors of interactive and educational exhibits, this spellbinding museum will mesmerise young and old.

The **Energy Hall**, on the ground floor, displays machines of the Industrial Revolution, including Stephenson's innovative *Rocket* (1829). Nostalgic parents will delight in the **Apollo 10 command module** in the **Making the Modern World gallery**.

An intriguing detour on the 1st floor is **Listening Post**, a haunting immersion into the 'sound' and chatter of the internet interspersed with thoughtful silence.

The **History of Computing** on the 2nd floor displays some intriguing devices, from Charles Babbage's analytical engine to hulking valve-based computers.

The 3rd-floor **Flight Gallery** (free tours 1pm most days) is a favourite place for children, with its gliders, hot-air balloon and varied aircraft. The hi-tech **Wellcome Wing** has an **IMAX Cinema** (tickets £10) showing the usual crop of travelogues, space adventures and dinosaur attacks in stunning 3D.

If you've kids under the age of five, pop down to the basement and **The Garden**,

*Napoleon as Mars the Peacemaker*, Antonio Canova, Apsley House
PAWEL LIBERA/ALAMY ©

ALEX SEGRE/ALAMY ©



where there's a fun-filled play zone, including a water-play area, besieged by tots in red waterproof smocks.

**Wellington Arch** Monument

**Map p150 (☎7930 2726; www.english-heritage.org.uk; Hyde Park Corner W1; adult/child £3.90/2.30, with Apsley House £7.90/4.70; 10am-5pm Wed-Sun Apr-Oct, to 4pm Nov-Mar; ; Hyde Park Corner)** This magnificent neo classical 1826 arch, facing Apsley House in the green space strangled by the Hyde Park Corner roundabout, originally faced the Hyde Park Screen, but was shunted here in 1882 for road widening. The same year saw the removal of the disproportionately large equestrian statue of the duke crowning it, making way some years later for Europe's largest bronze sculpture: *Peace Descending on the Quadriga of War* (1912), three years in the casting.

Until the 1960s part of the monument served as a tiny police station (complete with pet moggy), but was restored and opened up to the public as a three-floor exhibition space, with exhibits on the **blue plaque scheme** of historical markers (on the 1st floor), the nearby Australian and New Zealand war memorials and triumphal arches around the world (3rd floor). The open-air balconies (accessible by lift) afford unforgettable views of Hyde Park, Buckingham Palace and the Houses of Parliament; the views get even better during the annual **Trooping the Colour** pageantry and the RAF fly-past.

**Apsley House** Historic Building

**Map p150 (www.english-heritage.org.uk; 149 Piccadilly W1; adult/child £6.30/3.80; 11am-5pm Wed-Sun Apr-Oct, to 4pm Nov-Mar; Hyde Park**

## Lonely Planet's Top Tip

Catch the Queen's Life Guard (Household Cavalry) departing for Horse Guards Parade at 10.32am (9.32am on Sunday) from Hyde Park Barracks for the daily Changing of the Guard, performing a ritual that dates back to 1660. They troop via Hyde Park Corner, Constitution Hill and the Mall.

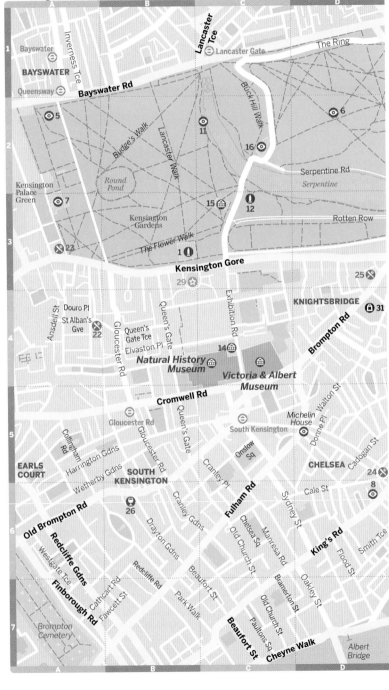

Bayswater

BAYSWATER

Queensway

Inverness Tce

Bayswater Rd

5

Lancaster Tce

Lancaster Gate

The Ring

Buck Hill Walk

6

11

16

Budge's Walk

Lancaster Walk

Round Pond

Kensington Palace Green

7

Serpentine Rd

Serpentine

15

12

Rotten Row

Kensington Gardens

The Flower Walk

23

1

Kensington Gore

29

25

Ansdell St

Douro Pl

St Alban's Gve

22

Queen's Gate Tce

Elvaston Pl

Gloucester Rd

Queen's Gate

Exhibition Rd

KNIGHTSBRIDGE

31

Brompton Rd

14

Natural History Museum

Victoria & Albert Museum

Cromwell Rd

Gloucester Rd

Queen's Gate

South Kensington

Michelin House

Walton St

Donne Pl

Collingham Rd

Harrington Gdns

Wetherby Gdns

Gloucester Rd

EARLS COURT

SOUTH KENSINGTON

Onslow Sq

Cranley Pl

CHELSEA

Cale St

Cadogan St

24

8

26

Old Brompton Rd

Redcliffe Gdns

Westgate Tce

Finborough Rd

Cathcart Rd

Fawcett St

Redcliffe Rd

Drayton Gdns

Cranley Gdns

Beaufort St

Park Walk

Fulham Rd

Chelsea Sq

Old Church St

Sydney St

Manresa Rd

King's Rd

Bramerton St

Oakley St

Flood St

Smith Tce

Old Church St

Paultons Sq

Beaufort St

Cheyne Walk

Albert Bridge

Brompton Cemetery

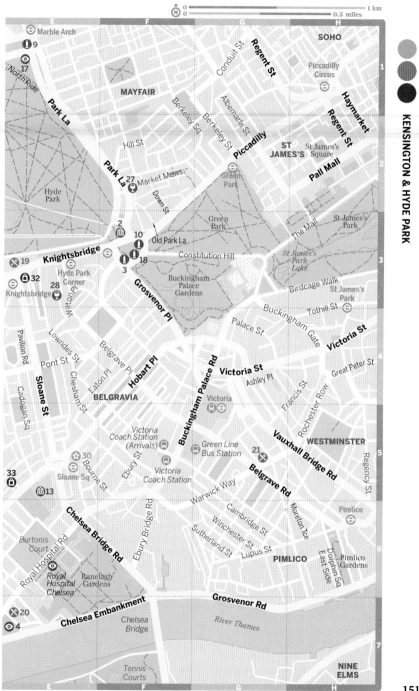

0    1 km
0    0.5 miles

Marble Arch
9
17

North Ride

Park La

MAYFAIR

Hill St

Park La

Hyde Park

27 Market Mews

Down St

Knightsbridge

19

32

28

Knightsbridge

Hyde Park
Corner

Milton Pl

2

10

3

18

Old Park La

Grosvenor Pl

Constitution Hill

Buckingham
Palace
Gardens

Pavilion Rd

Lowndes St

Pont St

Sloane St

Cadogan Sq

Belgrave Pl

Eaton Pl

Chesham St

Hobart Pl

BELGRAVIA

Victoria
Coach Station
(Arrivals)

Buckingham Palace Rd

Ebury St

Victoria
Coach Station

30

Bourne St

Sloane Sq

33

13

Chelsea Bridge Rd

Burtonis
Court

Royal Hospital Rd

Royal
Hospital
Chelsea

Ranelagh
Gardens

Ebury Bridge Rd

Chelsea Embankment

20

4

Chelsea
Bridge

Tennis
Courts

Conduit St

Regent St

SOHO

Piccadilly
Circus

Haymarket

Berkeley Sq

Berkeley St

Albemarle St

Piccadilly

ST
JAMES'S

St James's
Square

Regent St

Pall Mall

Green
Park

Green
Park

The Mall

St James's
Park

St James's
Park
Lake

Birdcage Walk

St James's
Park

Buckingham Gate

Tothill St

Palace St

Victoria St

Great Peter St

Victoria St

Ashley Pl

Francis St

Rochester Row

Victoria

Green Line
Bus Station

21

Belgrave Rd

WESTMINSTER

Vauxhall Bridge Rd

Regency St

Warwick Way

Cambridge St

Winchester St

Sutherland St

Lupus St

Moreton Tce

PIMLICO

Pimlico

Pimlico
Gardens

Dolphin Sq
East Side

Grosvenor Rd

River Thames

NINE
ELMS

# Kensington & Hyde Park

**Corner)** Still one of London's finest, Apsley House was designed by Robert Adam for Baron Apsley in the late 18th century, but later sold to the first Duke of Wellington, who lived here until he died in 1852.

In 1947 the house was given to the nation, which must have come as a surprise to the duke's descendants, who still live in a flat here; 10 of its rooms are open to the public. Wellington memorabilia, including his death mask, fills the basement gallery, while there's an astonishing collection of china and silver, including a stunning Egyptian service, a divorce present from Napoleon to Josephine (she declined it).

The stairwell is dominated by Antonio Canova's staggering 3.4m-high statue of a fig-leafed Napoleon with titanic shoulders, adjudged by the subject as 'too athletic'. The 1st-floor Wellington Gallery contains paintings by Velasquez, Rubens, Van Dyck, Brueghel, Murillo and Goya. Don't miss the elaborate Portuguese silver service, presented to Wellington in honour of his triumph over 'Le Petit Caporal'.

## Hyde Park                                    Park

Map p150 ( ☎ 7298 2000; www.royalparks.org.uk; ◎ 5.30am-midnight; ⦵ Hyde Park Corner, Marble Arch, Knightsbridge or Lancaster Gate) London's largest royal park spreads itself over 142 hectares of neatly manicured gardens, wild expanses of overgrown grass and magnificent trees.

It was the first royal park to open to the public in the early 17th century, the famous venue of the Great Exhibition in 1851, and it became an enormous potato bed during WWII.

Hyde Park is separated from Kensington Gardens by the L-shaped **Serpentine**, a small lake that will host the Olympic triathlon and marathon swimming events in 2012. Rent a paddle boat from the **Serpentine boathouse** ( ☎ 7262 1330; adult/child per 30min £8/4, per hr £10/5). The **Serpentine solar shuttle boat** (adult/child £2.50/1.50) harnesses solar power to ferry you from the boathouse to the Princess Diana Memorial Fountain in Kensington Gardens.

KIMBERLEY COOLE/LONELY PLANET IMAGES ©

## ✓ Don't Miss
# Natural History Museum

One of London's most-loved museums, this colossal landmark building is infused with the irrepressible Victorian spirit of collecting, cataloguing and interpreting the natural world. The main museum building, with its blue- and sand-coloured brick and terracotta, is as much a reason to visit as the world-famous collection within.

Your first impression is the dramatically over-arching **diplodocus skeleton** as you enter, which inspires children to yank their parents to the fantastic **dinosaur gallery**, with its impressive overhead walkway culminating in the museum's star attraction: the roaring animatronic T-rex.

The **Life galleries** are stuffed with fossils and glass cases of taxidermic birds. Ponder the enormity of the extinct giant ground sloth, visit the excellent **Creepy Crawlies** room, and admire the architecture. The vast **Darwin Centre** focuses on taxonomy, and showcases 28 million insects and six million plants in 'a giant cocoon'.

The **Earth galleries** swap Victorian fustiness for sleek, modern design, the black walls of its **Earth Hall** lined with crystals, gems and precious rocks. Ride out a tremor in the **Restless Surface gallery**, where the **mock-up of the Kobe earthquake** (a facsimile of a small Japanese grocery shop) shudders in replication of the 1995 earthquake where 6000 people perished.

A slice of English countryside in SW7, the beautiful **Wildlife Garden** (⊙ Apr-Oct) displays a range of British lowland habitats, even including a meadow with farm gates and a bee tree where a colony of honey bees fills the air.

### NEED TO KNOW

Map p150; ☏ 7942 5000; www.nhm.ac.uk; Cromwell Rd SW7; admission free; ⊙ 10am-5.50pm; ⊖ South Kensington

**FREE** **Serpentine Gallery**     Gallery
Map p150 ( ☎7402 6075; www.serpentine
gallery.org; Kensington Gardens W2; ☺10am-
6pm; 🛜; ⊖Knightsbridge) What resembles
an unprepossessing 1930s tearoom in the
midst of leafy Kensington Gardens is one
of London's most important contemporary art galleries.

Every year a leading architect
(who has never built in the UK) is
commissioned to build a new 'Summer
Pavilion' nearby, open from May to
October. A new 880-sq-metre exhibition
space, the **Serpentine Sackler Gallery**,
will open in 2012 in the Magazine, a
former Palladian villa–style gunpowder
depot on the far side of the Serpentine
Bridge, built in 1805.

### Kensington Gardens     Park
Map p150 ( ☎7298 2000; www.royalparks.org.uk;
☺6am-dusk; ⊖Queensway, High St Kensington or Lancaster Gate) Immediately west of
Hyde Park and across the Serpentine
lake, these gardens are technically part
of Kensington Palace. If you have kids,
the **Diana, Princess of Wales Memorial
Playground**, in the northwest corner of
the gardens, has some pretty ambitious
attractions for children.

George Frampton's celebrated **Peter
Pan statue** is close to the lake.

### Kensington Palace     Palace
Map p150 ( ☎0844 482 7777; www.hrp.org.
uk; adult/child £12.50/6.25, park & gardens
free; ☺10am-6pm Mar-Sep, to 5pm Oct-Feb;
⊖Queensway, Notting Hill Gate or High St Kensington) Built in 1605, the palace became
the favourite royal residence under
William and Mary of Orange in 1689, and
remained so until George III became king
and relocated to Buckingham Palace.

In the 17th and 18th centuries,
Kensington Palace was variously
renovated by Sir Christopher Wren and
William Kent. At the time of writing the
palace and its garden were undergoing
costly restoration in preparation for a
grand reopening in late March 2012. For
most visitors the highlight is the **Royal
Ceremonial Dress Collection**.

Most beautiful of all the quarters is the **Cupola Room**. The **Queen's Apartments** nearby are where Queen Mary entertained her visitors.

The **King's Gallery** displays some of the royal art collection, including the only known painting of a classical subject by Van Dyck.

The **King's Drawing Room** is dominated by a painting of **Cupid and Venus** by Giorgio Vasari (1511–74). There are lush views of the park and gardens from here.

The **Sunken Garden** near the palace is at its prettiest in summer; the nearby Orangery is a bright, rather formal place for tea. A new cafe will be added to the palace once renovations are complete in 2012.

**FREE** **Albert Memorial**    Monument
Map p150 ( ☎ 7495 0916; 45min tours adult/concession £6/5; ⏰ tours 2pm & 3pm 1st Sun of the month Mar-Dec; ⊖ Knightsbridge or Gloucester Rd) This splendid Victorian confection on the southern edge of Kensington Gardens, facing the Royal Albert Hall, is as ostentatious as the subject, Queen Victoria's German husband Albert (1819–61), was purportedly humble. Albert explicitly insisted he did not want a monument; ignoring the good prince's wishes, the Lord Mayor instructed George Gilbert Scott to build the 53m-high, gaudy Gothic memorial in 1872. An eye-opening blend of mosaic, gold leaf, marble and Victorian bombast, the renovated monument is topped with a crucifix. To step beyond the railings for a close-up of the 64m-long *Frieze of Parnassus* along the base, hop on one of the 45-minute tours.

**Royal Albert Hall**    Historic Building
Map p150 ( ☎ 7589 3203, box office 0207 589 8212, tours 7959 0558; www.royalalberthall.com; Kensington Gore SW7; tours adult/concession £11/10; ⏰ tours hourly 10.30am-4.30pm most days ☎; ⊖ South Kensington) This huge,

155

domed, red-brick amphitheatre, adorned with a frieze of Minton tiles, is Britain's most famous concert venue (see p159) and home to the BBC's Promenade Concerts (the Proms) every summer. Built in 1871 the hall was never intended as a concert venue but as a 'Hall of Arts and Sciences', so it spent the first 133 years of its existence tormenting everyone with shocking acoustics. You can take a one-hour front-of-house guided tour of the hall from the box office at door 12.

### Princess Diana Memorial Fountain
Memorial

Map p150 (Kensington Gardens W2; Knightsbridge) Opposite Kensington Gardens' Serpentine Gallery and across West Carriage Dr is this memorial fountain dedicated to the late Princess of Wales.

### Marble Arch
Monument

Map p150 (Marble Arch) Lending its name to the surrounding area, this huge white arch was designed by John Nash in 1827. Facing Speakers' Corner, it was moved here from its original spot in front of Buckingham Palace in 1851, when adjudged too unimposing an entrance to the royal manor. The arch contains three rooms (inaccessible to the public) and was used as a police hideout.

# Chelsea & Belgravia

### King's Road
Street

Map p150 (Sloane Sq or South Kensington) In the 17th century Charles II fashioned a love nest here for himself and his mistress Nell Gwyn, an orange seller turned actress at the Drury Lane Theatre. Heading back to Hampton Court Palace at eventide, Charles would employ a farmer's track that inevitably came to be known as the King's Rd. The street was at the forefront of London fashion during the technicolour '60s and anarchic '70s, and continues to be trendy now, albeit in a more self-conscious way.

Near the Sloane Sq end, the **Saatchi Gallery** (7823 2363; www.saatchi-gallery.co.uk; Duke of York's HQ, King's Rd SW3 4SQ; admission free; 10am-6pm) offers 6500 sq metres of space for temporary exhibitions.

### Chelsea Physic Garden
Garden

Map p150 (7352 5646; www.chelseaphysicgarden.co.uk; 66 Royal Hospital Rd SW3; adult/child £8/5; noon-5pm Tue-Fri, to 10pm Wed Jul & Aug, noon-6pm Sun Apr-Oct); Sloane Sq) This walled pocket of botanical enchantment was established by the Apothecaries' Society in 1676 for students working on medicinal plants and healing. One of Europe's oldest of its kind, the small grounds are a compendium of botany from carnivorous pitcher plants to rich yellow flag irises, a cork oak from Portugal, delightful ferns and a treasure trove of rare trees and shrubs. Enter from Swan Walk.

Princess Diana Memorial Fountain
PHILIP GAME/LONELY PLANET IMAGES ©

# Detour: Notting Hill

## PORTOBELLO ROAD MARKET

Like Camden and Spitalfields, **Portobello Road Market** (Portobello Rd W10; ☺8am-6pm Mon-Wed, 9am-1pm Thu, 7am-7pm Fri & Sat, 9am-4pm Sun; ⊖Notting Hill Gate or Ladbroke Grove) is an iconic London attraction with the usual mix of street food, fruit and veg, antiques, colourful fashion, and trinkets you'd never thought you'd need. Although the shops along Portobello Rd open daily and the fruit and veg stalls (from Elgin Cres to Talbot Rd) only close on Sunday, the busiest day by far is Saturday, when antique dealers set up shop (from Chepstow Villas to Elgin Cres). This is also when the fashion market (beneath Westway from Portobello Rd to Ladbroke Rd) is in full swing – although you can also browse for fashion on Friday and Sunday.

## NOTTING HILL CARNIVAL

Every August, trendy Notting Hill throws a big, long and loud party. Europe's leading street festival is a vibrantly colourful three-day celebration of Afro-Caribbean music, culture and food. Over a million people visit each year, taking part in the celebrations, thronging the streets and letting their hair down. The festival is a must if you want a spirited glimpse of multicultural London and its cross-pollination of music, food, clothing, language and heritage.

## MUSEUM OF BRANDS, PACKAGING & ADVERTISING

This **unexpected find** (www.museumofbrands.com; 2 Colville Mews, Lonsdale Rd W11; adult/child £6.50/2.25; ☺10am-6pm Tue-Sat, 11am-5pm Sun; ⊖Notting Hill Gate) is fairly low-tech but very eye-catching, with sponsored displays at the end of the gallery and exhibits showing the evolution of packaging of some well-known products including Johnson's Baby Powder and Guinness.

# Eating

Quality gravitates to where the money is, and you'll find some of London's finest establishments in the swanky hotels and ritzy mews of Chelsea, Belgravia and Knightsbridge.

## Knightsbridge, Kensington & Hyde Park

### Launceston Place
Modern European ££

Map p150 (☎7937 6912; www.launcestonplace-restaurant.co.uk; 1a Launceston Pl W8; 3-course lunch/Sun lunch/dinner £18/24/42; ☺closed lunch Mon; ⊖Gloucester Rd or Kensington High St) This exceptionally handsome restaurant on a picture-postcard Kensington street of Edwardian houses is super-chic. The food, prepared by chef Tristan Welch, a protégé of Marcus Wareing, tastes as divine as it looks. The adventurous (and flush) will go for the tasting menu (£52).

### Zuma
Japanese £££

Map p150 (☎7584 1010; www.zumarestaurant.com; 5 Raphael St SW7; mains £15-75; ⊖Knightsbridge) A modern-day take on the traditional Japanese *izakaya* ('a place to stay and drink sake'), where drinking and eating go together in relaxed unison, Zuma oozes style and sophistication. Traditional Japanese materials – wood and stone – combine with modern pronunciation for a highly contemporary feel. The private *kotatsu* room is the place for large dinner groups, or dine alongside the open-plan kitchen at the sushi counter.

## Speakers' Corner

The **northeastern corner of Hyde Park** (Map p150; ⊖ Marble Arch) is traditionally the spot for oratorical acrobatics and soapbox ranting. It's the only place in Britain where demonstrators can assemble without police permission, a concession granted in 1872 as a response to serious riots 17 years. About 150,000 people had gathered to demonstrate against the Sunday Trading Bill before Parliament only to be unexpectedly ambushed by police concealed within Marble Arch. If you've got something to get off your chest, do so on Sunday, although you'll mainly have fringe dwellers, religious fanatics and hecklers for company.

### Dinner by Heston Blumenthal
Modern British £££

Map p150 ( ✆ 7201 3833; www.dinnerby heston.com; Mandarin Oriental Hyde Park, 66 Knightsbridge SW1; set lunch £28, mains £32-72; ☺ lunch & dinner; ⊖ Knightsbridge) The most eagerly awaited restaurant opening of recent years, sumptuously presented Dinner, on the ground floor of the Mandarin Oriental, is a gastronomic tour de force, taking diners on a tour of British culinary history (with inventive modern inflections). Dishes carry historical dates to provide context and a sense of tradition, while the restaurant interior is a design triumph, from the glass-walled kitchen and its overhead clock mechanism to the large windows onto the park. Book ahead.

### Min Jiang
Chinese £££

Map p150 (www.minjiang.co.uk; 10th fl, Royal Garden Hotel, 2-24 Kensington High St W8; mains £10.50-48; ⊖ Kensington High St) Min Jiang serves up seafood, excellent Peking duck (half/whole £27.50/53.50) – cooked in a wood-burning stove – and has sumptuously regal views over Kensington Palace and Gardens. The menu is diverse, with a sporadic accent on spice (the Min Jiang is a river in Sichuan), but vaults alarmingly across China from dim sum to stir-fried Mongolian-style ostrich.

### Kazan
Turkish ££

Map p150 (www.kazan-restaurant.com; 93-94 Wilton Rd SW1; mains £11.95-15.95, set meals £25.95-39.95; ⊖ Victoria) Excellent and enjoyable, Kazan gets repeated thumbs up for its set meze platters, shish kebabs and *karniyarik* (lamb-stuffed aubergines). Flavours are rich and full, service is attentive and the refreshingly unaffected setting allows you to focus on dining, with one eye on the evening belly dancers that occasionally swivel into view.

## Chelsea & Belgravia

### Gordon Ramsay
Modern European £££

Map p150 ( ✆ 7352 4441; www.gordonramsay .com; 68 Royal Hospital Rd SW3; 3-course lunch/ dinner £45/90; ☺ lunch & dinner Mon-Fri; ⊖ Sloane Sq) One of Britain's finest restaurants and London's longest-running with three Michelin stars, this is hallowed turf for those who worship at the altar of the stove. It's true that it's a treat right from the taster to the truffles, but you won't get much time to savour it all. Bookings are made in specific sittings and you dare not linger; book as late as you can to avoid that rushed feeling.

### Rasoi Vineet Bhatia
Indian £££

Map p150 ( ✆ 7225 1881; www.rasoi-uk.com; 10 Lincoln St SW3; 2-/3-/4-course lunch £21/27/32; ☺ lunch Sun-Fri, dinner daily; ⊖ Sloane Sq) When you eventually locate this gorgeous restaurant off the King's Rd and ring the doorbell, it's like being invited round for dinner at someone's Chelsea residence with a handful of other guests. High on hospitality, seductively decorated and home to stunningly presented Indian cuisine (including a seven-course vegetarian gourmand menu for £79), this is truly what a fine dining experience should be. Book ahead.

# Drinking & Nightlife

### Galvin at Windows  Cocktail Bar
Map p150 (www.galvinatwindows.com; London Hilton on Park Lane, 28th fl, 22 Park Lane W1; ⊙10am-1am Mon-Wed, to 3am Thu-Sat, to 11pm Sun; ⊖Hyde Park Corner) This swish bar on the edge of Hyde Park opens onto stunning views, especially at dusk. Cocktail prices reach similar heights (£13.50 to £15.25) but the leather seats are comfortable and the marble bar is gorgeous.

### Drayton Arms  Pub
Map p150 (www.thedraytonarmssw5.co.uk; 153 Old Brompton Rd SW5; ⊙noon-midnight Mon-Fri, 10am-midnight Sat & Sun; ⊖West Brompton or South Kensington, ⊒430) This vast Victorian corner boozer is delightful inside and out, with some bijou art nouveau features (sinuous tendrils and curlicues above the windows and the doors), contemporary art on the walls and a fabulous coffered ceiling.

### Nag's Head  Pub
Map p150 (53 Kinnerton St SW1; ⊖Hyde Park Corner) Located in a serene mews not far from bustling Knightsbridge, this gorgeously genteel early-19th-century drinking den has eccentric decor (think 19th-century cricket prints), traditional wood-panelled charm, a sunken bar and a no-mobile-phones rule.

# ⭐ Entertainment

### Royal Albert Hall  Concert Venue
Map p150 (🎵information 7589 3203, bookings 7589 8212; www.royalalberthall.com; Kensington Gore SW7; tickets £5-150, Proms tickets £5-75; ⊖South Kensington) This splendid Victorian concert hall hosts classical music, rock and other performances, but is most famously the venue for the BBC-sponsored Proms. Booking is possible, but from mid-July to mid-September Proms punters also queue for £5 standing (or 'prom-enading') tickets that go on sale one hour before curtain-up.

### Royal Court Theatre  Theatre
Map p150 (🎵7565 5000; www.royalcourttheatre.com; Sloane Sq SW1; tickets free-£25; ⊖Sloane Sq) Equally renowned for staging innovative new plays and old classics, the Royal

Royal Albert Hall

CHRISTER FREDRIKSSON/LONELY PLANET IMAGES ©

Court is among London's most progressive theatres and has continued to discover major writing talent across the UK under its inspirational artistic director, Dominic Cooke.

Tickets for concessions are £6 to £10, and £10 for everyone on Monday (four 10p standing tickets sold at the Jerwood Theatre Downstairs); tickets for under-26-year-olds are £8. Standby tickets are sold an hour before performances, but normally at full price.

### 606 Club                                    Jazz
( ☏ 7352 5953; www.606club.co.uk; 90 Lots Rd SW10; ⏱ 7pm-late Mon-Thu & Sun, 8pm-late Fri & Sat, 12.30-4pm some Sun; ⊖ Fulham Broadway or Earl's Court) Named after its old address on Kings Rd, which cast a spell over jazz lovers London-wide back in the '80s, this fantastic, tucked-away basement jazz club and restaurant gives centre stage to contemporary British-based jazz musicians nightly. Hidden behind a nondescript brick wall, the club frequently opens until 2am, although at weekends you have to dine to gain admission (booking is advised). There is no entry charge, but a music fee (£10 during the week, £12

Friday and Saturday, £10 Sunday) will be added to your food/drink bill at the end of the evening.

# 🛍 Shopping

**Frequented by models and celebrities and awash with new money (much from abroad), this well-heeled part of town is all about high fashion, glam shops, groomed shoppers and iconic top-end department stores.**

### Harrods                          Department Store
Map p150 ( ☏ 7730 1234; www.harrods.com; 87-135 Brompton Rd SW1; ⏱ 10am-8pm Mon-Sat, 11.30am-6pm Sun; ⊖ Knightsbridge) Both garish and stylish at the same time, perennially crowded Harrods is an obligatory stop for London's tourists, from the cash strapped to the big, big spenders. Piped opera will be thrown at you as you recoil from the price tags: after an hour of browsing, you may just want to lie down on one of the doubles in the 2nd-floor bedroom department. But the stock is astonishing and you'll swoon over the spectacular food hall.

Harrods

# Detour:
# Kew Gardens

As well as being a public garden, Kew is a pre-eminent **research centre** (www.kew.org; adult/under 17yr/senior & student £13.90/free/11.90; ☺gardens 9.30am-6.30pm Mon-Fri, to 7.30pm Sat & Sun Apr-Aug, 9.30am-6pm Sep & Oct, 9.30am-4.15pm Nov-Feb, glasshouses 9.30am-5.30pm Apr-Oct, 9.30am-3.45pm Nov-Feb; ⊖ ⊠ Kew Gardens), maintaining its reputation as the most exhaustive botanical collection in the world.

Assuming you come by tube and enter via Victoria Gate, you'll come almost immediately to a large pond overlooked by the enormous and iconic 700-glass-paned Palm House, a domed hothouse of metal and curved sheets of glass dating from 1848 and housing a splendid display of exotic tropical greenery; the aerial walkway offers a parrots'-eye view of the lush vegetation.

The beautiful Temperate House in the southeast of Kew Gardens (north of the pagoda) is the world's largest surviving Victorian glasshouse, an astonishing feat of architecture housing an equally sublime collection of plants.

In the **Arboretum**, a short walk from Temperate House, this fascinating and much-enjoyed walkway takes you underground and then 18m up in the air into the tree canopy, for closer angles on tree anatomy.

### John Sandoe Books    Books
Map p150 ( ☎7589 9473; www.johnsandoe.com; 10 Blacklands Tce SW3; ☺9.30am-5.30pm Mon-Sat, to 7.30pm Wed, noon-6pm Sun; ⊖Sloane Sq) The perfect antidote to impersonal book superstores, this atmospheric little bookshop is a treasure trove of literary gems and hidden surprises. In business for decades, loyal customers swear by it and the knowledgeable booksellers spill forth with well-read pointers.

### Harvey Nichols    Department Store
Map p150 ( ☎7235 5000; www.harveynichols.com; 109-125 Knightsbridge SW1; ☺10am-8pm or 9pm Mon-Sat, 11.30am-6pm Sun; ⊖Knightsbridge) At London's temple to high fashion, you'll find Chloé and Balenciaga bags, the city's best denim range, a massive make-up hall with exclusive lines, great jewellery and the fantastic restaurant, Fifth Floor.

# Clerkenwell, Hoxton & Spitalfields

**Come here for throbbing nightlife, hip shopping and innovative dining.** The three adjoining but very different districts are Clerkenwell, just north of the City; Shoreditch and its northern extension Hoxton, an area (roughly) between Old St tube station and just east of Shoreditch High St; and Spitalfields, centred on its eponymous market and Brick Lane, its heaving main thoroughfare. This remains London's creative engine room and, for night owls, *the* place in town to wing to for wining, dining and a good time either side of midnight. There are sights and shops you'll want to explore in daytime, but they don't get too overrun so there's no compulsion to head out particularly early.

All three neighbourhoods have a glut of excellent cafes, restaurants, bars and clubs, but Shoreditch remains the centre of late-night gravity. Sunday is excellent for a leisurely stroll through Spitalfields.

St John's Gate (p168)
S R VEEJAY/ALAMY ©

# Clerkenwell, Hoxton & Spitalfields Highlights

## Geffrye Museum (p169)

An institution devoted to interiors may seem out of the ordinary and idiosyncratic, but this charming museum succeeds on all levels and affords a fascinating insight into the evolution of interiors in Britain. It's also housed in a beautiful old row of 18th-century almshouses, well worth seeing for themselves alone, along with a charming herb garden.

### Clubbing in Shoreditch (p175)

Nowhere in London can rival the creative maelstrom of the capital's coolest quarter. True, prices have risen over the past decade, but you can't beat an evening out in Shoreditch, where the best and most exciting of the capital's clubs – including XOYO and Cargo (p176) – rule. Cargo

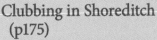

JULIO ETCHART/ALAMY ©

## Shopping at Spitalfields Market (p177) 3

The market at Spitalfields has long been a London favourite – and even though (inevitably, given its position on some of London's prime real estate) the developers moved in and 'regenerated' much of the old market, this place still has its fair share of excellent shopping, eating and atmosphere.

## Brick Lane (p172) 4

Wander through wonderfully preserved Georgian Spitalfields (p169), before emerging onto exuberant and cacophonous Brick Lane to explore Banglatown and the hip bars, shops and cafes of the Old Truman Brewery. Grab a cheap and filling spicy meal, peek into some of the many interesting shops or just soak up the atmosphere. You might want to steer clear of Brick Lane at the weekends though, as crowds can be immense.

## Drinking in a Local Pub 5

Serve up your poison according to taste in this well-stocked neighbourhood, from the historic, traditional pubs of Clerkenwell to the hip and fashionable bars of Shoreditch and Hoxton. Make a start with the Jerusalem Tavern (p174) and then see out the night taking your pick from some of London's coolest watering holes. Ye Old Mitre (p175)

# Spitalfields & Shoreditch Walk

*This two-mile walk takes you through one of London's most exciting and creative neighbourhoods. You can do it anytime, but for the best experience aim for Sunday mornings when two of the biggest markets are in full swing.*

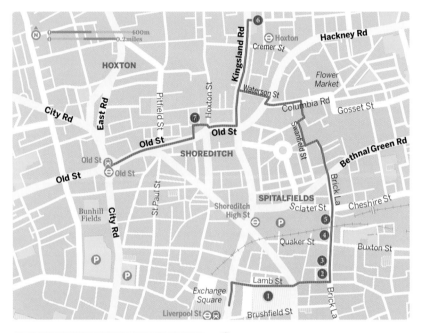

## ❶ Spitalfields Market

One of London's best **markets** (p177), this is a great weekend treat for clothing, records and food. Walk here from Liverpool St tube station, enter the old market building and get lost among its many stalls.

## ❷ Sunday UpMarket

From 10am to 5pm on Sundays inside the Old Truman Brewery, this **market** is relatively uncrowded, with wonderful clothes, music and crafts from young designers. The excellent food hall (at the Brick Lane end) is a tempting array of global grub, from Ethiopian vegie dishes to Japanese delicacies.

## ❸ Old Truman Brewery

This was the biggest brewery in London by the mid-18th century, and the Director's House on the left dates from 1740. Next to the 19th-century Vat House is the 1830 Engineer's House and a row of former stables. The brewery shut down over 20 years ago and is now part of Sunday UpMarket.

### 4 Brick Lane

In 1550 this was just a country road leading to brickyards; by the 18th century it had been paved and lined with houses and cottages inhabited by the Spitalfields weavers. Today the southern part of this vibrant **street** (p172) is full of touristy curry houses (with all street names in Bengali as well as English).

### 5 Brick Lane Market

On Sundays, around the Shoreditch tube station, you'll find good bargains on clothes, but the market (from 8am to 3pm Sundays) is good for furniture, household goods, bric-a-brac, secondhand clothes and cheap fashion. Saunter down Cheshire St for little boutiques featuring new designers and vintage collections.

### 6 Geffrye Museum

A small estate of Victorian houses, this fascinating **museum** (p169) is devoted to English interiors through the ages. End your walk in the lovely glass cafe in the back, and have a look at the museum's aromatic herb garden.

### 7 White Cube Gallery

Pop into Hoxton Sq on the way to Old St tube. Check out the small park where there's always something going on and join the crowds having a drink outside in good weather. Don't miss the **White Cube gallery** (p169) where there's always something intriguing or controversial hanging on the pristine white walls.

 **The Best...**

## PLACES TO EAT

**Moro** Excellent Moorish menu, still winning plaudits. (p173)

**Leila's Shop** Lovely Shoreditch cafe, strong on rustic charm and thoughtfully prepared food. (p173)

**St John** For British cuisine, St John remains one of London's best. (p173)

**Les Trois Garçons** Over-the-top decor, terrific Modern French menu. (p173)

## PLACES TO DRINK

**Jerusalem Tavern** Tiny but delightful, with original beers from a Norfolk brewery. (p174)

**Book Club** A modern temple to good times, with great offbeat events. (p175)

**Golden Heart** Fun, fantastic pub drawing an arty, trendy clientele (p176)

**Mason & Taylor** Designer bar with a connoisseur's range of beers. (p176)

## PLACES TO DANCE

**Fabric** Hip Clerkenwell club for hedonists: a warren of three floors, three bars and unisex toilets. (p175)

**Cargo** Creative music menu and trendy Shoreditch locale. (p176)

**XOYO** Diverse music menu and an eclectic crowd of dancers. (p176)

Hoxton Square
IAIN CHAMBERS/ALAMY ©

# Discover Clerkenwell, Hoxton & Spitalfields

## Getting There & Away

○ **Underground** Farringdon and Barbican are stops for Clerkenwell, on the Circle, Hammersmith & City and Metropolitan Lines. Old St is on the Bank branch of the Northern Line. Liverpool St is on the Central Line.

○ **Overground** Shoreditch High St and Hoxton are handy stops on the overground running north to Dalston and Highbury & Islington, and south to Wapping.

○ **Bus** Clerkenwell and Old St are connected with Oxford St by the 55, and with Waterloo by the 243. The 38 up Rosebery Ave goes to Exmouth Market. The 8 and 242 zip through the city and up Shoreditch High St.

*Suspended*, Mona Hatoum, 2011, at White Cube
HUGO GLENDINNING. COURTESY WHITE CUBE ©

## ◉ Sights

### Clerkenwell

**Charterhouse**  Historic Building
Map p170 (www.thecharterhouse.org; Charterhouse Sq EC1; admission £10; ◷ guided tours 2.15pm Wed Apr-Aug; ⊖ Barbican or Farringdon) You need to book six months in advance to see inside this former Carthusian monastery, where the centrepiece is a Tudor hall with a restored hammerbeam roof. Its incredibly popular two-hour guided tours begin at the 14th-century gatehouse on Charterhouse Square, before going through to the Preachers' Court, the Master's Court, the Great Hall and the Great Chamber, where Queen Elizabeth I stayed on numerous occasions.

For tickets, you need to send a stamped, self-addressed envelope, a covering letter giving the dates of three Wednesdays between April and August when you would like to visit, and a cheque made payable to 'Charterhouse', to Tour Bookings, Charterhouse, Charterhouse Square, London EC1M 6AN.

**FREE St John's Gate**
Museum, Historic Building
Map p170 ( ⊖ Farringdon) During the 12th century, the crusading Knights of St John of Jerusalem (a religious and military order with a focus on providing care to the sick) established a priory on this site that originally covered around 4 hectares. The gate, off Clerkenwell Rd, was built in 1504 as a grand entrance to the priory and although most of the buildings were destroyed when Henry VIII dissolved every monastery in the country between 1536 and 1540, the gate lived on. Inside

# Georgian Spitalfields

Crowded around its eponymous market and the marvellous Hawksmoor Christ Church, Spitalfields is a layer cake of immigration from all over the world. Waves of French Huguenots, Jews, Irish and, more recently, Indian and Bangladeshi immigrants have made Spitalfields home, and it remains one of the capital's most multicultural areas. A walk down Brick Lane is the best way to get a sense of today's Bangladeshi community, but to get a taste of what Georgian Spitalfields was like, branch off to Princelet, Fournier, Elder and Wilkes Sts. Having fled persecution in France, the Huguenots set up shop here from the late 1600s, practising their trade of silk weaving. The attics of these grand town houses were once filled with clattering looms and the area became famous for the quality of its silk – even providing the material for Queen Victoria's coronation gown. To see inside one of these wonderful old buildings, visit **Dennis Severs' House**.

is the small **Museum of the Order of St John** (www.museumstjohn.org.uk; St John's Lane EC1; ⊙10am-5pm Mon-Sat), which covers the history of the Order (including rare examples of the knights' armour), as well as the foundation of St John's Ambulance, set up in the 19th century to promote first aid and revive the Order's ethos of caring for the sick.

Across the road from the gate is the fine Norman crypt of the original **priory church** (admission free; ⊙10am-3pm Mon-Sat), which houses a sturdy alabaster effigy of a Castilian knight (1575) and a battered monument portraying the last prior, William Weston, as a skeleton in a shroud.

Try to time your visit for one of the comprehensive **guided tours** (donation suggested; ⊙11am & 2.30pm Tue, Fri & Sat) of the gate and the restored church.

## Shoreditch & Hoxton

### Geffrye Museum · Museum

Map p170 (www.geffrye-museum.org.uk; 136 Kingsland Rd E2; admission free; ⊙10am-5pm Tue-Sat, noon-5pm Sun; ⊖Hoxton) This series of beautiful 18th-century ivy-clad almshouses, with an extensive and well-presented herb garden, was first opened as a museum in 1914, in a spot that was then in the centre of the furniture industry. The museum inside is devoted to

domestic interiors, with each room of the main building furnished to show how the homes of the relatively affluent middle class would have looked from Elizabethan times right through to the end of the 19th century.

Be sure to time your visit in order to see the exquisite restoration of a historic **almshouse interior.** The setting is so fragile, however, that **tours** (£2.50; ⊙hourly tours 11am-3pm 1st Sat, 1st & 3rd Wed, 2nd & 4th Thu) run only a few times a month.

### FREE White Cube · Gallery

Map p170 (www.whitecube.com; 48 Hoxton Sq N1; ⊙10am-6pm Tue-Sat; ⊖Old St) This Hoxton Sq cube is aptly named and, while the gallery is now part of Britain's 'new establishment', it's always worth a visit just to have a look at the latest shows. There's another White Cube (p64) in St James's.

## Spitalfields

### Dennis Severs' House · Museum

Map p170 (☎7247 4013; www.dennissevers house.co.uk; 18 Folgate St E1; Sun/Mon/Mon evening £8/5/12; ⊙noon-4pm Sun, noon-2pm Mon following 1st & 3rd Sun of the month, 6-9pm Mon; ⊖Liverpool St) This quirky hotchpotch of a cluttered house is named after the late American eccentric who restored it and turned it into what he called a 'still-life

# Clerkenwell, Hoxton & Spitalfields

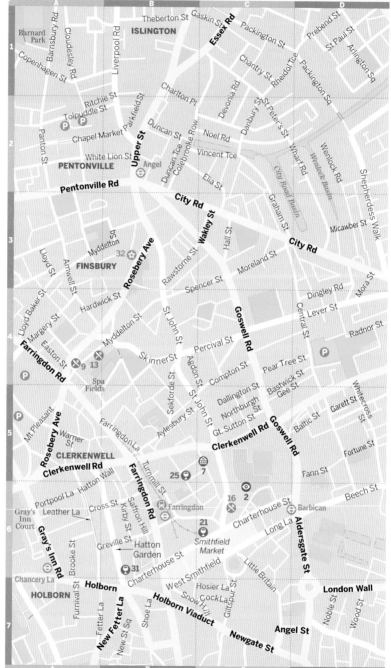

0 500 m
0 0.25 miles

DE BEAUVOIR TOWN

Orsman St

Dunston Rd

Queensbridge Rd

Baring St

Poole St

Penn St

Hyde Rd

Phillipp St

Laburnum St

Whiston Rd

How's St

Shoreditch Park

Pitfield St

Hemsworth St

Nuttall St

Thurtle Rd

Appleby St

Geffrye St

Ormsby St

New North Rd

Mintern St

Ivy St

Purcell St

Stanway St

Hoxton St

5

Dunloe St

Dunloe St

Wenlock St

Crondall St

Falkirk St

15

Hoxton

Cremer St

Kingsland Rd

Hackney Rd

Diss St

Ravenscroft St

HOXTON

Provost St

Nile St

Nile St

Bevenden St

Fanshaw St

Haberdasher St

Pitfield St

SHOREDITCH

18

Columbia Rd

East Rd

Britannia Wk

Chart St

Bowling Green Walk

24

8

City Rd

Brunswick Pl

Old St

20

22

Virginia Rd

Brick La

35

Peerless St

Bath St

Old St

Curtain Rd

11

Boundary St

Club Row

Bateman's Row

27

Old St

30

Leonard St

19

26

12

Bethnal Green Rd

Featherstone St

Clere St

Luke St

Holywell La

Sclater St

Bunhill Fields

Epworth St

Paul St

Shoreditch High St

SPITALFIELDS

Dufferin St

Bunhill Row

Finsbury Square

City Rd

29

28

Quaker St

1

33

6

Chiswell St

Worship St

Clifton St

Appold St

10

4

Folgate St

23

14

17

Earl St

Sun St

Exchange Square

Spital Sq

Lamb St

34

3

Silk St

Moor La

Wilson St

Spitalfields Market

Brushfield St

Moorfields

South Pl

Eldon St

Liverpool St

Bishopsgate

Artillery La

Brune St

Fashion St

Moorgate

Moorgate

Finsbury Circus

Liverpool St

New St

Middlesex St

Brick La

London Wall

Wormwood St

Houndsditch

Wentworth St

Coleman St

Moorgate

Petticoat Lane Market

Old Castle St

Gouston St

Aldgate East

Gresham St

Bevis Marks

171

# Clerkenwell, Hoxton & Spitalfields

drama'. Severs was an artist, and lived in the house (in a similar way to the original inhabitants) until his death in 1999.

Visitors today find they have entered the home of a 'family' of Huguenot silk weavers, who were common to the Spitalfields area in the 18th century. Each of the 10 rooms recreates a specific time in the house's history from 1724 to 1914. From the cellar to the bedrooms, the interiors demonstrate both the original function and design of the rooms, as well as the highs and lows of the area's history. It's a unique and intriguing proposition by day, but 'Silent Night' tours by candlelight every Monday evening (bookings essential) are even more memorable.

## Brick Lane                    Street
Map p170 ( ◎ Shoreditch High St or Liverpool St)
Full of noise, colour and life, Brick Lane is a vibrant mix of history and modernity, and a palimpsest of cultures. Today it is the centrepiece of a thriving Bengali community in an area nicknamed Banglatown. The southern part of the lane is one long procession of curry and balti houses intermingled with fabric shops and Indian supermarkets.

Just past Hanbury St is the converted **Old Truman Brewery**, a series of buildings on both sides of the lane that was once London's largest brewery.

## Christ Church Spitalfields    Church
Map p170 (www.christchurchspitalfields.org; Commercial St E1; ◎11am-4pm Tue, 1-4pm Sun; ◎Shoreditch High St or Liverpool St) Diagonally opposite Spitalfields Market, on the corner of Commercial and Fournier Sts, is this restored church, where many of the area's weavers worshipped. The magnificent English baroque structure, with a tall spire sitting on a portico of four great Tuscan columns, was designed by Nicholas Hawksmoor and completed in 1729.

# ◎ Eating

As well as a wealth of fantastic cafes and restaurants, this area also hosts a number of food markets where you can grab a real variety of dishes and cuisines, from deliciously moist chocolate brownies to fiery Thai curries and overflowing burritos. Streets to check out include **Exmouth Market** (✪noon-3pm Thu & Fri; ⊖Farringdon or Angel), **Whitecross St Market** (✪11am-3pm Mon-Fri; ⊖Old St) and **Brick Lane and the surrounding streets.**

# Clerkenwell

## Moro
Fusion ££

Map p170 (☑7833 8336; www.moro.co.uk; 34-36 Exmouth Market EC1; mains £15.50-19.50; ☎; ⊖Farringdon or Angel) Still a frequent award winner 15 years after it launched, Moro serves Moorish cuisine, a fusion of Spanish, Portuguese and North African flavours. The restaurant is always full and buzzing, and the food is generally fabulous, with such dishes on its constantly evolving menu as wood-roasted chicken with chermoula, and charcoal-grilled lamb with garlic purée. Reservations are essential.

## St John
British ££

Map p170 (☑3301 8069; www.stjohnrestaurant.co.uk; 26 St John St EC1; mains £17-23.80; ✪closed dinner Sun; ⊖Farringdon) This London classic is wonderfully simple – its light bar and cafe area giving way to a surprisingly small dining room where 'nose to tail eating' is served up courtesy of celebrity chef Fergus Henderson.

## Caravan
Brasserie ££

Map p170 (☑7833 8115; www.caravanonexmouth.co.uk; 11-13 Exmouth Market EC2; small plates £4.50-8, big plates £12.50-16; ✪8am-10.30pm Mon-Fri, 10am-10.30pm Sat & Sun; ☎; ⊖Farringdon) Perfect for a sunny day when the sides of the restaurant are opened onto bustling Exmouth Market, this place is a relaxed affair, offering all-day dining and drinking.

# Shoreditch & Hoxton

## Leila's Shop
Cafe £

Map p170 (17 Calvert Ave E2; dishes £5-7; ✪10am-6pm Wed-Sun; ⊖Shoreditch High St) Tucked away on up-and-coming Calvert Ave, Leila's Shop feels like a bohemian country kitchen. For breakfast, go for the eggs and ham, which come beautifully cooked in their own little frying pan. Sandwiches are freshly made with superior produce, and there's homemade lemonade and great coffee.

## Les Trois Garçons
Modern French £££

Map p170 (☑7613 1924; www.lestroisgarcons.com; 1 Club Row E1; 2/3 courses £39.50/45.50; ✪closed dinner Sun; ⊖Shoreditch High St) The name may prepare you for the French menu, but nothing on Earth could prepare you for the camp decor inside this made-over Victorian pub. The food is excellent, if a tad overpriced, and the small army of waiters unobtrusively delivers complimentary bread and tasty gifts from the kitchen.

---

# The Pho Mile

The Kingsland Rd has become famous for its string of Vietnamese cafes and restaurants, many of which are BYO and serve authentic and great-value cuisine.

**Viet Grill** (Map p170; ☑7739 6686; www.vietnamesekitchen.co.uk; 58 Kingsland Rd E2; mains £6.50-10; ⊖Hoxton) One of the more upmarket options along the road, Viet Grill is a low-lit, modern restaurant over two floors with a buzzy atmosphere and colonial decor.

**Sông Quê** (Map p170; ☑7613 3222; www.songque.co.uk; 134 Kingsland Rd E2; mains £6.70-8.60; ⊖Hoxton) With the kind of demand for seats that most London restaurants can only dream of, this perennial favourite always has a line of people waiting for a table.

## Spitalfields

### St John Bread & Wine
British ££

Map p170 (☏ 3301 8069; www.stjohnbreadand
wine.com; 94-96 Commercial St E1; mains £14-19;
⏰ 9am-10.30pm Mon-Sat, to 9pm Sun; ⊖ Liverpool St) Little sister to St John (p173), this
place is cheaper and more relaxed but
offers similar 'nose to tail' traditional fare
(potted pork, venison and trotter pie,
blood cake) in a simple, clean and bright
space popular with Spitalfields creative
types.

### Poppies
Fish & Chips ££

Map p170 (www.poppiesfishandchips.co.uk; 6-8
Hanbury St E1; mains £9-13; ⏰ 11am-11pm; 🛜;
⊖ Shoreditch High St or Liverpool St) This is a
glorious recreation of a 1950s East End
chippy, complete with waitresses in pin-
nies and hairnets, and retro memorabilia.
As well as the usual fishy suspects, it
also does jellied eels, homemade tartare
sauce and mushy peas, and you can
wash it all down with a glass of wine or
beer.

### Hawksmoor
Steak £££

Map p170 (☏ 7247 7392; 157 Commercial St
E1; mains £20-30; ⏰ closed dinner Sun; 🛜;
⊖ Shoreditch High St or Liverpool St) You could
easily miss discreetly signed Hawksmoor,
on an unlovely stretch of Commercial St,
but carnivores will find this impressive
steak restaurant worth seeking out. Make
sure you try one of the equally impressive
cocktails.

## 🍷 Drinking & Nightlife

### Clerkenwell

### Jerusalem Tavern
Pub

Map p170 (www.stpetersbrewery.co.uk; 55 Britton
St EC1; ⏰ Mon-Fri; 🛜; ⊖ Farringdon) One of
the first London coffee houses (1703), with
the 18th-century decor of occasional tile
mosaics still visible, the JT is an absolute
stunner. Sadly it's both hugely popular and
tiny, so get here early for a seat.

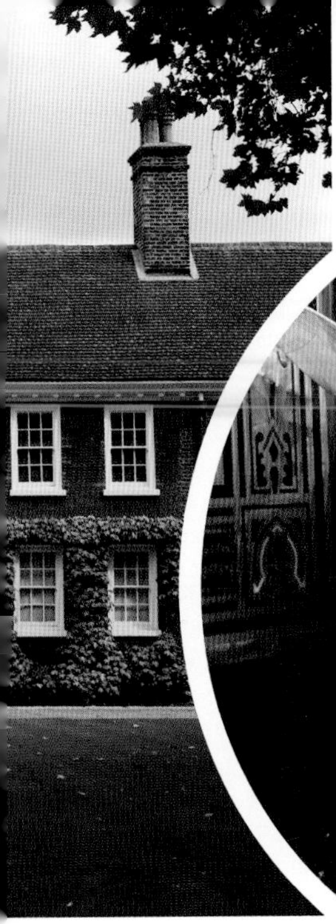

**Left:** Geffrye Museum (p169);
**Below:** Sculpture at Les Trois Garçons (p173)
(LEFT) NEIL SETCHFIELD/LONELY PLANET IMAGES ©; (BELOW) JONATHAN SMITH/LONELY PLANET IMAGES ©

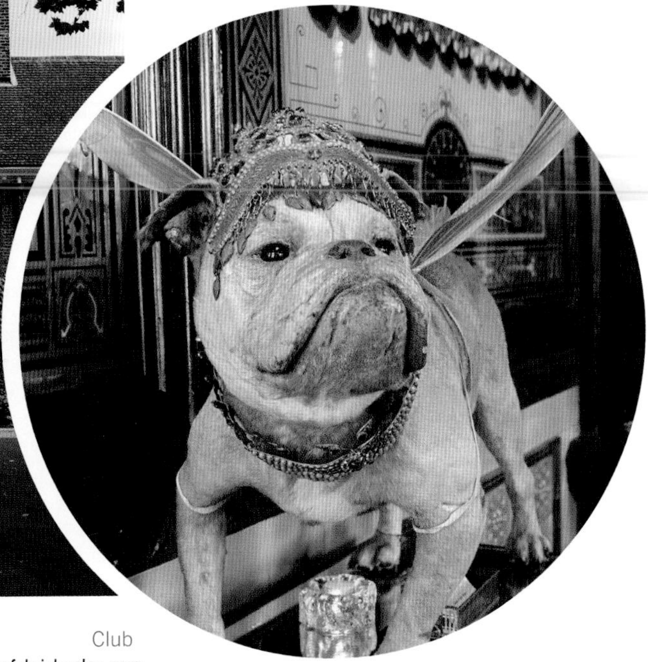

### Fabric — Club

**Map p170 (www.fabriclondon.com; 77a Charterhouse St EC1; 10pm-6am Fri, 11pm-8am Sat, 11pm-6am Sun; Farringdon)** This most impressive of superclubs is still the first stop on the London scene for many international clubbers, as the lengthy queues attest. The crowd is hip and well dressed without overkill, and the music – mainly electro, techno, house, drum and bass and dubstep – is as superb as you'd expect from London's top-rated club.

### Ye Olde Mitre — Pub

**Map p170 (1 Ely Ct EC1; Mon-Fri; ; Chancery Lane or Farringdon)** This is a delightfully cosy historic pub, tucked away in a backstreet off Hatton Garden – look for a Fullers sign above a low archway on the left. Ye Olde Mitre was originally built for the servants of Ely Palace and there is still a memento of Elizabeth I – the stump of a cherry tree around which she once danced.

## Shoreditch & Hoxton

### Book Club — Bar, Club

**Map p170 (www.wearetbc.com; 100 Leonard St EC2; 8am-midnight Sun-Wed, to 2am Thu-Sat; ; Old St)** This former Victorian warehouse has been transformed into an innovative temple to good times. Spacious and whitewashed with large windows upstairs and a basement bar below, it hosts a real variety of offbeat events, such as spoken word, dance lessons and life drawing, as well as a varied program of DJ nights (from punk, ska and '60s pop to electro, house and disco).

### George & Dragon — Gay

**Map p170 (2-4 Hackney Rd E2; Shoreditch High St or Old St)** Once a scuzzy local pub, the George was taken over and decorated with the owner's grandma's antiques (antlers, racoon tails, old clocks), cardboard cutouts of Cher and fairy lights, turning this one-room pub into what has remained the

epicentre of the Hoxton scene for more than a decade. Some of the best DJ nights in London are on offer here, with cabaret performances taking place on window sills.

### Mason & Taylor    Bar
Map p170 (www.masonandtaylor.co.uk; 51-55 Bethnal Green Rd E1; 🔊; ⊖Shoreditch High St) On a corner where Banglatown grinds up against Shoreditch, this designer beer bar offers an extraordinary range of cask and bottled beers. The selection is sourced from some interesting breweries, with welcome support for London's new breed of craft brewers, such as Kernel and Camden Town.

### Cargo    Club
Map p170 (www.cargo-london.com; 83 Rivington St EC2; ⏲noon-1am Mon-Thu, noon-3am Fri, 6pm-3am Sat, noon-midnight Sun; ⊖Old St or Shoreditch High St) Cargo is one of London's most eclectic clubs. Under its brick railway arches you'll find a dance-floor room, bar and outside terrace.

### XOYO    Club
Map p170 (www.xoyo.co.uk; 32-37 Cowper St EC2; ⊖Old St) Run by a group of music professionals, this lofty venue plays host to a finely chosen selection of gigs and club nights, as well as exhibiting art. The varied program – expect indie bands, hip hop, electro, dubstep and much in between – attracts a mix of clubbers from skinny-jeaned hipsters to more mature hedonists.

### Queen of Hoxton    Bar
Map p170 (www.thequeenofhoxton.co.uk; 1-5 Curtain Rd EC2; ⏲to 2am Thu-Sat; 🔊; ⊖Liverpool St) Industrial-chic bar with a games room, basement and varied music nights. However, the real drawcard is the vast rooftop bar, decked out with flowers, fairy lights and even a fish pond, with fantastic views across the city and a popular **outdoor film club** (www.rooftopfilmclub.com; ⏲Jun-Sep).

## Spitalfields

### Golden Heart    Pub
Map p170 (110 Commercial St E1; ⊖Liverpool St) It's an unsurprisingly trendy Hoxton crowd that mixes in the surprisingly untrendy interior of this brilliant Spitalfields boozer. While it's famous as the watering hole for the cream of London's art crowd, our favourite part about any visit is a chat with Sandra, the landlady-celebrity who talks to all comers and ensures the bullshit never outstrips the fun.

---

# The Cocktail Hour

While mojitos and caipirinhas are these days two-a-penny in Shoreditch bars, there are some places that take their shaking far more seriously. Here is a list of our favourites. It's worth booking ahead at them all.

**Worship St Whistling Shop** (Map p170; ☎7247 0015; www.whistlingshop.com; 63 Worship St EC2; ⏲noon-1am Mon-Thu, to 2am Fri & Sat; ⊖Old St or Liverpool St) A 'Victorian' drinking den that takes cocktails to a molecular level, the Whistling Shop (as Victorians called a place selling illicit booze) serves expertly crafted and highly unusual concoctions using potions conjured up in its on-site lab.

**Happiness Forgets** (Map p170; ☎7613 0325; www.happinessforgets.com; 8-9 Hoxton Sq N1; ⏲5-11pm Mon-Sat; 🔊; ⊖Old St or Hoxton) The menu promises mixed drinks and mischief at this low-lit bar with good-value cocktails in an intimate setting.

**Loungelover** (Map p170; ☎7012 1234; www.lestroisgarcons.com; 1 Whitby St E1; ⏲6pm-midnight Sun-Thu, to 1am Fri & Sat; 🔊; ⊖Liverpool St or Shoreditch High St) The drinks and the look are both faultless at this Shoreditch institution, where it's all about the superb cocktails and the junk-shop chic of the decor.

RICHARD I'ANSON/LONELY PLANET IMAGES ©

# ⭐ Entertainment

### Sadler's Wells                     Dance
Map p170 (📞0844 412 4300; www.sadlerswells.com; Rosebery Ave EC1; 🚇Angel) The theatre site dates from 1683 but was completely rebuilt in 1998; today it is the most eclectic and modern dance venue in town, with experimental dance shows of all genres and from all corners of the globe. The Lilian Baylis Studio stages smaller productions.

# 🔒 Shopping

There are tonnes of shops off Brick Lane, especially in burgeoning Cheshire St, Hanbury St and the Old Truman Brewery on Dray Walk. Clerkenwell is mostly known for its jewellery. For classic settings and unmounted stones, visit London's traditional jewellery and diamond trade area, **Hatton Garden** (www.hatton-garden.net; 🚇Chancery Lane).

### Spitalfields Market               Market
Map p170 (www.oldspitalfieldsmarket.com; Commercial St, btwn Brushfield & Lamb Sts E1; 🕐10am-4pm Sun-Fri; 🚇Liverpool St) One of London's best markets, with traders hawking their wares here since the early 17th century. The market is open six days a week, with a particular focus on each day, but the best days to come are Thursdays (for antiques), Fridays (fashion) and Sundays, when the market is at its bustling best and filled with fashion, jewellery, food and music stalls.

### Rough Trade East                 Music
Map p170 (www.roughtrade.com; Dray Walk, Old Truman Brewery, 91 Brick Lane E1; 🕐8am-8pm Mon-Fri, 11am-7pm Sat & Sun; 🚇Liverpool St) This vast record store has an impressive selection of CDs and vinyl across all genres, as well as an interesting offering of books.

### Tatty Devine                    Jewellery
Map p170 (www.tattydevine.com; 236 Brick Lane E2; 🕐11am-6pm Tue-Sun; 🚇Shoreditch High St) Harriet Vine and Rosie Wolfenden make hip and witty jewellery that's become the favourite of many young Londoners. Their original designs feature all manner of fauna-and-flora inspired necklaces, as well as creations sporting moustaches, dinosaurs and bunting.

# The East End & Docklands

**Traditional, yet in flux, this is a stimulating multicultural neighbourhood.** Despite immigrants settling here unbroken for several centuries, the East End remains home to London's best known denizen, the cockney. Because of its immigrant communities, however, it's also a diverse area to eat, drink and explore.

There may be few standout sights but exploration really pays dividends in these unique neighbourhoods. South of the East End is Docklands, once the hub of the British Empire then later a post-industrial wasteland. After massive regeneration it captures a vision of London's future as well as its history.

The recent opening of overground lines has made East London much easier to traverse. The three main areas to target are the all-new Olympic Park (and neighbouring Hackney), Docklands itself (and adjoining waterside Limehouse and Wapping) and Whitechapel (from which Bethnal Green is just a short hop away).

Canary Wharf tube station
DBURKE/ALAMY ©

# East End & Docklands Highlights

## Olympic Park (p187)

The main draw of Olympic Park is its architectural attractions: the Olympic Stadium and the striking Aquatics Centre. The award-winning Velodrome (aka the 'Pringle') has also been praised for its fine lines, sustainable credentials and functional appeal, while an admirable ethos of regeneration has guided the entire transformation of this once-neglected area of East London. Olympic Stadium (p187), designed by Populous

**1**

**2** ## Whitechapel Gallery (p184)

It's not surprising you'll find one of the city's most ambitious and eventful art galleries in one of London's most diverse and culturally vibrant neighbourhoods and thoroughfares. With cutting-edge exhibits, and the attention it gives to both luminaries and up-and-coming names in international art, this is a great place to check the pulse of contemporary art.

## Docklands Skyline

You'd probably never guess it from the ultramodern and postmodern skyscrapers dominating the Isle of Dogs and Canary Wharf, but from the 16th century until the mid-20th century this was the centre of the world's greatest port, the hub of the British Empire. From the late 1980s, Docklands was regenerated from its post-industrial decline into a top financial centre, with riveting pockets of history.

## Columbia Road Flower Market (p193)

London's markets are perfect for catching the character of this vibrant city, in all its many facets and moods. Locals simply love to trawl through markets – browsing, chatting, socialising and searching for shopping ideas. It may be a colourful celebration of flowers and plants but a visit to Columbia Road Flower Market is also fun and perfect for seeing locals in their outdoor element.

## Victoria Park (p185)

Around a quarter of London is gorgeous parkland, and it's not just the big royal parks that deserve attention. Often overlooked by visitors, this 86-hectare park – more intimately called 'Vicky Park' by locals – is highly popular with Londoners who flock here in fine weather. Undergoing redevelopment for 2012, the park is receiving an attractive spruce up.

# East End Walk

*This easy stroll offers insight into the old and new of the East End, taking you through historic streetscapes, over Regent's Canal, and through green parkland to Hackney Wick and the impressive Olympic Park.*

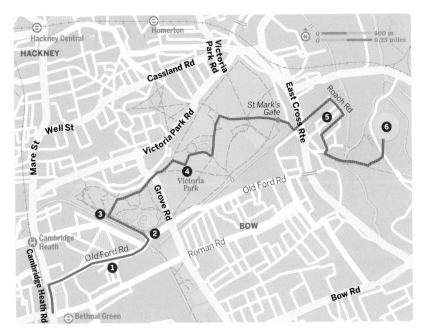

**WALK FACTS**

- **Start** Bethnal Green tube station
- **Finish** Olympic Park
- **Distance** 3 miles
- **Duration** Two hours

## 1 Cyprus St

Exit the tube station towards the Museum of Childhood and head north. Take the first right and continue until you can take a right into Cyprus Pl. The surrounding area here was heavily bombed during WWII (due to its industry and proximity to the docks) and the tower blocks you can see if you raise your eyes skyward are a product of postwar redevelopment. But beautifully preserved Cyprus St gives a taste of what Victorian Bethnal Green would have looked like. Continue left down Cyprus St and back onto Old Ford Rd.

## 2 Victoria Park

Just over marvellous Regent's Canal lies Victoria Park (p185), designed in the 1840s to improve East Enders' quality of life. The park is a glorious place for a wander, with several lakes and acres of greenery to explore.

## 3 Dogs of Alcibiades

Take the path down to the road around the lake and head left to the Dogs of Alcibiades howling on plinths, replicas of originals that stood here from 1912.

### 4 Burdett-Coutts Memorial

Turn right here and then again at the end of the road and continue to the grand Royal Inn on the Park. Cross the road into the eastern section of the park and take a right towards the recently restored Burdett-Coutts Memorial (1862), a gift of Angela Burdett-Coutts, once the richest woman in England and a prominent philanthropist.

### 5 Hackney Wick

From here, ramble on to the east lake and exit through St Mark's Gate at the park's eastern tip. Cross the road and pick up the canal path next to the Top O the Morning pub, crossing the canal at the first bridge you come to. Undergoing extensive redevelopment for the Olympic Games, Hackney Wick is home to a warren of warehouses and a growing community of artists. Stop off at the Counter Cafe (Map p186) or Formans for views of the stadium, and check out their latest art exhibits.

### 6 Olympic Park

From here you're a mere shot-put from the Olympic Park (p187), heralding a whole new era for the East End. Even if you haven't got tickets for the games in 2012, the park is definitely worth a visit and will be re-branded the Queen Elizabeth Olympic Park in 2013.

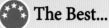

# The Best...

## PLACES TO EAT

**Wapping Food** Industrial decor meets haute cuisine. (p191)

**Formans** Top-notch seafood and Olympian views. (p190)

**Tayyabs** Deservedly popular, ever-busy Punjabi restaurant. (p189)

**E Pellici** Traditional East End cafe. (p189)

## PLACES TO DRINK

**Dove Freehouse** Excellent range of brews. (p191)

**Grapes** Super-cosy with bags of history; titchy but overflowing with charm. (p192)

**Carpenter's Arms** Good-looking pub with a notorious history. (p191)

**Royal Inn on the Park** A solid all-rounder. (p192)

## PLACES FOR EAST END HISTORY

**Museum of London Docklands** Stuffed with riveting nuggets of local dockside history and lore. (p188)

**Ragged School Museum** Eye-opening display of Victorian teaching utensils. (p185)

**V&A Museum of Childhood** Dedicated to the culture of childhood. (p185)

Dogs of Alcibiades, Victoria Park
GLYN THOMAS PHOTOGRAPHY/ALAMY ©

# Discover the East End & Docklands

## 🔄 Getting There & Away

○ **Underground** Central Line runs to Bethnal Green, Mile End and Stratford.

○ **Overground** A quick link from Camden and Highbury to Hackney, Hackney Wick and Stratford.

○ **DLR** A scenic link to Limehouse and Docklands; joins the dots with Stratford Domestic and International stations.

○ **Bus** Catch the 55 from Oxford St or the 38 from Victoria. The 277 runs from Hackney to the Docklands via Victoria Park.

○ **Rail** A quick ride to London Fields, Cambridge Heath or Stratford from Liverpool St.

○ **Boat** During the Games, catch a barge from Limehouse to Olympic Park.

Whitechapel Bell Foundry
MICHAEL FREEMAN/CORBIS ©

## ◎ Sights

### Whitechapel

**Whitechapel Gallery**  Gallery

Map p186 (www.whitechapelgallery.org; 77-82 Whitechapel High St E1; admission free; ⊙11am-6pm Tue-Sun, to 9pm Thu; ⊖Aldgate East) This ground-breaking gallery, which moved into its main art nouveau building in 1899, extended into the library next door in 2009, doubling its exhibition space to 10 galleries. Founded by the Victorian philanthropist Canon Samuel Barnett at the end of the 19th century to bring art to the people of East London, it has made its name by putting on exhibitions by both established and emerging artists, cartoonists and architects, including Jackson Pollock (his first UK show), Gary Hume, Robert Crumb, Mies van der Rohe and Picasso (whose *Guernica* was exhibited here in 1939). The gallery's ambitiously themed shows change every couple of months – check the program online – and there's also live music, poetry readings, talks and films till late on Thursday. Don't miss the phenomenal 'social sculptures' in various (and ephemeral) spaces throughout – there's even one on the roof of the building. Other features are an excellent bookshop, the Whitechapel Gallery Dining Room and an uberdesigned cafe on the mezzanine level.

**Whitechapel Bell Foundry**  Historic Building

Map p186 (www.whitechapelbellfoundry.co.uk; 32-34 Whitechapel Rd E1; tours per person £11; ⊙tours 10am & 1.30pm selected Wed & Sat, shop 9.30am-4.15pm Mon-Fri; ⊖Aldgate East or Whitechapel) The Whitechapel Bell Foundry has been standing on this site since 1738, although an earlier foundry nearby is known to have been in business in 1570. Both Big Ben (1858) and the Liberty Bell (1752) in Philadelphia were cast here, and the foundry also cast a new bell for New York City's Trinity Church, damaged in the terrorist attacks of 11 September 2001. The 1½-hour guided tours (maximum 25 people) are conducted on particular Saturdays and Wednesdays (check the website) but are often booked out a year in advance.

**Whitechapel Road**                    Street

Map p186 (⊖Whitechapel) The East End's main thoroughfare, Whitechapel Rd hums with a cacophony of Asian, African and Middle Eastern languages. Its busy shops and market stalls sell everything from Indian snacks to Nigerian fabrics and Turkish jewellery, as the East End's multitudinous ethnic groupings rub up against each other more or less comfortably. It's a chaotic and poor place, but it's full of life.

# Bethnal Green & Hackney

FREE **V&A Museum of Childhood**                    Museum

Map p186 (www.vam.ac.uk/moc; cnr Cambridge Heath & Old Ford Rds E2; ⏰10am-5.45pm; 📷; ⊖Bethnal Green) Housed in a renovated Victorian-era building moved from South Kensington in 1866, this branch of the Victoria & Albert Museum is aimed at both kids (with activity rooms and inter-active exhibits, including a dressing-up box and sandpit) and nostalgic grown-ups who come to admire the antique toys. From teddies, doll's houses and dolls (one dating from 1300 BC) to Meccano, Lego and computer games, it's a wonderful toy-cupboard trip down memory lane.

# Mile End & Victoria Park

**Victoria Park**                    Park

Map p186 (www.towerhamlets.gov.uk; ⏰dawn-dusk; ⊖Mile End, 🚌277 or 425) The 'Regent's Park of the East End', Victoria Park is an 86-hectare leafy expanse opened in 1845 – the first public park in the East End that came about after a local MP

## Exploring the East End

### BY BICYCLE

The most genial way to get around the East End is along the water. Cyclists and pedestrians can drop down to Regent's Canal at the bottom of Broadway Market and follow the waterway to Limehouse. Branching east of this at Victoria Park, the Hertford Union Canal will deliver you to Hackney Wick and the Olympic Park. From Limehouse Basin you can also pick up the Thames Path and follow it along the river to St Katharine Docks.

### BY BARGE

A great way to see a different side of the East End is to climb aboard a barge and tour the canals and waterways. **Water Chariots** (www.water-chariots.co.uk; ⏰approx Apr-Oct) offers a program of pleasure cruises and, during the Olympic Games, a shuttle service for passengers travelling up the canal from Limehouse.

presented Queen Victoria with a petition of 30,000 signatures. At the time of writing, the park was undergoing a £12-million revamp, which will improve both the lakes, introduce a skate park and create a hub building housing a cafe, community room and park offices in the eastern section of the park.

FREE **Ragged School Museum**                    Museum

Map p186 (www.raggedschoolmuseum.org.uk; 46-50 Copperfield Rd E3; ⏰10am-5pm Wed & Thu, 2-5pm 1st Sun of month; ⊖Mile End) Both adults and children are inevitably charmed by this combination of mock Victorian schoolroom – with hard wooden benches and desks, slates, chalk, inkwells

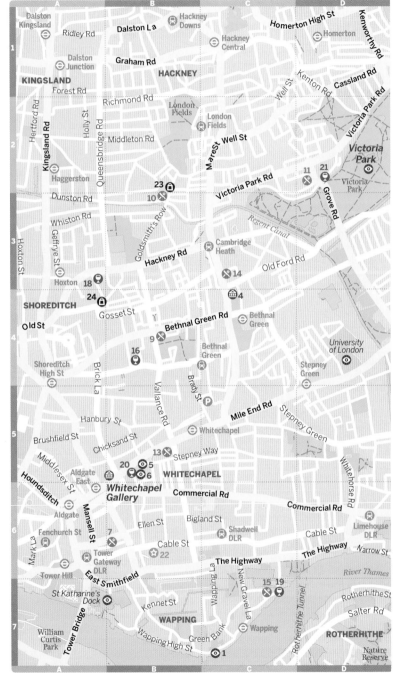

# The East End

Dalston Kingsland

Ridley Rd

Dalston La

Hackney Downs

Homerton High St

Homerton

Kenworthy Rd

Hackney Central

Dalston Junction

Graham Rd

HACKNEY

Well St

Kenton Rd

Cassland Rd

Victoria Park Rd

KINGSLAND

Forest Rd

Hertford Rd

Holly St

Kingsland Rd

Queensbridge Rd

Richmond Rd

London Fields

London Fields

Mare St

Well St

Victoria Park

Victoria Park

Middleton Rd

Haggerston

23

10

Dunston Rd

Goldsmith's Row

Victoria Park Rd

11

21

Grove Rd

Regent Canal

Whiston Rd

Geffrye St

Hoxton St

Hoxton

18

Hackney Rd

Cambridge Heath

Old Ford Rd

14

SHOREDITCH

24

Gosset St

4

Bethnal Green Rd

Bethnal Green

Old St

Shoreditch High St

Brick La

9

Bethnal Green

16

Valance Rd

Brady St

University of London

Stepney Green

Hanbury St

Mile End Rd

Stepney Green

Brushfield St

Chicksand St

Whitechapel

Middlesex St

13

Stepney Way

Houndsditch

20

5

6

WHITECHAPEL

Aldgate East

Whitechapel Gallery

Commercial Rd

Commercial Rd

Whitehorse Rd

Aldgate

7

Ellen St

Bigland St

Shadwell DLR

Cable St

Limehouse DLR

Fenchurch St

Mansell St

Mark La

Cable St

22

Narrow St

Tower Gateway DLR

The Highway

Tower Hill

East Smithfield

The Highway

River Thames

Rotherhithe Tunnel

Rotherhithe St

St Katharine's Dock

Wapping La

New Gravel La

15

19

Salter Rd

Tower Bridge

William Curtis Park

Kennet St

Green Bank

Wapping High St

WAPPING

1

Wapping

ROTHERHITHE

Nature Reserve

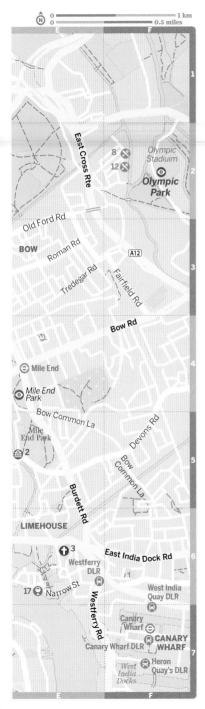

## The East End

and abacuses – recreated East End kitchen and social history museum below. 'Ragged' was a Victorian term used to refer to pupils' usually torn, dirty and dishevelled clothes, and the museum celebrates the legacy of Dr Thomas Barnardo, who founded this school for destitute East End children in the 1870s.

# Hackney Wick & Stratford

## 📷 Olympic Park — Park

Map p186 (www.london2012.com/olympic-park; ⊖Stratford or Hackney Wick) From the mills of Cistercian monks in the 1st century, to the railway hub of the 1880s (from which goods from the Thames were transported all over Britain), the tidal Lower Lea Valley had long been the source of what Londoners required to fuel their industries. But until building work on the Olympic Park began in 2008, this vast area of East London had become derelict, polluted and largely ignored. Creating world-class sporting facilities for the 2012 Games was, of course, at the forefront of the development, but this was well balanced with the aim of regenerating this area for generations to come.

The main focal point of the Queen Elizabeth Olympic Park, as it will be known from 2013, is the **Olympic Stadium**, with a Games capacity of 80,000, scaling back to approximately 60,000 seats post-Games. The striking **Aquatics Centre**, which will greet park visitors entering from Stratford, is the work of Clerkenwell-based architect Zaha Hadid and houses two 50m swimming pools and a diving pool. The equally impressive and award-winning **Velodrome** (aka the 'Pringle') has been praised for its aesthetic qualities, as well as its sustainable credentials and functional appeal. The 114m, spiralling red structure is Anish Kapoor's **ArcelorMittal Orbit**, or the 'Hubble Bubble Pipe', offering a vast panorama from its viewing platform.

The north of the park has been given over to wetlands, which provide a much wilder environment than the gardens and landscaping of the southern half of the park, which is home to the main venues. Set to open to the public in phases from 2013, the developments to transform the park into its promised legacy will take at least another 25 years to complete.

# Wapping & Limehouse

## Wapping                        Neighbourhood
Map p186 ( Ⓤ Wapping) Once notorious for slave traders, drunk sailors and prostitutes, Wapping's towering warehouses, built at the beginning of the 19th century, still give an atmospheric picture of the area's previous existence. Although there's nothing to actually mark it, down

on the riverside below Wapping New Stairs (near the marine police station) was **Execution Dock**, where convicted pirates were hanged and their bodies chained to a post at low tide, to be left until three tides had washed over their heads.

## Limehouse                        Neighbourhood
Map p186 (DLR Limehouse or Westferry) There isn't much to Limehouse, although it became the centre of London's Chinese community – its first Chinatown – after some 300 sailors settled here in 1890. The most notable attraction here is **St Anne's Limehouse** (www.stanneslimehouse. org; cnr Commercial Rd & Three Colt St E1). This was Nicholas Hawksmoor's earliest church (1725) and still boasts the highest church clock in the city.

# Docklands

## Museum of London Docklands                        Museum
(www.museumindocklands.org.uk; No 1 Warehouse, West India Quay E14; admission free; ⊙10am-6pm; Ⓤ Canary Wharf or DLR West India Quay) Housed in a converted warehouse dating from 1802, this museum offers a comprehensive overview of the entire history of the Thames from the arrival of the Romans in AD 43. Well-organised with knowledgeable and helpful staff, it's at its best when dealing with specifics such as the docks during WWII, as well as their controversial transformation into the Docklands during the 1980s.

The tour begins on the 3rd floor (take the lift to the top) with the Roman settlement of Londinium and works its way downwards through the ages. Keep an eye out for the scale model of old London Bridge. Other highlights include Sailortown (a recreation of the cobbled streets, bars and lodging houses of a mid-19th-century dockside community) and nearby Chinatown, and more detailed galleries such as London, Sugar & Slavery, which examines the capital's role in the transatlantic slave trade.

The museum has special exhibitions every few months, for which there is usually a charge.

# Eating

The East End's multiculturalism has ensured that its ethnic cuisine stretches far and wide, with some fantastic low-key eateries serving authentic and value-for-money fare. But the area's gentrification has introduced a slew of gastropubs and more upmarket eateries – the latest even earning a Michelin star.

## Whitechapel

### Tayyabs
Indian, Pakistani £
Map p186 (☏7247 9543; www.tayyabs.co.uk; 83-89 Fieldgate St E1; mains £6.50-10; ⊗noon-midnight; ⊖Whitechapel) This buzzing (OK, crowded) Punjabi restaurant is in another league to its Brick Lane equivalents. *Seekh* kebabs, masala fish and other starters served on sizzling hot plates are delicious, as are accompaniments such as dal, naan and raita. Daily specials are also available.

### Café Spice Namasté
Indian ££
Map p186 (☏7488 9242; www.cafespice.co.uk; 16 Prescot St E1; mains £14-19, 2-course set lunch £15.95; ⊗closed lunch Sat & all day Sun; ⊖Tower Hill or DLR Tower Gateway) Chef Cyrus Todiwala has taken an old magistrates court, just a 10-minute walk from Tower Hill and decorated it in carnival colours; the service and atmosphere are as bright as the walls.

## Bethnal Green & Hackney

### E Pellici
Cafe £
Map p186 (332 Bethnal Green Rd E2; dishes £5-7.80; ⊗7am-4pm Mon-Sat; ⊖Bethnal Green, ☐8) There aren't many reasons to recommend a stroll down Bethnal Green Rd, but stepping into this diminutive, but larger-than-life, Anglo-Italian cafe is one of them. You're likely to be met by a warmer-than-average greeting as you squeeze onto a table among an amiable collection of East Enders. Opened in 1900 the wood-panelled caff is bedecked with museum-quality original fittings.

### Viajante
Fusion £££
Map p186 (www.viajante.co.uk; Patriot Sq E2; tasting menu lunch £28-70, dinner £65-90; ⊗lunch Wed-Sun, 6-9.30pm Mon-Sun; ☎; ⊖Bethnal Green) Part of the Town Hall Hotel & Apartments (but with a completely separate entrance on Cambridge Heath Rd), this is an unexpected spot to find a Michelin-starred restaurant. The elegant

*Jack the Ripper and the East End* exhibition, Museum of London Docklands

AFP/GETTYIMAGES ©

THE EAST END & DOCKLANDS EATING

dining room marries contemporary design with the original Edwardian features, and the very open kitchen (where food is 'assembled') offers only blind tasting menus. Chef Nuno Mendes' dishes are inventive, beautifully put together and a well-crafted and exciting fusion of flavours.

### F Cooke
Pies £

Map p186 (9 Broadway Market; mains £3-4; ⊙10am-7pm; ⓡCambridge Heath, �🚌55) If you want a glimpse of what eating out was like in Broadway Market before the street was gentrified, head to F Cooke pie-and-mash shop. This family business has been going strong since 1900, and the shop has the original signage and tiles, along with plenty of family photographs around the walls and sawdust on the floor.

## Mile End & Victoria Park

### Fish House
Fish & Chips £

Map p186 (www.fishouse.co.uk; 126-128 Lauriston Rd E9; mains £8.50-12.50; ⊙noon-10pm ⊖Mile End, then 🚌277) This combination seafood restaurant and chippy is just the sort of place you wish you had in your own neighbourhood. The freshest of fresh fish and crustaceans are dispensed from both a busy takeaway section (where a blackboard tells you from where your fish has come) and a cheerful sit-down restaurant.

## Hackney Wick & Stratford

### Formans
Seafood ££

Map p186 (☎8525 2365; www.formans.co.uk; Stour Rd E3; mains £12-19.50; ⊙dinner Thu & Fri, lunch & dinner Sat, noon-5pm Sun; 🛜; ⊖Hackney Wick) H Forman & Son have been curing fish here since 1905, and are notable for developing the much-celebrated London cure. Obliged to move to make way for the Olympic developments, they're now housed in appropriately salmon-pink premises that comprise their smokery, restaurant, bar and art gallery. The diminutive restaurant, with unrivalled views over the Olympic stadium, serves a fantastic variety of smoked salmon (the wild smoked salmon is exceptional), as well as an interesting range of dishes with ingredients sourced from within the British Isles.

**Left:** Cafe at Victoria Park (p185); **Below:** Pie and mash, F Cooke
(LEFT) HOWARD BARLOW/ALAMY ©; (BELOW) GIDEON MENDEL/CORBIS ©

# Wapping & Limehouse

**Wapping Food** Modern European ££
Map p186 ( ☏7680 2080; www.thewapping
project.com; The Wapping Project, Wapping
Hydraulic Power Station, Wapping Wall E1; mains
£14-21; ☎; ⊖Wapping) Stylish dining room
set in the innards of a disused power station, creating a spectacular and unexpectedly romantic atmosphere. A high-quality,
seasonal menu changes daily but might
include guinea fowl wrapped in pancetta,
or onglet with beetroot and horseradish.

# 🍷 Drinking & Nightlife

## Whitechapel

**Rhythm Factory** Club
Map p186 (www.rhythmfactory.co.uk; 16-18
Whitechapel Rd E1; ⊖Aldgate East) Perennially
hip and popular, the Rhythm Factory is a
club and venue hosting a variety of bands
and DJs of all genres that keep the up-for-
it crowd happy until late.

## Bethnal Green & Hackney

**Dove Freehouse** Pub
Map p186 (www.belgianbars.com; 24-28 Broadway
Market E8; ☎; ☒Cambridge Heath, ☒55)
Attractive pub with its rambling rooms
and wide range (21 on draught) of Belgian
Trappist, wheat and fruit-flavoured beers.
Drinkers spill out onto the street in warmer
weather, or hunker down in the low-lit back
room with board games when it's chilly.

**Carpenter's Arms** Pub
Map p186 (www.carpentersarmsfreehouse.
com; 73 Cheshire St E2; ☎; ⊖Shoreditch High
St, ☒Bethnal Green) After a browse in the
shops along Cheshire St, you'll probably
end up outside this gorgeous corner pub.
Once notorious – the pub was owned in
the '60s by the Kray brothers, who gave it

191

over to their mother – it has been well restored to a trendy, yet cosy and intimate pub combining traditional pub architecture with contemporary touches.

### Nelsons Head
Gay

Map p186 (www.nelsonshead.com; 32 Horatio St E2; ⊙from 4pm Mon-Sat, 9am-11pm Sun; ⊖Hoxton) Small, down-to-earth locals' pub with quirky decor, a fun and friendly mixed clientele, and plenty of camp tunes.

## Mile End & Victoria Park

### Royal Inn on the Park
Pub

Map p186 (111 Lauriston Rd E9; 🛜; ⊖Mile End, then 🚊277) On the northern border of Victoria Park, this excellent place, once a poster pub for Transport for London, has a half-dozen real ales and Czech lagers on tap, outside seating to the front and a recently made-over garden at the back.

## Hackney Wick & Stratford

### King Edward VII
Pub

(www.kingeddie.co.uk; 47 Broadway E15; ⊖Stratford) Built in the 19th century, this lovely old boozer is a series of handsome rooms set around a central bar. The front bar and saloon are the most convivial, and there's a little leafy courtyard at the back.

## Wapping & Limehouse

### Grapes
Pub

Map p186 (www.grapeslondon.co.uk; 76 Narrow St E14; DLR Limehouse) One of Limehouse's renowned historic pubs – there's apparently been a drinking house here since 1583 – the Grapes is tiny, especially the riverside terrace, which can only really comfortably fit about a half-dozen close friends. However, it's cosy inside and exudes plenty of olde-worlde charm.

### Prospect of Whitby
Pub

Map p186 (57 Wapping Wall E1; 🛜; ⊖Wapping) Once known as the Devil's Tavern, the Whitby is said to date from 1520, making it the oldest riverside pub in London. Check out the wonderful pewter bar – Samuel Pepys once sidled up to it to sup.

## ☆ Entertainment

### Wilton's
Theatre

Map p186 (📞7702 2789; www.wiltons.org.uk; 1 Graces Alley E1; ⊖Tower Hill or DLR Tower Gateway) A gloriously atmospheric example of one of London's Victorian public-house music halls, Wilton's hosts a real variety of shows, from comedy and classical music to literary theatre and opera. You can also take a one-hour guided **tour** (£6; ⊙3pm & 6pm Mon) of the building to hear more about its fascinating history. The hall's **Mahogany Bar** (⊙5-11pm Mon-Fri) is a great way to get a taste of the place if you're not attending a performance.

Broadway Market
ORIEN HARVEY/LONELY PLANET IMAGES ©

DOUG MCKINLAY/LONELY PLANET IMAGES ©

# 🔒 Shopping

The boutiques and galleries lining Columbia Rd (which are usually open at the weekend only) and the shops along Broadway Market and Cheshire St are part of London's up-and-coming independent retail scenes. If you're after something a little more mainstream, Westfield Stratford City, currently Europe's largest urban shopping centre, can't fail to satisfy.

### Columbia Road Flower Market
Market

Map p186 (www.columbiaroad.info; ⏲8am-3pm Sun; ⊖Hoxton) A real explosion of colour and life, this weekly market sells a beautiful array of flowers, pot plants, bulbs, seeds and everything you might need for the garden. A lot of fun, even if you don't buy anything. The market gets really packed so go as early as you can, or later on, when the vendors sell off the cut flowers cheaply. It stretches from Gossett St to the Royal Oak pub.

### Broadway Market
Market

Map p186 (www.broadwaymarket.co.uk; ⏲9am-5pm Sat; ⏍London Fields, 🚌55 or 277) There's been a market down this pretty street since the late 19th century, the focus of which has these days become artisanal food, arty knick-knacks, books, records and vintage clothing.

# Hampstead & North London

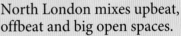

### North London mixes upbeat, offbeat and big open spaces.

Hampstead Heath and Camden Market should top your list; Camden is a major sight and its energy is intoxicating, while Hampstead Heath will offer you a glorious day out and an insight into how North Londoners spend their weekend.

You could spend an eternity here exploring the sights and nightlife, so you'll have to pick and choose carefully (which we have done for you).

Because this part of London is predominantly residential, it is at its busiest at the weekend. This means that most sights are relatively quiet during the week, with the exception of the Wellcome Collection and the British Library.

North London is largely a wealthy area, full of 20- or 30-somethings, young families and celebrities (Primrose Hill). The nightlife is excellent with great pubs in Hampstead or Islington and fab live music in Camden.

Camden Market (p205)

# Hampstead & North London Highlights

## British Library (p200)

Bibliophiles will have a field day discovering the treasures of this library and marvelling at the accumulated wisdom stored within its walls. An impressive shrine to the written word and the nation's principal copyright library, there's not only one copy of every British and Irish publication but, for antiquarians and historians, a rare wealth of ancient manuscripts, maps and documents.

**1**

## Highgate Cemetery (p206)

**2** London's Victorian cemeteries can be extraordinarily sublime places. Highgate Cemetery – the king of kings in the Victorian Valhalla look – is fascinating whether you're a name hunter, an architecture buff, a photographer or just someone in search of the ruins-reclaimed-by-nature look. If you're a communist, you'll probably ignore all of the above and simply come to lay flowers at the grave of Karl Marx.

## Kenwood House (p205)

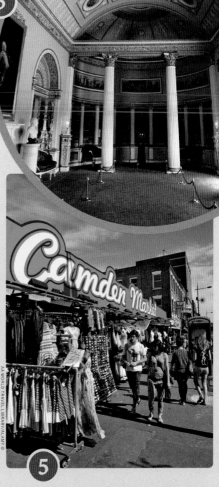

ROCCO FASANO/LONELY PLANET IMAGES ©

There's no better conclusion to a walk across Hampstead Heath than arriving at this simply sublime house on a sunny day. Kenwood House – in its stunning Hampstead Heath setting – is a magnificent piece of stately villa architecture. Transformed by Robert Adam in the 18th century, the house's beautiful exterior also contains a breathtaking art collection and a gorgeous library.

## Parliament Hill (p205)

London's heath land is a chance to escape the synthetic urban environment for a while, or at least, view it from a pleasantly buffered distance. Few views of London are as choice as the one unfolding before you from Parliament Hill in epic Hampstead Heath. Our advice is to prepare a simple picnic, throw a blanket on the grass and enjoy the panorama. As all North Londoners do.

## Camden Market (p205)

London's scattered markets are a must for those on the hunt for shopping ideas and a confluence of goods from all over the place. This famous North London market has an astonishing variety of goods, from vintage clothing through to food, ornaments, antiques, musical instruments and more. And when you have had your fill of picking through the stalls, there are fantastic pubs, canal views and knockout live music venues.

# Hampstead Heath Walk

*Sprawling Hampstead Heath, with its rolling woodlands and meadows, feels a million miles away from the City of London. Covering 320 hectares it's home to about 180 bird species, a rich array of flora and expansive views.*

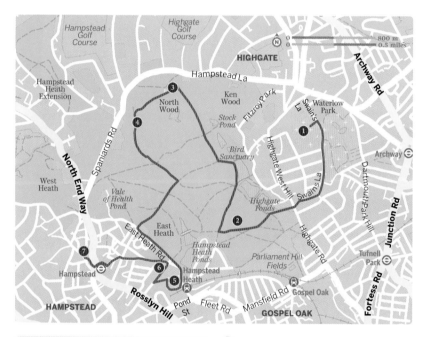

## WALK FACTS

- **Start** Highgate Cemetery
- **Finish** Holly Bush
- **Distance** 6 miles
- **Duration** Three hours

### ❶ Highgate Cemetery

The final resting place of Karl Marx, George Eliot and other notables, this supreme cemetery (p206) is divided into Eastern and Western sections. There are some magnificent images of nature relentlessly overwhelming Gothic headstones but to visit the overgrown, atmospheric West Cemetery, you'll need to take a tour.

### ❷ Parliament Hill

From the cemetery head down Swain's Lane to the roundabout with Highgate West Hill, and climb up to Parliament Hill (p205) – a Hampstead Heath high point – for some all-inclusive views south over town. Have a picnic prepared for lunch and some sustenance before continuing your walk.

### ❸ Kenwood House

Traverse the heath to this magnificent neoclassical 18th-century mansion (p205), a glorious sweep of perfectly landscaped gardens leading down to a picturesque lake, the setting for summer concerts. It contains a magnificent art collection, with paintings by Rembrandt, Constable, Turner and others.

### 4 Henry Moore & Barbara Hepworth Sculptures

London is dotted with pieces from Moore and Hepworth, and not far from Kenwood House are two of their sculptures that complement their open-air setting. The tall *Monolith (Empyrean)* by Hepworth dates from 1953, carved from blue Corrib limestone; the *Two Piece Reclining Figure No 5* by Moore is fashioned from bronze.

### 5 Keats House

Cross the heath to this elegant Regency house (Map p212) on Wentworth Pl, once home to the golden boy of the Romantic poets. Keats wrote *Ode to a Nightingale* while sitting under a plum tree (now vanished, but a new tree has been planted) in the garden in 1819.

### 6 No 2 Willow Road

Modern architecture fans will want to swing past this property (Map p212) at 2 Willow Rd, the central house in a block of three, designed by Ernö Goldfinger in 1939. Entry to the then path-breaking property is by guided tour until 3pm (after which non-guided viewing is allowed).

### 7 Holly Bush

This beautiful pub (Map p212), at 22 Holly Mount, is a fitting conclusion to your journey, with an antique Victorian interior, a secluded hilltop location, open fires in winter and a knack for making you stay longer than you had intended. Set above Heath St, it's reached via the Holly Bush Steps.

## ★ The Best...

### PLACES TO EAT

**Ottolenghi** An Italian culinary sensation. (p210)

**Manna** Manna from a delightful vegetarian heaven. (p209)

**Mangal Ocakbasi** A full-on Turkish meat feast. (p211)

**Gaucho Grill** Only place for a Hampstead steak-out. (p210)

**Market** Straightforward but excellent British food. (p207)

### PLACES TO DRINK

**Edinboro Castle** Laid-back pub with a great garden. (p211)

**Garden Gate** Stuffed with old English charm. (p213)

**Proud Camden** Housed in an erstwhile horse hospital, with live music. (p212)

**Boogaloo** Leaves other jukeboxes sounding like your great-grandmum's collection of 78s. (p212)

### PARKS & GARDENS

**Hampstead Heath** London's most famous heathland, with astonishing views. (p205)

**Regent's Park** Vast John Nash–designed expanse of green. (p203)

Keats House
GREG BALFOUR EVANS/ALAMY ©

# ✓ Don't Miss
## British Library

In 1998 the British Library moved to its current premises between King's Cross and Euston stations. At a cost of £500 million, it was Britain's most expensive building, and not one that is universally loved; Colin St John Wilson's exterior of straight lines of red brick, which Prince Charles reckoned was akin to a 'secret-police building', is certainly not to all tastes. But even those who don't like the building from the outside will be won over by the spectacularly cool and spacious interior.

Map p204

www.bl.uk

96 Euston Rd NW1

admission free

⊗9.30am-6pm Mon & Wed-Fri, to 8pm Tue, to 5pm Sat, 11am-5pm Sun

⊖King's Cross St Pancras

## King's Library

At the centre of the building is the wonderful King's Library, the 65,000-volume collection of King George III, displayed in the eerily beautiful six-storey, 17m-high glass-walled tower.

The collection is considered one of the most significant of the Enlightenment period, and it was bequeathed to the nation by George III's son, George IV, in 1823. It was decided that the volumes would be kept at the British Museum, but after a bomb fell on the collection during WWII, it was moved to the Bodleian Library in Oxford and only moved back to London in 1998, when the new British Library opened.

## Sir John Ritblat Gallery

The highlight of a visit to the British Library is the Sir John Ritblat Gallery where the library keeps its most precious and high-profile documents. The collection spans almost three millennia of history and contains manuscripts, religious texts, maps, music scores, autographs, diaries and more.

Rare texts from all the main religions are represented, including the *Codex Sinaiticus*, the first complete text of the New Testament; a Gutenberg *Bible* (1455), the first Western book printed using movable type; and the stunningly illustrated Jain sacred texts.

There are historical documents, including one of four remaining copies of *Magna Carta* (1215), the charter credited with setting out the basis of human rights in English law. Not so important, but poignant, is Captain Scott's final diary including an account of explorer Lawrence Oates's death.

Literature is well represented, with Shakespeare's *First Folio* (1623) and manuscripts by some of Britain's best-known authors (such as Lewis Carroll, Jane Austen and Thomas Hardy).

Music fans will love the Beatles' earliest handwritten lyrics and original scores by Handel, Mozart and Beethoven.

## The Philatelic Exhibition

The Philatelic Exhibition, next to the Sir John Ritblat Gallery, is based on collections established in the 19th century and now consists of more than 80,000 items, including postage and revenue stamps and postal stationery from almost every country and from all periods.

## Tours

There are one-hour **guided tours** (☏ 01937 546 546; adult/child £8/6.50) of the library's public areas at 3pm Monday, Wednesday and Friday and at 10.30am and 3pm Saturday, and another that includes a visit to one of the reading rooms at 11.30am and 3pm Sunday. Further tours, including tours of the conservation studios, are also regularly available. Bookings are recommended for all tours.

### One for the Books

The British Library is the nation's principal copyright library: it stocks one copy of every British and Irish publication as well as historic manuscripts, books and maps from the British Museum. As well as hosting excellent permanent collections, the British Library runs regular temporary exhibitions of various authors, genres and themes, all connected to its records.

### Library Cafes

All the catering at the British Library comes courtesy of the wonderful Peyton & Byrne, the progeny of Irish chef Oliver Peyton. There are three main outfits: the 1st floor **restaurant** (☺ 9.30am-5pm Mon-Fri, to 4pm Sat), with spectacular views of the King's Library Tower and treats such as made-to-order stir-fries; the **cafe** (☺ daily) on the ground floor, which serves hot drinks, pastries and sandwiches; and the **Espresso Bar** (Euston Rd; ☺ daily).

# Discover Hampstead & North London

## 🔁 Getting There & Away

○ **Underground** The Northern Line has stops in Camden, Hampstead, Highgate and Islington (Angel).

○ **Overground** The Overground crosses North London from east to west and is useful for areas such as Dalston that are not connected to the tube.

○ **Bus** There is a good network of buses in North London connecting various neighbourhoods together, and with the centre of town.

## ◉ Sights

North London is a collection of small neighbourhoods, ancient villages that were slowly drawn into London as the metropolis expanded. King's Cross has historically been a blight on the capital's landscape, but the opening of the beautiful St Pancras International train terminal and the urban renewal behind the station (the University of London will move there in 2014) is making this part of town more attractive. The rest of North London certainly doesn't suffer from an image problem: with wonderful parks, amazing views and some of the best pubs around, it's a great place for a more sedate day out.

### King's Cross & Euston

**British Library** Cultural Building
See p200.

**Wellcome Collection** Museum
Map p208 (www.wellcomecollection.org; 183 Euston Rd NW1; admission free; ⏰10am-6pm Tue-Sat, to 10pm Thu, 11am-6pm Sun; 🚇Euston Sq or Euston) The Wellcome Collection styles itself as a 'destination for the incurably curious', an accurate tag for an institution that seeks to explore the links between medicine, science, life and art. It's a serious topic but the genius of the museum is its accessibility.

The heart of the permanent collection is Sir Henry Wellcome's collection of objects from around the world. Wellcome (1853–1936), a pharmacist, entrepreneur and collector, was fascinated with medicine and amassed more than a million objects from different civilisations associated with life, birth, death and sickness.

Barges on Regent's Canal, which runs along Regent's Park
PHILIP GAME/LONELY PLANET IMAGES ©

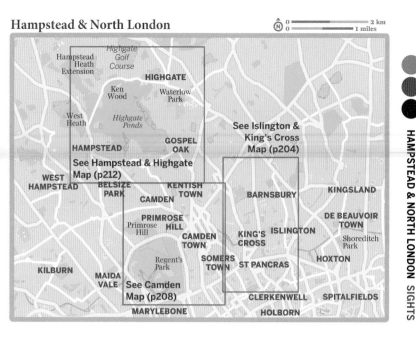

### London Canal Museum    Museum

Map p204 (www.canalmuseum.org.uk; 12-13 New Wharf Rd N1; adult/child £4/2; ☺10am-4.30pm Tue-Sun & bank holidays; ⊖King's Cross/St Pancras) This quirky but fascinating museum is in an old ice warehouse (with a deep well where the frozen commodity was stored) dating from the 1860s. It traces the history of Regent's Canal, the ice business and the development of ice cream via models, photographs, exhibits and documentaries from the archives.

## Regent's Park

### London Zoo    Zoo

Map p208 (www.zsl.org/london-zoo; Outer Circle, Regent's Park NW1; adult/child £19/15 plus optional £2 donation to protect endangered species; ☺10am-4pm Nov-Mar, to 5.30pm Apr–mid-Jul, Sep & Oct, to 6pm mid-Jul–Aug; ⊖Regent's Park or Camden Town) Established in 1828, these zoological gardens are among the oldest in the world. This is where the word 'zoo' originated but the emphasis nowadays is firmly placed on conservation, education and breeding, with fewer species and more spacious conditions.

The newest development is **Penguin Beach**, a huge and beautifully landscaped enclosure featuring a pool with cool underwater viewing areas.

Another highlight is **Gorilla Kingdom**, a project that involves a gorilla conservation program in Gabon and the Democratic Republic of Congo in central Africa.

### Regent's Park    Park

Map p208 (www.royalparks.gov.uk; ☺5am-dusk; ⊖Baker St or Regent's Park) The most elaborate and ordered of London's many parks, this one was created around 1820 by John Nash, who planned to use it as an estate to build palaces for the aristocracy.

Among its many attractions are the London Zoo, Regent's Canal along its northern side, an ornamental lake, an open-air theatre in Queen Mary's Gardens where Shakespeare is performed during the summer months, ponds and colourful flowerbeds, rose gardens that look spectacular in June, and sports pitches where Londoners regularly meet to play football, rugby and volleyball.

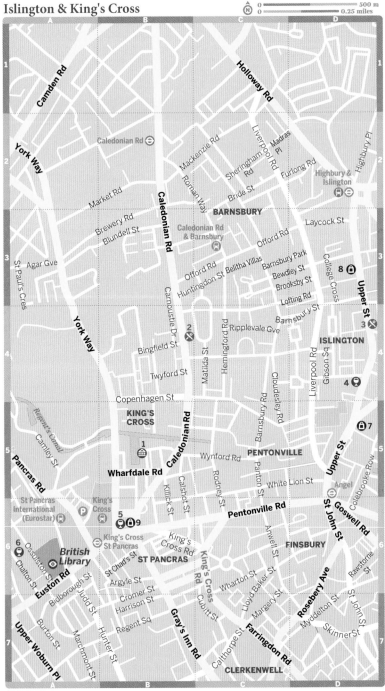

0   500 m
0   0.25 miles

Camden Rd

York Way

Holloway Rd

Caledonian Rd ⊖

Mackenzie Rd

Liverpool Rd

Madras Pl

Sheringham Rd

Furlong Rd

Highbury & Islington

Highbury Pl

Roman Way

Bride St

BARNSBURY

Caledonian Rd

Market Rd

Brewery Rd

Blundell St

St Paul's Cres

Agar Gve

Caledonian Rd & Barnsbury

Laycock St

Offord Rd

Offord Rd

Huntingdon St Belitha Villas

Barnsbury Park

Bewdley St

Brooksby St

Lofting Rd

College Cross

8

Upper St

York Way

Carnoustie Dr

Bingfield St

2

Matilda St

Hemingford Rd

Ripplevale Gve

Barnsbury St

3

ISLINGTON

Twyford St

Liverpool Rd

Gibson Sq

4

Copenhagen St

Cloudesley Rd

Barnsbury Rd

KING'S CROSS

Regent's Canal

Camley St

1

Caledonian Rd

Wynford Rd

PENTONVILLE

7

Pancras Rd

Wharfdale Rd

Calshot St

Killick St

Rodney St

Panton St

White Lion St

Upper St

Colebrooke Row

St Pancras International (Eurostar) 🚇

P

King's Cross

5

9

King's Cross St Pancras

King's Cross Rd

Pentonville Rd

Anwell St

Angel

St John St

Goswell Rd

British Library

6

Ossulston St

Chalton St

Euston Rd

St Chad's St

ST PANCRAS

Bidborough St

Judd St

Argyle St

Cromer St

Harrison St

Wharton St

Lloyd Baker St

Margery St

FINSBURY

Rosebery Ave

Rawstorne St

St John St

Upper Woburn Pl

Burton St

Marchmont St

Regent Sq

Hunter St

Gray's Inn Rd

Cubitt St

Calthorpe St

Farringdon Rd

Myddelton St

Skinner St

CLERKENWELL

# Camden

## Camden Market     Market

Map p208 (Camden High St NW1; ⏱10am-6pm, closed 25 Dec; ⊖Camden Town or Chalk Farm, ℝCamden Rd) In spite of – or perhaps because – it stopped being cutting-edge several thousand cheap leather jackets ago, Camden Market receives a whopping 10 million visitors every year making it one of the city's most popular attractions.

What started out as a collection of attractive craft stalls by Camden Lock on the Regent's Canal now extends in various shapes or forms most of the way from Camden Town tube station to Chalk Farm tube station. Camden Market consists of four main market areas – **Buck Street Market**, **Lock Market**, **Canal Market** and **Stables Market** – although they all seem to blend into one with the crowds snaking along and the 'normal' shops lining the streets. You'll find a bit of everything here: clothes (of variable quality) in profusion, bags, jewellery, arts and crafts, candles, incense and myriad decorative titbits. For a more detailed breakdown of what you might find, see p214.

There are dozens of food stalls at the Lock Market and the Stables Market;

virtually every type of cuisine is offered, from French to Argentinian, Japanese and Caribbean.

## Primrose Hill     Neighbourhood

Map p208 Wedged between well-heeled Regent's Park and edgy Camden, the little neighbourhood of Primrose Hill is high on the wish list of most Londoners – but is utterly unaffordable to many.

The proximity of the gorgeous, eponymous **park**, with fabulous views of London, is another draw.

# Hampstead & Highgate

## Hampstead Heath     Park

Map p212 ( ⊖Hampstead, ℝGospel Oak or Hampstead Heath, 🚌214 or C2 to Parliament Hill Fields) Sprawling Hampstead Heath, with its rolling woodlands and meadows, feels a million miles away – despite being approximately four – from the City of London. It covers 320 hectares, most of it woods, hills and meadows, and is home to about 180 bird species, 23 species of butterflies, grass snakes, bats and a rich array of flora. It's a wonderful place for a ramble, especially to the top of **Parliament Hill**, which offers expansive views across the city and is one of the most popular places in London to fly a kite. Alternatively head up the hill in North Wood or lose yourself in the West Heath.

Those of a more artistic bent should make a beeline for Kenwood House but stop to admire the **sculptures by Henry Moore and Barbara Hepworth** on the way.

## Kenwood House     Historic House

Map p212 (Hampstead Lane NW3; admission free; ⏱11.30am-4pm; ⊖Archway or Golders Green, then 🚌210) This magnificent neoclassical mansion stands at the northern end of the heath in a glorious sweep of landscaped gardens leading down to a picturesque lake, around which concerts take place during the summer months (see p213).

The house was remodelled by Robert Adam in the 18th century, and rescued from developers by Lord Iveagh Guinness, who donated it to the nation in 1927,

including the wonderful collection of art it contains. The Iveagh Bequest, as it is known, contains paintings by such greats as Rembrandt (one of his many self-portraits), Constable, Turner, Hals, Vermeer and Van Dyck and is one of the finest small collections in Britain.

Robert Adam's Great Stairs and the library, one of 14 rooms open to the public, are especially fine. There are **guided tours** (adult/concession £2/1) of the house daily at 2.30pm.

### Highgate Cemetery     Cemetery

Map p212 ( 8340 1834; www.highgate -cemetery.org; Swain's Lane N6; adult/child £3/ free; 10am-5pm Mon-Fri, 11am-5pm Sat & Sun Apr-Oct, closes 4pm daily Nov-Mar; Highgate) Most famous as the final resting place of Karl Marx, George Eliot (pseudonym of Mary Ann Evans) and other notable mortals, Highgate Cemetery is set in 20 wonderfully wild and atmospheric hectares, with dramatic and overdecorated Victorian family crypts. It is divided into two parts on either side of Swain's Lane. On the eastern side you can visit the **grave of Karl Marx**. The real draw however is the overgrown western section of this Victorian Valhalla. To visit it, you'll have to take a one-hour **tour** ( 8340 1834; adult/child £7/3; 1.45pm Mon-Fri, hourly from 11am to 3pm Sat & Sun Nov-Mar, to 4pm Apr-Oct). Note that children under eight are not allowed to join. It is a maze of winding paths leading to the **Circle of Lebanon**, rings of tombs flanking a circular path and topped with a majestic cedar of Lebanon tree.

# Eating

**North London is full of eating gems. From historic pubs to smart eateries catering for some of the capital's most sought-after residential neighbourhoods, this is not a place where you'll be left without options.**

**Left:** Kenwood House (p205); **Below:** Hampstead Heath (p205)

# King's Cross & Euston

### Mestizo
Mexican ££

Map p208 (www.mestizomx.com; 103 Hampstead Rd NW1; mains £10-20; ☺lunch & dinner; ⊖Warren St) At this large and very attractive restaurant and tequila bar you'll find everything from *quesadillas* (cheese-filled tortillas) to filled corn enchiladas. But go for the specials: *pozole* (a thick fresh corn soup with meat) and several different preparations of *mole* (chicken or pork cooked in a rich chocolate sauce).

### Diwana Bhel Poori House
Vegetarian £

Map p208 (www.diwanabhelpoori.co.uk; 121-123 Drummond St; mains £7-9; ☺noon-midnight; ⊖Euston or Euston Sq) Arguably one of the best Indian vegetarian restaurants in London, Diwana specialises in Bombay-style *bhel poori* (a sweet-and-sour, soft and crunchy 'party mix' snack) and dosas (filled pancakes made from rice flour). You can try thalis, which offer a selection of tasty treats (£7 to £9), and the all-you-can-eat lunchtime buffet (£7) is legendary.

### Ravi Shankar
Indian £

Map p208 (133-135 Drummond St NW1; mains £6-10; ☺lunch & dinner; ⊖Euston or Euston Sq) Another reliable *bhel poori* house (a vegetarian restaurant named after the dish of the same name containing puffed rice and a mix of vegetables) on Drummond St, this place with the memorable name is a good second choice if you can't get a table at Diwana.

# Camden

### Market
Modern British ££

Map p208 (www.marketrestaurant.co.uk; 43 Parkway NW1; mains £10-14; ☺closed dinner Sun; ⊖Camden Town) This fabulous restaurant

# Camden

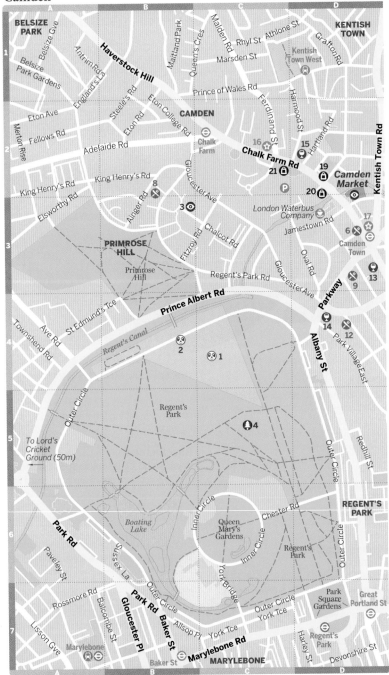

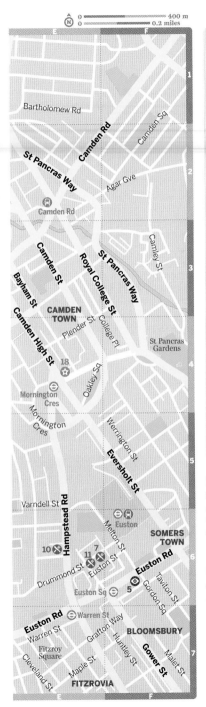

## Camden

### ◎ Top Sights
Camden Market ...................................D3

### ◎ Sights
1 London Zoo...........................................C4
2 London Zoo (Entrance).....................B4
3 Primrose Hill.......................................B3
4 Regent's Park......................................C5
5 Wellcome Collection..........................F6

### ✪ Eating
6 Bar Gansa ...........................................D3
7 Diwana Bhel Poori House ..................E6
8 Manna...................................................B2
9 Market ..................................................D3
10 Mestizo.................................................E6
11 Ravi Shankar ......................................E6
12 York & Albany.....................................D4

### ◉ Drinking & Nightlife
13 Black Cap.............................................D3
14 Edinboro Castle...................................D4
15 Lock Tavern.........................................D2
Proud Camden ..........................(see 21)

### ✪ Entertainment
16 Barfly ....................................................C2
17 Electric Ballroom ...............................D3
18 Koko.......................................................E4

### ⌂ Shopping
Buck Street Market ..................(see 17)
19 Canal Market.......................................D2
20 Lock Market.........................................D2
21 Stables Market....................................C2

is an ode to great, simple British food with a hint of European thrown in. The light and airy space with bare brick walls, steel tables and basic wooden chairs reflects this simplicity.

**Manna**  Vegetarian ££
Map p208 (☏7722 8082; www.mannav.com; 4 Erskine Rd NW3; mains £11-14; ⊗lunch Sat & Sun, dinner Tue-Sun; ⊖Chalk Farm) Tucked away on a side street in Primrose Hill, this little place does a brisk trade in inventive vegetarian cooking. The menu features such mouth-watering dishes as green korma, wild garlic and pea risotto cake and superb desserts. Reservations are usually essential.

209

### York & Albany
Brasserie ££

Map p208 (www.gordonramsay.com/yorkand albany; 127-129 Parkway NW1; mains £13-19; ⏱ breakfast, lunch & dinner; ⊖ Camden Town) This chic brasserie, part of chef Gordon Ramsay's culinary empire, serves classics with a Mediterranean twist such as roast leg of rabbit with potatoes and lemony anchovies, and confit lamb shoulder with soft polenta. The restaurant also does divine pizzas in its wood-fired oven.

### Bar Gansa
Spanish ££

Map p208 (☎ 7267 8909; www.bargansa.co.uk; 2 Inverness St NW1; tapas £5; ⏱ 10am-12.30am Sun-Wed, to 1.30am Thu-Sat; ⊖ Camden Town) Decked out in loud yellow and red, Bar Gansa is a focal point of the Camden scene and is howlingly popular. The menu is mostly tapas, which makes it very popular with small groups of friends.

## Hampstead & Highgate

### Gaucho Grill
Steakhouse £££

Map p212 (☎ 7431 8222; www.gauchorestau rants.co.uk; 64 Heath St NW3; mains £15-52; ⏱ noon-11pm Mon-Sat, from 10am Sun; ⊖ Hampstead) Carnivores, rejoice: this is one of the finest places for steak in London. The

Gaucho sampler (£89.95) is well worth sharing between three or four to taste the different cuts of meat (rump, sirloin, fillet and rib eye).

### Wells Tavern
Gastropub ££

Map p212 (☎ 7794 3785; www.thewellshamp stead.co.uk; 30 Well Walk NW3; mains £10-16; ⏱ lunch & dinner; ⊖ Hampstead) This popular gastropub, with a surprisingly modern interior (given its traditional exterior), is a real blessing in good-restaurant-deprived Hampstead. The menu is proper posh English pub grub – Cumberland sausages, mash and onion gravy, or just a full roast with all the trimmings. At the weekends you'll need to fight to get a table or, more wisely, book.

## Islington

### Ottolenghi
Italian ££

Map p204 (☎ 7288 1454; www.ottolenghi.co.uk; 287 Upper St N1; mains £7-12; ⏱ 8am-11pm Mon-Sat, 9am-7pm Sun; ⊖ Highbury & Islington or Angel) This is the pick of Upper St's many eating options – a brilliantly bright, white space that's worth a trip merely to see the eye-poppingly beautiful cakes in the deli. Reservations are essential in the evenings.

Ottolenghi

# Walking Along Regent's Canal

The canals that were once a trade lifeline for the capital have now become a favourite escape for Londoners, providing a quiet walk away from traffic and crowds. For visitors, an added advantage of Regent's Canal towpath is that it provides an easy (and delightful) shortcut across North London.

You can, for instance, walk from Little Venice to Camden (p205) in less than an hour; on the way, you'll pass Regent's Park (p203), London Zoo (p203), Primrose Hill (p205), beautiful villas designed by architect John Nash as well as redevelopments of old industrial buildings into trendy blocks of flats. Allow 15 to 20 minutes between Camden and Regent's Park, and 25 to 30 minutes between Regent's Park and Little Venice.

### Georgian Iberian Restaurant
Russian ££

Map p204 (www.iberiarestaurant.co.uk; 294-296 Caledonian Rd; mains £8.50-16; ⊘dinner Tue-Sun, lunch Sat & Sun; ⊖Caledonian Rd or Highbury & Islington) There isn't much going on in the area but this place justifies the 10-minute walk from Islington. Georgian food is infused with flavours from neighbouring Russia (smoked ingredients, beans, walnuts, cabbage, dill) and the Middle East (mezes, flatbread and lots of spices).

## Dalston

### Mangal Ocakbasi
Turkish £

(www.mangal1.com; 10 Arcola St E8; mains £5-12; ⊘noon-midnight; ☒Dalston Kingsland) Mangal is the quintessential Turkish *ocakbasi* (open-hooded grill, the mother of all BBQs) restaurant: cramped and smoky and serving superb meze, grilled lamb chops, quail and a lip-smacking assortment of kebabs. There's no menu as such: you choose from the meat counter and then go and sit down.

 # Drinking & Nightlife

Camden Town is one of North London's favoured drinking areas, with more bars and pubs pumping music than you can manage to crawl between. The hills of Hampstead are a real treat for old-pub aficionados, while painfully hip Dalston is currently London's coolest place to drink.

## King's Cross

### Somers Town Coffeehouse
Pub

Map p204 (www.somerstowncoffeehouse.co.uk; 60 Chalton St NW1; ⊖King's Cross/St Pancras) French bistro meets English pub is perhaps the best way to describe this gorgeous 'bistro pub'. As you would expect from such a mix, there is an equally good selection of beers and wines (all French, *bien sûr*).

### Camino
Bar

Map p204 (www.camino.uk.com; Regent Quarter, N1; ⊖King's Cross/St Pancras) This new venture in the Regent Quarter development is very popular with London's Spanish community and therefore feels quite authentic. Drinks, too, are representative of what you'd find in Spain: Cava, Estrella on tap, and a long, all-Spanish wine list. It's off Caledonian Rd.

## Camden

### Edinboro Castle
Pub

Map p208 (www.edinborocastlepub.co.uk; 57 Mornington Tce NW1; ⊖Camden Town) A reliable Camden boozer, the large and relaxed Edinboro has a refined Primrose Hill atmosphere. It boasts a full menu, gorgeous furniture designed for slumping and a fine bar. Where the pub comes into its own, however, is in its huge beer

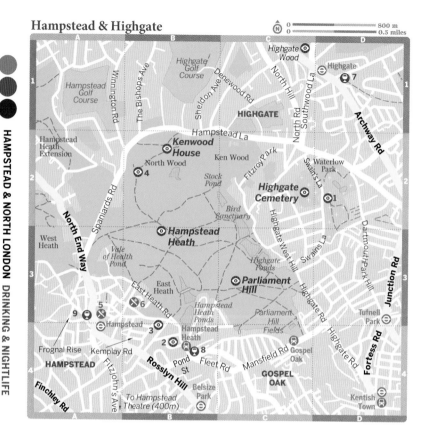

garden, complete with BBQ and table football and adorned with fairy lights for long summer evenings.

### Proud Camden                     Bar
Map p208 (www.proudcamden.com; The Horse Hospital, Stables Market, Chalk Farm Rd NW1; ⏱to 1.30am Mon-Wed, to 2.30am Thu-Sat, to 12.30am Sun; ⊖Camden Town or Chalk Farm) The former Horse Hospital, which looked after horses injured pulling barges on nearby Grand Union Canal, is now one of Camden's most brilliant bars. There are live bands and DJs in the large main room, and art exhibits adorn the walls. It's fantastic in summer, when the terrace is open.

### Lock Tavern                      Pub
Map p208 (www.lock-tavern.co.uk; 35 Chalk Farm Rd NW1; ⏱to 1am Fri & Sat; ⊖Chalk Farm or Camden Town) An institution in Camden, the black-clad Lock Tavern rocks for several reasons: it's cosy inside, has an ace roof terrace from where you can watch the market throngs, the food is good, the beer plentiful and it also has a roll-call of guest bands and DJs at the weekend to spice things up.

### Black Cap                        Gay
Map p208 (www.faucetinn.com/blackcap; 171 Camden High St NW1; ⏱noon-2am Mon-Thu, to 3am Fri & Sat, to 1am Sun; ⊖Camden Town) This friendly, sprawling place is Camden's premier gay venue, and attracts people from all over North London.

## Hampstead & Highgate

### Boogaloo                         Bar
Map p212 (www.theboogaloo.org; 312 Archway Rd N6; ⏱to 1am Thu, to 2am Fri & Sat;

⊖Highgate) 'London's Number 1 Jukebox' is how Boogaloo flaunts itself and how it's been described in the local media: its celebrity-musician-fiddled-with jukebox playlists feature the favourite 10 songs of the likes of Nick Cave, Sinead O'Connor, Howie B and Bobbie Gillespie, to name but a few. There's plenty to boogie to, with live music on every night of the week.

### Garden Gate — Pub
Map p212 (www.thegardengatehampstead.co.uk; 14 South End Rd NW3; ⊙noon-11pm; ⊠Hampstead Heath) At the bottom of the heath hides this gem of a pub, a 19th-century cottage with a gorgeous beer garden. The interior is wonderfully cosy, with dark wood tables, upholstered turquoise chairs and an assortment of distressed sofas.

## Islington

### Bull — Pub
Map p204 (www.thebullislington.co.uk; 100 Upper St N1; ⊙to midnight Wed & Thu, to 1am Fri & Sat; ⊖Angel or Highbury & Islington) One of Islington's liveliest pubs, Bull serves 27 different kinds of draught lager, real ales, fruit beers, ciders and wheat beer, plus a large selection of bottled drinks and wine.

## Dalston

### Passing Clouds — Club
(www.passingclouds.org; 1 Richmond Rd E8; ⊙10pm-4am Fri & Sat, hours vary Mon-Fri; ⊠Dalston Junction or Dalston Kingsland, ⊠243, 76) One of those little flickers of nightlife brilliance, Passing Clouds throws legendary parties that go on until the early hours of the morning. The music is predominantly world oriented, with a lot of African influence and regular Afrobeat bands, and a reputed jam session on Sunday nights (from 9pm); the parties are a healthy mix of DJs and live music with a multicultural crowd that really makes you feel you're in London.

## ☆ Entertainment

North London is the home of indie rock; many a famous band started playing in the area's grungy bars. Here's where to go for some of the best gigs in town.

### Proud Camden — Live Music
Map p208 (www.proudcamden.com; The Horse Hospital, Stables Market, Chalk Farm Rd NW1; ⊙ to 1.30am Mon-Thu, 2.30am Fri & Sat, 12.30am Sun; ⊖Camden Town or Chalk Farm) It's very trendy indeed at Proud, with gorgeous Camdenites heading to the sunset-watching terrace for outdoor gigs in summer or indoor booths in winter. Proud is a great venue in North London that combines live music and exhibitions, and it's really best in summer, when the terrace is open.

### Kenwood House — Live Music
Map p212 (www.picnicconcerts.com; Hampstead Lane NW3; ⊖Archway or Golders Green, then ⊠210) Attending an outdoor concert in the grounds of Hampstead's Kenwood House has been a highlight of any good summer in London for years. These days the so-called Picnic Concerts sponsored by English Heritage focus as much on jazz (Ray Davies, Gypsy Kings, Jools Holland) and pop (Simply Red) as they do classical music and opera.

Concerts take place on Friday and Saturday evenings from late June to late August; bring your picnic and bubbles to make it a brilliant night.

### Barfly
Live Music

Map p208 (www.barflyclub.com; Monarch, 49 Chalk Farm Rd NW1; ⊖ Chalk Farm or Camden Town) This typically grungy, indie-rock Camden venue is well known for hosting small-time artists looking for their big break. The venue is small, so you'll feel like the band is just playing for you and your mates.

### Koko
Concert Venue

Map p208 (www.koko.uk.com; 1a Camden High St NW1; ⊘7-11pm Sun-Thu, to 4am Fri & Sat; ⊖Mornington Cres) Once the legendary Camden Palace, where Charlie Chaplin, the Goons, the Sex Pistols and Ryan Adams have all performed in the past, Koko is keeping its reputation as one of London's better gig venues – Madonna played a *Confessions on a Dance Floor* gig here in 2006 and Prince gave a surprise gig in 2007. There are live bands almost every night of the week.

### Electric Ballroom
Live Music

Map p208 (www.electricballroom.co.uk; 184 Camden High St NW1; ⊖ Camden Town) One of Camden's historic venues, the Electric Ballroom has been entertaining North Londoners since 1938. Many great bands and musicians have played here, from Blur to Paul McCartney, The Clash and U2. There are club nights on Fridays (Sin City: metal music) and Saturdays (Shake: a crowd pleaser of dance anthems from the 1970s, '80s and '90s).

# 🔒 Shopping

Shopping in Camden is more about cheap, disposable fashion and made-for-tourist trinkets at the huge market, although you might occasionally be tempted to pop into one of the many clothes boutiques lining the high street.

### Camden Market
Market

Map p208 Camden Market comprises four distinct market areas; they tend to sell similar kinds of things although each has its own specialities and quirks. Just beyond the railway arches, opposite Hartland Rd, the **Stables** (Chalk Farm Rd NW1; ⊘10am-6pm daily; ⊖Chalk Farm) is the best part of the market, with antiques, Asian artefacts, rugs and carpets, pine furniture and vintage clothing. **Lock Market** (www.camdenlockmarket.com; Camden Lock Pl NW1; ⊘10am-6pm daily; ⊖Camden Town) is right next to the canal lock, with diverse food, ceramics, furniture, oriental rugs, musical instruments and designer clothes. Just over the canal bridge, **Canal Market** (cnr Chalk Farm Rd & Castlehaven Rd NW1; ⊘10am-6pm Thu-Sun; ⊖Chalk Farm or Camden Town) has bric-a-brac

Camden Market
FERNANDO CARNIEL MACHADO/DREAMSTIME ©

Warpaint performing at Barfly

REDFERNS/GETTYIMAGES ©

from around the world. **Buck Street Market** (cnr Camden High & Buck Sts NW1; ⏰9am-5.30pm Thu-Sun; 🚇Camden Town) is a covered market housing stalls for fashion, clothing, jewellery and tourist tat. It's the closest to the station but the least interesting.

### Gill Wing                                   Gifts
Map p204 (www.gillwing.co.uk; 190 Upper St N1; 🚇Highbury & Islington) Gill Wing's three wonderfully individual boutiques are a must-see on this strip of Upper St – her shoe shop is much loved, and the gift shop is full of amusing and garishly designed presents, but the real favourite is her stylish cook shop that has launched the dreams of many an aspirant Islington homemaker.

### Annie's Vintage Costumes & Textiles          Vintage
Map p204 (www.anniesvintageclothing.co.uk; 12 Camden Passage N1; 🚇Angel) One of London's most enchanting vintage shops, Annie's has costumes to make you look like Greta Garbo.

### Housmans                                    Books
Map p204 (www.housmans.com; 5 Caledonian Rd N1; 🚇King's Cross/St Pancras) This long-standing, not-for-profit bookshop, where you'll find books unavailable on the shelves of the more mainstream stockists, is a good place to keep up to date with all sorts of progressive, political and social campaigns, and with your more radical reads.

# Greenwich

**Greenwich is packed with gorgeous architecture, parkland and standout museums.** The existential divide between North and South London may remain as stark as ever, but growing numbers of North Londoners have warmed to South London's more affordable property prices, leafy charms and relaxed tempo. And nowhere typifies this atmosphere more successfully than Greenwich, with its eye-catching blend of stately, royal architecture, charming side streets, two-storey cottages and riverside pubs.

From a sightseeing perspective, there are some beautiful views from Greenwich Park's high point, and there's the world-famous Royal Observatory (p222), the fabulous National Maritime Museum (p225) and the magnificent Old Royal Naval College (p230). Greenwich Market (p227) is a must for those shopping and snacking. Ticket-holders are also queuing up to come here for some South London venues of the 2012 Games.

Greenwich is one of the highlights of any visit to London so allow a day to do it justice.

Greenwich Park (p222)

ROBERT STAINFORTH/ALAMY ©

# Greenwich Highlights

## Royal Observatory (p222)

Time is a largely intangible and abstract concept, but it's fair to say that the closest you can get to touching it is by paying a visit to the Royal Observatory in Greenwich, and straddling hemispheres and time zones as you stand on the actual meridian line. Get here for 1pm on any day of the week to see the red time ball at the top of the Royal Observatory drop. Interior of the Royal Observatory

**1**

**2**

## Greenwich Park (p222)

By any standards Greenwich Park, designed by Le Nôtre, the man responsible for the gardens at Versailles, is a pretty special place. The panoramic London views from the top of the hill are spectacular and the entire place is wonderful for a long walk or a picnic when the weather's good. Don't miss the deer park in the southeast corner and come here in October for edible chestnuts that litter the ground.

## National Maritime Museum (p225) 3

With its handsome naval heritage and good-looking riverside perch, Greenwich is ideally suited for a definitive glance back at Britain's nautical history. Steer a course through the world's largest maritime museum and explore a simply riveting collection of artefacts.

## Old Royal Naval College (p230) 4

A visit to Greenwich is totally incomplete without a visit to this former naval hospital, designed by Christopher Wren at the end of the 17th century. The colourful details of the murals within the glorious Painted Hall can draw you into hours of exploration and discovery, while the nearby chapel is simply outstanding. This is one of Greenwich's top sights, so don't rush through it.

## Greenwich Market (p227) 5

Packed with stalls, Greenwich's famous market is perfect browsing territory for gift ideas, but it also cooks up some excellent snacks three days a week, when you can savour flavours from around the world. Dotted around the perimeter of the market are some excellent shops, rounding out a highly appetising picture.

# Greenwich Walk

*This genteel and charming neighbourhood, magnificently placed by a bend in the Thames, has heaps to offer beyond its drawcard sights. This itinerary links together more discreet attractions tucked away from the main drag.*

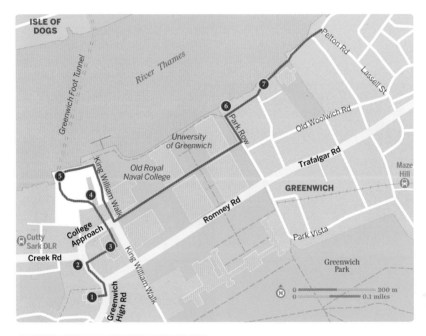

## 1 St Alfege Church

Designed by Nicholas Hawksmoor in 1714 to replace a 12th-century building, this glorious parish **church** (www.st-alfege.org; Church St SE10; ⊙10am-4pm Mon-Sat, 1-4pm Sun; ☒Greenwich or DLR Cutty Sark) features a restored mural by James Thornhill, a largely wood-panelled interior and an intriguing 'Tallis' keyboard with middle keyboard octaves from the Tudor period. Pop into lovely St Alfege Passage, behind the church, for a stunning little stone-paved alley running past the churchyard.

## 2 Beehive

Wander down Greenwich Church St to join the Greenwich vinyl junkies at this funky meeting ground of old records and retro togs at this fascinating shop (p231). Pop in for a glance and leave with a mod-print dress, vintage Bakelite telephone and a copy of Bowie's *Hunky Dory*.

## 3 Greenwich Market

Cross the road to dive into this lively and well-stocked market (p227). Rub shoulders with the crowds looking for gifts and souvenirs from the stalls, pick up tasty snacks from the stalls or browse through its absorbing choice of shops.

### 4 Cutty Sark

One of Greenwich's signature icons, this historic clipper ship (p224) should have reopened by the time you read this, after a conflagration in 2007 caused serious damage.

### 5 Greenwich Foot Tunnel

Completed in 1902, the 370m-long **Greenwich Foot Tunnel** running under the Thames from the Isle of Dogs is fun to explore. The lifts down to the tunnel run between 7am and 7pm Monday to Saturday and 10am to 5.30pm on Sunday. Otherwise it's between 88 to 100 steps down and – shudder – up (open 24 hours).

### 6 Trafalgar Tavern

Head south along King William Walk and cross the grounds of the Old Royal Naval College to this cavernous and historic **pub** (www.trafalgartavern.co.uk; 6 Park Row SE10; ☺noon-11pm Mon-Thu, to midnight Fri & Sat, to 10.30pm Sun; DLR Cutty Sark, ☒Maze Hill), with big windows onto the river. Dickens drank here (using it as the setting for the wedding breakfast scene in *Our Mutual Friend*) and prime ministers Gladstone and Disraeli dined on the pub's celebrated whitebait.

### 7 Walking by the River

A short walk east along the Thames puts Greenwich's riverside character into clear definition. This section of the Thames Path is most attractive closer to Greenwich, with fantastic views of Canary Wharf and the river. Do what locals do and have an evening drink at the Cutty Sark Tavern (p228).

## ✶ The Best...

### PLACES TO EAT

**Nevada Street Deli** Great for some uniquely flavoured homemade sausages and mash, or caffeine replacement. (p226)

**Inside** Smart restaurant with a deservedly popular Modern European menu. (p227)

**Old Brewery** Handy cafe by day, commendable restaurant by night. (p227)

### PLACES TO DRINK

**Greenwich Union** Good-looking, fantastic pub with a great range of Meantime brews and a congenial interior. (p228)

**Cutty Sark Tavern** History, riverside perch and decent beer all rolled into one. (p228)

**Old Brewery** Mouth-watering range of ales and a central location. (p228)

### SIGHTS

**Greenwich Park** Get lost in lovely Greenwich Park. (p222)

**National Maritime Museum** Engrossing collection of pieces from Britain's nautical heritage, great for kids and adults. (p225)

**Royal Observatory** Stand on the Meridian and plant a foot in both east and west. (p222)

**Old Royal Naval College** Beautiful interior of decorative artwork and lavish design. (p230)

# Don't Miss
# Royal Observatory & Greenwich Park

One of London's most-visited attractions and part of the National Maritime Museum, the Royal Observatory is where the study of the sea and the stars converge. The Prime Meridian charts its line through the grounds of the observatory, chosen quite arbitrarily in 1884, cleaving the globe into the eastern and western hemispheres. The observatory sits on a hill within leafy and regal Greenwich Park, London's oldest royal park, with its fabulous views, 72 hectares of trees and lush greenery.

Map p226

📞 8858 4422

www.nmm.ac.uk/places/royal-observatory

Greenwich Park, Blackheath Ave SE10

adult/child/concession £10/free/7.50

🕙 10am-5pm

🚉 Greenwich or DLR Cutty Sark

# Flamsteed House

Following an ambitious £15-million reno-vation, the excellent Royal Observatory is divided into two sections.

You now need to pay to access the sites of the northern portion, dedicated to horology. Charles II ordered the construction of the Christopher Wren–designed Flamsteed House – the original observatory building – in 1675; it contains the magnificent Octagon Room, where timepieces are housed. It also has absorbing galleries dedicated to timekeeping and longitude.

Outside Flamsteed house, the globe is decisively sliced into east and west, where visitors can delightfully straddle both hemispheres in the Meridian Courtyard, with one foot either side of the meridian line. Every day at 1pm the red time ball at the top of the Royal Observatory continues to drop as it has done since 1833.

# Astronomy Centre

The southern half contains the highly informative and free Astronomy Centre, where you can touch the oldest object you will ever encounter: part of the Gibeon meteorite, a mere 4.5 billion years old! Other engaging exhibits include an orrery (mechanical model of the solar system, minus Uranus and Neptune) from 1780, astronomical documentaries, a first edition of Newton's *Principia Math-ematica* and the opportunity to view the Milky Way in multiple wavelengths.

Also here is the state-of-the-art **Peter Harrison Planetarium** ( ☎ 8312 8565; www.nmm.ac.uk/astronomy; adult/child/family £6.50/4.50/17.50; ⏰ hourly shows 12.45-3.45pm Mon-Fri, 11am-4.15pm Sat & Sun), London's sole planetarium, with a digital laser projector that can cast entire heavens onto the inside of its roof.

# Greenwich Park

Handsome venue of the 2012 Olympic Games equestrian events, this **park** ( ☎ 8858 2608; www.royalparks.gov.uk; ⏰ dawn-dusk; 🚉 Greenwich or Maze Hill, DLR Cutty Sark) is one of London's loveliest expanses of green, with a rose garden, picturesque walks and astonishing views from the crown of the hill. Covering a full 73 hectares, this is the oldest enclosed royal park and is partly the work of André Le Nôtre, the landscape architect who designed the gardens of Versailles. The park is rich in historic sights, including a teahouse near the Royal Observatory, a cafe behind the National Maritime Museum, a deer park, tennis courts in the southwest and a boating lake at the Queen's House end. In October, look out for edible chestnuts.

# Ranger's House

This elegant **Georgian villa** ( ☎ 8853 0035; www.english-heritage.org.uk; Greenwich Park, Chesterfield Walk SE10; adult/child/concession £6.30/3.80/5.70; ⏰ tours 11.30am & 2.30pm Mon-Wed, 11am-5pm Sun early Apr-Sep), built in 1723, once housed the park's ranger and now contains a collection of 700 works of art (medieval and Renaissance paint-ings, porcelain, silverware, tapestries) amassed by Julius Wernher (1850–1912), a German-born railway engineer's son who struck it rich in the diamond fields of South Africa in the 19th century. The Spanish Renaissance jewellery collection is the best in Europe, and the rose garden fronting the house defies description.

## Prime Meridian

The Greenwich Meridian was selected as the global Prime Meridian at the International Meridian Conference in Washington DC in 1884. Greenwich thereafter became the world's common zero for longitude and standard for time calculations, replacing the multiple meridians that had previously existed. Greenwich was assisted in its bid by the earlier US adoption of Greenwich Mean Time for its own national time zones. Furthermore, the majority of world trade already used sea charts that identified Greenwich as the Prime Meridian.

# Discover Greenwich

## Getting There & Away

○ **Underground, DLR & Train** Most sights in Greenwich can be easily reached from the Cutty Sark DLR station; a quicker way from central London is via one of the mainline trains from Charing Cross or London Bridge to Greenwich railway station.

○ **Walking** If coming from Docklands to Greenwich, consider walking under the river.

○ **Boat** Thames Clipper (p283) boats run to Greenwich and Woolwich Arsenal from London Eye Millennium Pier.

## ◎ Sights

### Royal Observatory & Greenwich Park    Museum, Park
See p222.

### FREE Queen's House    Historic Building
Map p226 ( ☏ 8858 4422, recorded information 8312 6565; www.nmm.ac.uk/places/queens-house; Romney Rd SE10; ⊙10am-5pm; ☒Greenwich or DLR Cutty Sark; 🛜) The first Palladian building by architect Inigo Jones after he returned from Italy is indeed far more enticing than the art collection it contains, even though it includes some Turners, Holbeins, Hogarths and Gainsboroughs. The house was begun in 1616 for Anne of Denmark, wife of James I, but was not completed until 1638, when it became the home of Charles I and his queen, Henrietta Maria. The ceremonial **Great Hall** is the principal room – a gorgeous cube shape, with an elaborately tiled floor dating back to 1637; the ceiling was originally decorated with nine paintings by Orazio Gentileshci. The beautiful helix-shaped **Tulip Staircase** (named for the flowers on the wrought-iron balustrade; sadly, no photos allowed) leads to a gallery on Level 2, hung with paintings and portraits with a sea or seafaring theme from the National Maritime Museum's fine-art collection.

### Cutty Sark    Ship
Map p226 ( ☏ 8858 2698; www.cuttysark.org.uk; Cutty Sark Gardens SE10; ☒Greenwich or DLR Cutty Sark) This Greenwich landmark, the last of the great clipper ships to sail between China and England in the 19th

Spiral staircase, Queen's House
GREG BALFOUR EVANS/ALAMY ©

JOHN HARPER/CORBIS ©

Don't Miss

## National Maritime Museum

Narrating the long and eventful history of seafaring Britain, this museum is one of Greenwich's top attractions.

The exhibits are arranged thematically and highlights include **Miss Britain III** (the first boat to top 100mph on open water) from 1933, the 19m-long **golden state barge** built in 1732 for Frederick, Prince of Wales, and the **huge ship's propeller** installed on Level 1. The museum also owns the uniform coat that Britain's greatest sea-faring hero, Horatio Nelson, was wearing when he was fatally shot (and the actual bullet), plus a replica of the lifeboat used by explorer Ernest Shackleton and some of his men after the *Endurance* sank on their epic mission in Antarctica.

The **Your Ocean** exhibit examines the science, history, health and future of the sea. Kids will love firing a cannon in the **All Hands** exhibit or manoeuvring a tanker into port using the Bridge Simulator. A branch of bakery-cafe Paul is on the upper deck, and museum space increased with the Sammy Ofer Wing, which opened in late 2011. Tours depart from the ship's propeller at noon, 1pm and 3pm.

NEED TO KNOW

Map p226; ☎8858 4422; www.nmm.ac.uk; Romney Rd SE10; admission free; ⏰10am-5pm; 🚉Greenwich or DLR Cutty Sark

century, was due to reopen in spring 2012 after serious fire damage. Luckily half of its furnishings and equipment, including the mast, had been removed for conservation at the time of the conflagration.

**Fan Museum** Museum

**Map p226 (☎8305 1441, 8858 7879; www.fan-museum.org; 12 Crooms Hill SE10; adult/7-16yr & concession/family £4/3/10; ⏰11am-5pm Tue-Sat, noon-5pm Sun; 🚉Greenwich or DLR**

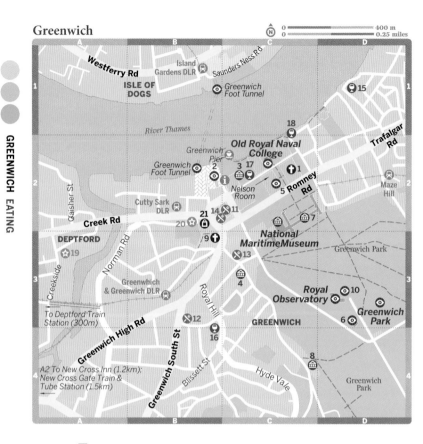

Cutty Sark; 📷) The world's only museum entirely devoted to fans has a wonderful collection of ivory, tortoiseshell, peacock-feather and folded-fabric examples alongside kitsch battery-powered versions and huge ornamental Welsh fans. The setting of an 18th-century Georgian town house also has a Japanese-style garden plus the **Orangery (half-/full tea £5/6;** ⏱ **3-5pm Tue & Sun)**, with lovely trompe l'œil murals and twice-weekly afternoon tea.

**O2**  Concert Venue
( 📞 8463 2000, bookings 0844 856 0202; www.theo2.co.uk; Millennium Way SE10; 🚇 North Greenwich) The 380m-wide circular O2 cost £750 million to build and costs more than £5 million a year just to keep it erect. Once the definitive white elephant, it has hosted big acts like Madonna, Prince, Justin Timberlake and Barbara Streisand in its 23,000-seat **O2 Arena** and soul, pop and jazz bands in the 2350-seat **IndigO2**. Massive exhibitions (Tutankhamen and the Golden Age of the Pharaohs, The Human Body) and sporting events have made their temporary homes here, as well as a slew of bars, clubs and restaurants. During the Olympics, this venue will host the basketball and gymnastics events as the North Greenwich Arena.

## ✕ Eating

### Nevada Street Deli  Deli **£**
Map p226 (www.nevadastreetdeli.co.uk; 8 Nevada St, SE10; sandwiches £3.75-4; ⏱ 9am-6pm; DLR Cutty Sark) There may be a sudden

# Greenwich

scramble for one of the few outside tables when the sun pops out, but this charming wedge-shaped space is a popular spot for sandwiches (especially bacon sandwiches), all-day breakfasts, mushrooms or gravlax on toast, a plate of scrumptious handmade sausages in a wealth of varieties (smoked salmon, spinach and fetta cheese) or merely a restorative cup of steaming coffee.

### Inside
Modern European ££
Map p226 (✆8265 5060; www.insiderestaurant.co.uk; 19 Greenwich South St SE10; mains £12.50-17.75, 2-/3-course set menu lunch £12.95/17.95, set menu early dinner £17.95/22.95; ⊙closed dinner Sun & all day Mon; DLR/🚃Greenwich) With white walls, modern art and linen tablecloths, Inside is a relaxed kind of place and one of Greenwich's best restaurant offerings.

### Greenwich Market
Market £
Map p226 (www.greenwichmarket.net; Greenwich Market, SE10; ⊙10am-5.30pm Wed, Sat & Sun; DLR Cutty Sark) Perfect for snacking your way through a world atlas of food while browsing the other market stalls. Come here on a Wednesday, Saturday or Sunday for delicious food-to-go, with everything from Spanish tapas to Thai curries, sushi, Polish doughnuts, French crêpes, Brazilian churros, smoked Louisiana sausages, chivitos and more. Follow your nostrils and make your choice, then you can wash it all down with a glass of fresh farmhouse cider.

### Old Brewery
Modern British ££
Map p226 (✆3327 1280; Pepys Bldg, Old Royal Naval College, SE10; mains £11.50-26; ⊙cafe 10am-5pm Mon-Sun, restaurant 6-11pm Mon-Sat & 6-10.30pm Sun; DLR Cutty Sark) A working brewery with splendidly burnished 1000-litre copper vats at one end and a high ceiling lit with natural sunlight, the Old Brewery is perfectly located after staggering around Greenwich's top sights. Right next to Discover Greenwich exhibition, it's a cafe by day, transforming into a restaurant in the evening, serving a choice selection of fine dishes carefully sourced from the best seasonal ingredients.

### Tai Won Mein
Chinese £
Map p226 (39 Greenwich Church St, SE10; ⊙11.30am-11.30pm; mains from £4.95) The staff may be a bit jaded but this great

snack spot – the Cantonese moniker just means 'Big Bowl of Noodles' – serves epic portions of carbohydrate-rich noodles to those overcoming Greenwich's titanic sights.

# 🍷 Drinking & Nightlife

**If you're looking for old school pubs, this part of London can oblige – and will throw in some wonderful views to boot.**

### Greenwich Union                    Pub
Map p226 (www.greenwichunion.com; 56 Royal Hill SE10; DLR Cutty Sark) The award-winning Union plies six or seven local microbrewery beers, including raspberry and wheat varieties, and a strong list of ales, plus bottled international brews. It's a handsome place, with duffed up leather armchairs and a welcoming long, narrow aspect that leads to the conservatory and beer garden at the rear.

### Cutty Sark Tavern                    Pub
Map p226 (www.cuttysarktavern.co.uk; 4-6 Ballast Quay SE10; DLR Cutty Sark, 🚌177 or 180) Housed in a delightful bow-windowed, wood-beamed Georgian building that sits directly on the Thames, the Cutty Sark Tavern is one of the few independent pubs that are left in Greenwich. The bar is lined with half a dozen cask-conditioned ales that are on tap, and there is an inviting riverside sitting-out area opposite.

### Old Brewery                    Bar
Map p226 (Pepys Bldg, Old Royal Naval College, SE10; 🕐11am-11pm Mon-Sat, noon-10.30pm Sun; DLR Cutty Sark) Conveniently situated within the grounds of the Old Royal Naval College, the brickwork bar at the Old Brewery is run by the Meantime Brewery, which sells its own brew draught Imperial Pale Ale (brewed on site), along with a heady range of more than 50 beers, ranging from Belgian Trappist ales to fruity and flavoured brews and smoked beers. There's also a wide-ranging menu

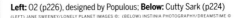
**Left:** 02 (p226), designed by Populous; **Below:** Cutty Sark (p224)
(LEFT) JANE SWEENEY/LONELY PLANET IMAGES ©; (BELOW) INSTINIA PHOTOGRAPHY/DREAMSTIME ©

of much more. There are extra tables outside in the courtyard.

# ⭐ Entertainment

Early September sees Greenwich play host to London's largest comedy festival, the Greenwich Comedy Festival (www.greenwichcomedyfestival.co.uk), which is set in the grounds of Old Royal Naval College.

## Laban
Dance

Map p226 (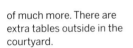information 8691 8600, bookings 8469 9500; www.laban.org; Creekside SE8; admission £6-15; Deptford Bridge, DLR Greenwich) This is an independent dance training school, which also presents student performances, graduation shows and regular pieces by the resident troupe, Transitions Dance Company, as well as other assorted dance, music and physical performances. Its stunning £23-million home was designed by Herzog & de Meuron, designers of the Tate Modern (see p124).

## Up the Creek
Comedy

Map p226 (8858 4581; www.up-the-creek. com; 302 Creek Rd SE10; admission £10-15; Fri & Sat; Greenwich, DLR Cutty Sark) Bizarrely enough, the hecklers can be funnier than the acts at this great club. Mischief, rowdiness and excellent comedy are the norm with open mic nights on Thursdays (£4) and Sunday specials (£6; www.sunday special.co.uk).

## 02
Live Music

(0871 984 0002; www.theo2.co.uk; Peninsula Sq SE10; North Greenwich) One of the city's major concert venues, hosting all the biggies – the Rolling Stones, Britney Spears, Prince and many others – inside the 20,000-capacity stadium. Ticket prices start at £25.

DOUG MCKINLAY/LONELY PLANET IMAGES ©

## ✓ Don't Miss
# Old Royal Naval College

When Christopher Wren was commissioned by William and Mary to construct a naval hospital here in 1692, he conceived it in two separate halves to protect the river views from the Queen's House, Inigo Jones' miniature masterpiece to the south. Built on the site of the Old Palace of Placentia, where Henry VIII was born in 1491, the hospital was initially intended for those wounded in the victory over the French at La Hogue. In 1869 the building was converted into a Naval College; today it is home to the University of Greenwich and Trinity College of Music, with two main rooms open to the public.

Designed as a dining hall for sailors, the **Painted Hall** ( ⏲10am-5pm) is one of Europe's greatest banquet rooms, dressed in decorative 'allegorical Baroque' murals by artist James Thornhill. The magnificent ceiling mural above the Lower Hall is a feast, showing William and Mary enthroned amid symbols of the Virtues.

With its mix of ancient Greek and naval motifs, the beautiful **chapel** ( ⏲10am-5pm Mon-Sat, 12.30-5pm Sun) in the Queen Mary Building is decorated in an elaborate rococo style. If possible come on the first Sunday of the month, when there's a free 50-minute **organ recital** at 3pm, or time your visit for sung Eucharist at 11am on Sunday.

The new **Discover Greenwich** (Pepys Bldg, King William Walk; ⏲10am-5pm; admission free) delves into the history of Greenwich with hands-on exhibits, many aimed at children.

A 90-minute **guided tour** ( ☏8269 4791; adult/under 16yr £5/free; ⏲tours 11.30am & 2pm) from the Painted Hall will take you to places not normally open to the public: the Jacobean undercroft of the former Placentia palace and the 140-year-old Victorian Skittle Alley, featuring enormous hand-carved wooden bowling balls and pins.

NEED TO KNOW

Map p226; ☏8269 4747; www.oldroyalnavalcollege.org; King William Walk SE10; admission free; ⊠Greenwich or DLR Cutty Sark

# 🔒 Shopping

Greenwich is a paradise for lovers of retro clothes stores and secondhand bookshops; endlessly fascinating Greenwich Market (p227) rewards both casual and determined browsing.

### Compendia                        Gifts, Souvenirs
Map p226 ( 📞8293 6616; www.compendia.co.uk; 10 Greenwich Market; ⏱11am-5.30pm; DLR Cutty Sark) Compendia's owners are madly enthusiastic about games – board or any other kind – and they'll look for the rarest of things if you ask them to. The shop is excellent for gifts you can enjoy with your mates – backgammon, chess, Scrabble, solitaire and more fringe interests such as Mexican Train Domino, which claims to be the world's fastest game, Carrom (popular in South Asia) and Go. Look out for the Escher jigsaws and if you're Greenwich Park–bound, pick up a Frisbee, a kite, some juggling balls or even a diabolo.

### Emporium                        Fashion, Jewellery
Map p226 ( 📞8305 1670; 330-332 Creek Rd SE10; ⏱10.30am-6pm Wed-Sun; DLR Cutty Sark) Each piece is individual at this lovely vintage shop (unisex), where glass cabinets are crammed with costume jewellery, old perfume bottles and straw hats, while gorgeous jackets and blazers intermingle on the clothes racks.

### Beehive                        Vintage
Map p226; 📞8858 1964; 320-322 Creek Rd, SE10; ⏱10.30am-6pm Tue-Sun, 10.30am-6.30pm Sat & Sun; DLR Cutty Sark) Funky meeting ground of old vinyl (Bowie, Rolling Stones, vintage soul) and retro togs (frocks, blouses, leather jackets and overcoats).

Oxford ○

100km
60ml

50km
30ml

**LONDON**
✪

Windsor ○

○ Hampton
Court

Ⓝ

English Channel

# Day Trips

## Hampton Court Palace (p234)

One of the best days out London has to offer, this palace should not be missed by anyone with an interest in British history, Tudor architecture or delicious landscaped gardens.

## Windsor (p236)

An affluent town dominated by that nerve centre of British royalty, Windsor Castle, Windsor is a pleasant place to wander.

## Oxford (p237)

Although the world's oldest university town, Oxford's allure does not rest solely with its prestigious colleges, but with its delightful architecture and world-class museums, too.

# ✅

## Don't Miss
# Hampton Court Palace

London's most spectacular Tudor palace, 16th-century Hampton Court Palace, concocts an imposing sense of history, from the kitchens where you see food being prepared and the grand living quarters of Henry VIII to the spectacular gardens, complete with a 300-year-old maze.

12 miles southwest of London

📞 0844 482 7777

www.hrp.org.uk

Hampton Court Rd, East Molesy KT8

adult/child/concession/family £15.95/8/13.20/43

🚉 Hampton Court
⚓ from Westminster Pier, Apr-Oct, 3hr

## Base Court & Clock Court

Passing through the magnificent main gate (Trophy Gate) you arrive first in the Base Court and then the Clock Court, named after the 16th-century astronomical clock that still shows the sun revolving round the earth. The second court is your starting point; from here you can follow any or all of the six sets of rooms in the complex.

## Great Hall

The stairs inside Anne Boleyn's Gateway lead up to Henry VIII's State Apartments, including the Great Hall, the largest single room in the palace, decorated with tapestries and what is considered the country's finest hammerbeam roof.

## Chapel Royal & Kitchens

Further along the corridor is the beautiful Chapel Royal, built in just nine months and still a place of worship after 450 years.

Also dating from Henry's day are the delightful Tudor kitchens, again accessible from Anne Boleyn's Gateway and once used to rustle up meals for a royal household of some 1200 people. The kitchens have been fitted out to resemble how they might have looked in Tudor days and palace 'servants' turn the spits, stuff the peacocks and frost the marzipan with real gold leaf. Don't miss the Great Wine Cellar, which handled the 300 barrels each of ale and wine consumed here annually in the mid-16th century.

## King's Apartments

West of the colonnade in the Clock Court is the entrance to the Wolsey Rooms and the Young Henry VIII Exhibition. A tour of the apartments takes you up the grand King's Staircase, painted by Antonio Verrio in about 1700 and flattering the king by comparing him to Alexander the Great. Highlights include the King's Presence Chamber, dominated by a throne backed with scarlet hangings. The King's Great Bedchamber, with a bed topped with ostrich plumes, and the King's Closet (where His Majesty's toilet has a velvet seat) should not be missed.

## Queen's Apartments

William's wife, Mary II, had her own Queen's Apartments, accessible up the Queen's Staircase, decorated by William Kent. When Mary died in 1694, work on these was incomplete; they were finished during the reign of George II. The rooms are shown as they might have been when Queen Caroline used them for entertaining between 1716 and 1737. Compared with the King's Apartments, those for the queen seem austere, although the Queen's Audience Chamber has a throne as imposing as that of the king.

## Gardens

Beyond the palace are the stunning gardens. No-one should leave Hampton Court without losing themselves in the famous 800m-long **maze**, made of hornbeam and yew and planted in 1690. The maze is included in entry, although those not visiting the palace can enter for £3.85 (£2.75 for children, £11 for families). Last admission is at 5.15pm in summer and 3.45pm in winter.

### Haunted Hampton Court

Arrested for adultery and detained in the palace in 1542, Henry's fifth wife, Catherine Howard, was dragged screaming down a gallery at the palace by her guards after an escape bid. Her ghost is said to do a repeat performance to this day in the Haunted Gallery (she must be a tireless ghost as she also haunts the Tower of London).

# Windsor

With its romantic architecture and superb state rooms, Windsor Castle is one of Britain's premier tourist attractions and, since it is so close to central London and easily accessible by rail and road, it crawls with tourists in all seasons.

## Getting There & Away

**Bus** Green Line buses (☎0844 801 7261; www.greenline.co.uk) 701 and 702 link Victoria coach station with Windsor (return from £10, 1¼ hours) at least hourly every day.

**Train** Trains (☎0845 748 4950; www.nationalrail.co.uk) from Waterloo station go to Windsor Riverside station every 30 minutes, or hourly on Sunday (return from £10, 50 minutes). Trains from Paddington go via Slough to Eton and Windsor Central station (return from £9, 45 minutes).

## Need to Know

○ **Area code** ☎01753

○ **Location** 25 miles west of London

○ **Tourist office** (☎743900; www.windsor.gov.uk; Old Booking Hall, Windsor Royal Station, Thames St; ◷9.30am-5.30pm Mon-Sat, 10am-4pm Sun May-Aug, 10am-5pm Mon-Sat, 10am-4pm Sun Sep-Apr)

## ◉ Sights

### Windsor Castle                          Castle

(www.royalcollection.org.uk; adult/child £16.50/9.90, when State Apartments closed £9/6; ◷9.45am-5.15pm Mar-Oct, 9.45am-4.15pm Nov-Feb) British monarchs have inhabited Windsor Castle for more than 900 years, and it is well known to be the Queen's favourite residence and the place she calls home after returning from her work 'week' (now just Tuesday to Thursday) at the 'office' (Buckingham Palace). A disastrous fire in 1992 nearly wiped out this incredible piece of English cultural heritage. Luckily damage, though severe, was limited and a £37-million restoration, completed in 1997, has returned the state apartments to their former glory.

Starting out as a wooden castle erected around 1080 by William the Conqueror, and rebuilt in stone in 1170, this is one of the world's greatest surviving medieval castles, and its longevity and easy accessibility from London guarantee its popularity.

The castle area, covering more than five hectares, is divided into three wards. In the Upper Ward, the **State Apartments**, which are closed to the public at certain times (check the website), reverberate with history. The self-paced audioguide tour starts with the impossibly opulent **Grand Staircase** and weapons-filled **Grand Vestibule** and leads into the **Waterloo Chamber**, created to commemorate the Battle of Waterloo and filled with portraits of the great and the good by Sir Thomas Lawrence (1769–1830).

From here you move to the **King's Rooms** and **Queen's Rooms**. These are lessons in how the other half lives, with opulent furniture, tapestries and paintings by Canaletto, Dürer, Gainsborough, Van Dyck, Hogarth, Holbein, Rembrandt and Rubens. Next is the extraordinary **St George's Hall**, the structure most affected by the 1992 fire but now brought back to life, including its signature hammerbeam roof. The tour ends in the **Garter Throne Room**.

Outside on the North Terrace you can't help noticing the queues that form for the impossibly intricate **Queen Mary's Dolls' House**, the work of architect Sir Edwin Lutyens.

Moving westward through the Middle Ward and past the distinctive **Round Tower**, rebuilt in stone from the original Norman keep in 1180, you enter the Lower Ward. Here one of Britain's finest examples of early English architecture, **St George's Chapel** (begun by Edward IV in 1475, but not completed until 1528), has a superb nave done in Perpendicular Gothic style, with gorgeous fan vaulting.

DAVID JOYNER/ISTOCKPHOTO ©

South of the castle is beautiful **Windsor Great Park** (⊙8am-dusk) covering an area of some 40 sq miles.

A must for any visitor is the **changing of the guard** (⊙11am Mon-Sat Apr-Jul, alternate days Aug-Mar), a fabulous spectacle of pomp and ceremony that draws large crowds to the castle gates. You'll get a better view if you stay to the right of the crowd, and if you're just interested in watching the marching bands, find a spot along High or Sheet Sts; the guards leave from Victoria Barracks on the latter at 10.45am and return an hour later.

# Eating & Drinking

### Gilbey's — Modern British £££

(☎854921; www.gilbeygroup.com; 82-83 High St, Eton; mains £16-24, 2-/3-course lunch £18.50/24; ⊙lunch & dinner Mon-Fri, afternoon tea Sat & Sun) This little restaurant just beyond the bridge in Eton is one of the area's finest. Terracotta tiling and a sunny courtyard garden lend a Continental cafe air, but the understated decor and menu are indisputably British. Excellent wine list.

### Tower — Brasserie ££

(☎848547; High St; mains £10.50-14.50; ⊙7am-11pm Mon-Fri, from 8am Sat & Sun) Giant windows with priceless views over Windsor Castle are the immediate allure at this eatery in the Harte and Garter Hotel. The menu is brasserie style with a choice of classic British dishes – grills, fish, steaks – simply and perfectly done.

### Two Brewers — Pub

(www.twobrewerswindsor.co.uk; 34 Park St) This 17th-century inn perched on the edge of Windsor Great Park and the Long Walk is close to the castle's tradesmen's entrance and supposedly frequented by staff from the castle. It's a quaint and cosy place, with dim lighting, obituaries to castle footmen and royal photographs with irreverent captions on the wall. Great pub grub, too.

# Oxford

Victorian poet Matthew Arnold called Oxford 'that sweet city with her dreaming spires'. These days the spires coexist with a flourishing commercial city that

237

# Oxford

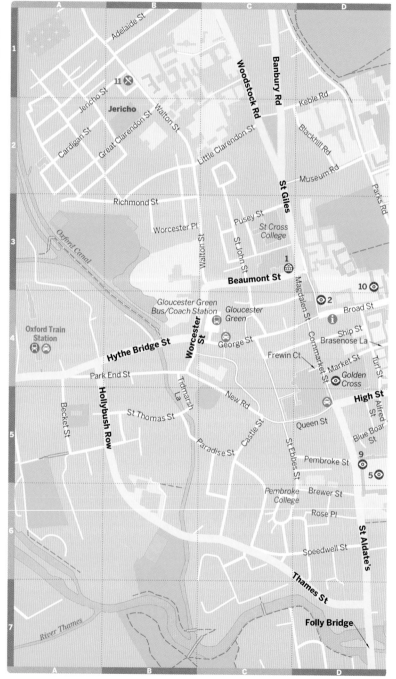

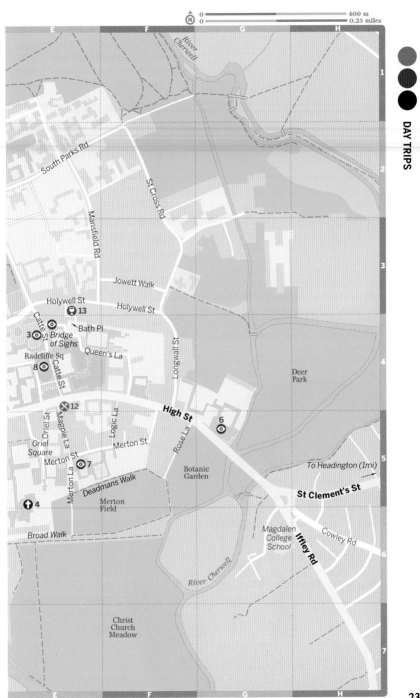

River Cherwell

South Parks Rd

St Cross Rd

Mansfield Rd

Jowett Walk

Holywell St

Holywell St 📍 13

Catte St

3 ⊙ Bath Pl

Bridge of Sighs

Queen's La

Radcliffe Sq

8 ⊙ Catte St

Longwall St

Deer Park

High St

❌ 12

6 ⊙

Oriel St

Magpie La

Logic La

Merton St

Oriel Square

Merton St

Merton La ⊙ 7

Rose La

To Headington (1mi) →

St Clement's St

Deadmans Walk

✝ 4

Merton Field

Botanic Garden

Magdalen College School

Cowley Rd

Iffley Rd

Broad Walk

River Cherwell

Christ Church Meadow

## Oxford

has some typical urban social problems. But for visitors, the superb architecture and the unique atmosphere of the more than three dozen colleges – synonymous with academic excellence – and their courtyards and gardens remain major attractions.

## Getting There & Away

**Bus** Oxford Tube (☎772250; www.oxfordtube.com) and Oxford Espress (☎785400; www.oxfordbus.co.uk) buses depart every 10 to 30 minutes round the clock from London's Victoria coach station (return from £16) and can be boarded at various other points in London, including Marble Arch, Notting Hill Gate and Shepherd's Bush. Journey time is an hour and 40 minutes.

**Train** There are two trains (☎0845 748 4950; www.nationalrail.co.uk) per hour from London's Paddington station (return from £16, one hour).

## Need to Know

○ **Area code** ☎01865

○ **Location** 59 miles northwest of London

○ **Tourist office** (☎252200; www.visitoxfordandoxfordshire.com; 15-16 Broad St; ⊙9.30am-5pm Mon-Sat, 10am-4pm Sun)

## ⊙ Sights

**Christ Church College**   University
Map p238 (www.chch.ox.ac.uk; St Aldate's; adult/child £7.50/6; ⊙9am-5.30pm Mon-Sat, 2-5.30pm Sun) Founded in 1525 and now massively popular with Harry Potter fans, having appeared in several of the films, Christ Church is the largest and grandest of all the 38 colleges. The main entrance is below **Tom Tower** (1681), designed by Christopher Wren and containing a 7-tonne bell called Great Tom. Visitors enter farther down St Aldate's via the wrought-iron gates of the War Memorial Gardens and Broad Walk. The college chapel is **Christ Church Cathedral**, the smallest in the country.

Radcliffe Camera
RAWDON WYATT/ALAMY ©

## Other Colleges University

If time and opening hours permit (check www.ox.ac.uk/colleges for details), consider visiting any of the following important colleges: **Magdalen College** (Map p238; www.magd.ox.ac.uk; High St; adult/child £4.50/3.50), pronounced *maud*-lin, with huge grounds bordering the River Cherwell; **Merton College** (Map p238; www.merton.ox.ac.uk; Merton St; adult/child £2/free), with a 14th-century library where JRR Tolkien wrote much of the *Lord of the Rings;* **Trinity College** (Map p238; www.trinity.ox.ac.uk; Broad St; adult/child £2/1), with an exquisitely carved chapel; and **Balliol College** (Map p238; www.balliol.ox.ac.uk; Broad St; adult/child £2/1), founded in 1263 and thought to be the oldest college in Oxford.

## Bodleian Library Library

Map p238 (www.bodleian.ox.ac.uk/bodley; Catte St; 30min/1hr tour £4.50/6.50; ⏰9am-5pm Mon-Fri, 9am-4.30pm Sat, 11am-5pm Sun) The early-17th-century Bodleian Library is one of the oldest public libraries in the world and one of just three copyright libraries in England. It is connected by tunnel with the Palladian-style **Radcliffe Camera** (1749), which functions as a reading room for the Bodleian and supports Britain's third-largest dome.

## FREE Ashmolean Museum Museum

Map p238 (www.ashmolean.org; Beaumont St; ⏰10am-6pm Tue-Sun) Britain's oldest public museum (1683) is now among the nation's finest after a massive £60-million redevelopment. It contains everything from Egyptian artefacts and Chinese art to European and British paintings by the likes of Rembrandt, Michelangelo, Turner and Picasso.

## 🍴 Eating & Drinking

### Quod International ££

Map p238 (📞202505; www.quod.co.uk; 92-94 High St; mains £12-16; ⏰7am-11pm Mon-Sat, 7am-10.30pm Sun) Perennially popular for its smart surroundings and buzzy atmosphere (not to mention its fine grills, fish dishes and pasta), this is the place Oxford students drag the rich uncle to when he's in town. Try their afternoon tea (£6.95 to £20.95) from 3pm to 5.30pm.

### Jericho Tavern Modern British ££

Map p238 (📞311775; www.thejerichooxford.co.uk; 56 Walton St; mains £8-12) Chilled out, with big leather sofas, a large beer garden and a live-music venue upstairs (supposedly Radiohead played their first gig here), this old coaching inn just outside the city gates in the trendy Jericho district has added gastropub to its CV, and it's a winner.

### Turf Tavern Pub

Map p238 (www.theturftavern.co.uk; 4 Bath Pl) Hidden away down a narrow alleyway off Holywell St, this tiny medieval pub is one of the town's best-loved and bills itself as 'an education in intoxication'.

# London

# In Focus

Changing of the Guard, Buckingham Palace (p56)
PAWEL LIBERA IMAGES/ALAMY ©

# London Today

Regent St, the West End (p47)

> *London has reaffirmed itself as a capital of transformative ideas*

## belief systems
(% of population)

**58** **8** **4** **2** **1** **27**

Christian    Muslim   Hindu   Jewish   Buddhist   Other

## if London were 100 people

60 would be white British

12 would be South Asian

11 would be white non-British

11 would be Africa or Afro-Caribbean

6 would be Other

## population per sq km

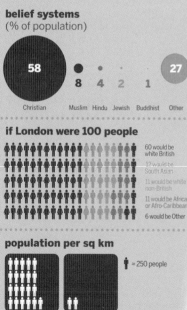

👤 ≈ 250 people

London      England

## The Olympic Games Effect

Since scooping its bid to host the 2012 Olympic Games, London has attracted a staggering amount of attention and scrutiny from talking heads, the media and the chattering classes. The city has been appraised, reappraised, examined and re-examined against a raft of expectations that would capsize a lesser city, especially one in the grip of recession. Yet London has reaffirmed itself as a capital of transformative ideas, cultural dynamism and staying power.

The recession may have double-dipped its way across the cityscape, leaving stalled projects and the occasionally immobile crane in its wake, but the Olympic project has proceeded according to plan, reshaping parts of the East End, expanding the city's transport network, rejuvenating squares and parks and adding a bit of fizz to even the most remote of urban backwaters.

Olympic Games work projects are notorious poisoned chalices, but London put its money on the massive regeneration of a derelict,

## Political Change

The UK political landscape endured great upheaval in the 2010 general election when the Labour Party – in power since 1997 – was unseated by public discontent over the economy, foreign policy and a seeming absence of dynamic leadership. The resulting hung parliament saw the Conservative Party and Liberal Democrats forced into the same bed, faced with the task of forging the first coalition cabinet since WWII, with David Cameron as prime minister. Rarely has a UK government taken charge in more economically blighted circumstances. With an economy essentially crippled by debt and overspending, a new Age of Austerity and unpopular public service cutbacks dawned, with rounds of belt-tightening gripping London and the UK. Some pundits linked the London riots of 2011 with the cutbacks and economic hardship, others blamed the erosion of social and personal responsibility in modern Britain.

GREG BALFOUR EVANS/ALAMY ©

polluted and neglected part of town, forging an emphasis on sustainability, the creation of wildlife and wetland habitats, and affordable housing.

## Multiculturalism

After the terrorist bombings by Muslim extremists on the London Transport network in 2005, multiculturalism became one of the fiercest debates in England's political history. Some say it all comes down to how Londoners, and British people, see themselves and their place in the world. Others lay the blame at the door of UK foreign policy. Others insist immigrants need to somehow conform to a national credo. Many Londoners are calling for greater efforts to promote integration of ethnic communities into British culture, but the subject remains a political minefield.

## Moving Forwards

An intelligent and nifty redesign of London's transport options is underway. The Barclays Cycle Hire Scheme (p283) has transformed the way a large number of people – including visitors – get about town. The East London Overground line has been extended and a cable car is planned across the Thames between Greenwich and the Royal Docks. Crossrail will bring high-frequency underground trains linking east and west London along two brand new lines costing £15.9 billion, due to commence service in 2018. The old Routemaster buses have largely vanished but are due to reappear in 2012 in modernised, more environmentally friendly form, replacing the much-mocked 'bendy buses'.

# History

St Paul's Cathedral (p102)

B.O'KANE/ALA

*The Romans are the real fathers of London and, amazingly, the Roman wall built around the settlement of Londinium still more or less demarcates the City of London from neighbouring London boroughs today. Through its history, London has endured a rollercoaster journey, experiencing conflict, apocalyptic plague, cataclysmic conflagrations and even bombardment with the world's first ever space rockets (the V-2).*

## The Romans

The empire-building Romans colonised Britain in AD 43, establishing the port of Londinium. They slung a wooden bridge over the Thames (near the site of today's London Bridge) and created a thriving colonial outpost before abandoning British soil for good in 410.

### AD 43

The Romans invade Britain and establish a base at Londinium on the River Thames.

## Saxon & Norman London

Saxon settlers, who colonised the southeast of England from the 5th century onwards, established themselves due west of Londinium in Lundenwic. Saxon London grew into a prosperous town segmented into 20 wards, each with its own alderman, and resident colonies of German merchants and French vintners. But Viking raids finally broke the weakening Saxon leadership, which was forced to accept the Danish leader Canute as king of England in 1016. With the death of Canute's son Harthacanute in 1042, the throne passed to the Saxon Edward the Confessor.

On his deathbed (1066) Edward anointed Harold Godwinson, the Earl of Wessex, as his successor, which enraged William, Duke of Normandy, who believed Edward had promised him the throne. William mounted a massive invasion from France and on 14 October defeated Harold at the Battle of Hastings, before marching on London to claim his prize. William the Conqueror was crowned king of England in Westminster Abbey on 25 December 1066, ensuring the Norman Conquest was complete.

**The Best...**
**Historical Treasures**

1 Tower of London (p98)

2 British Museum (p54)

3 Westminster Abbey (p52)

4 St Paul's Cathedral (p102)

5 Hampton Court Palace (p234)

**IN FOCUS HISTORY**

## Medieval & Tudor London

Successive medieval kings were happy to let the City of London keep its independence as long as its merchants continued to finance their wars and building projects. Later London became one of the largest and most important cities in Europe during the reign of the Tudors, which coincided with the discovery of the Americas and thriving world trade.

Henry VIII reigned from 1509 to 1547, built palaces at Whitehall and St James's, and bullied his lord chancellor, Cardinal Thomas Wolsey, into giving him Hampton Court. The most momentous event, however, was the split with the Catholic Church in 1534 after the Pope refused to annul his marriage to Catherine of Aragon, who had given him no heirs.

The 45-year reign (1558–1603) of his daughter Elizabeth I is still regarded as one of the most extraordinary periods in English history. During these four decades English literature reached new and still unsurpassed heights, and religious tolerance gradually became accepted doctrine. England became a naval superpower, having defeated the Spanish Armada in 1588, and the city established itself as the premier world trade market with the opening of the Royal Exchange in 1566.

**122**
Emperor Hadrian pays a visit to Londinium – this is the height of Roman London.

**852**
Vikings settle in London, having attacked the city a decade previously.

**1066**
After his victory at Hastings, William the Conqueror is crowned in Westminster Abbey.

# Great Fire of London

The Great Fire of London broke out in Thomas Farriner's bakery in Pudding Lane on the evening of 2 September 1666. Initially dismissed by London's dilatory lord mayor as 'something a woman might pisse out', the fire spread uncontrollably and destroyed 89 churches and more than 13,000 houses, raging for days.

The fire changed London forever. Many Londoners left for the countryside or to seek their fortunes in the New World, while the city itself rebuilt its medieval heart with grand buildings such as Wren's St Paul's Cathedral (p102). Wren's magnificent Monument (p105) stands as a memorial to the fire and its victims.

## Civil War, Plague & Fire

The English Civil Wars culminated with the execution of Charles I on 30 January 1649, and saw Oliver Cromwell rule the country as a republic for the next 11 years. During the Commonwealth of England, as the English republic was known, Cromwell banned theatre, dancing, Christmas and just about anything remotely entertaining. After Cromwell's death, parliament restored the exiled Charles II to the throne in 1660.

Charles II's reign witnessed two great tragedies in London: in 1665 the Great Plague devastated the population and the following year the Great Fire of London swept ferociously through the city's densely packed streets.

The wreckage of the inferno at least allowed master architect Christopher Wren to build his magnificent churches. The crowning glory of the 'Great Rebuilding', Wren's St Paul's Cathedral, was completed in 1710. One of the largest cathedrals in Europe, it remains one of the city's most prominent and visible landmarks.

## Victorian London

While the growth and achievements of the previous century were impressive, they were overshadowed by the dazzling Victorian era, dating from Queen Victoria's coronation in 1838. During the Industrial Revolution London became the nerve centre of the largest and richest empire the world has witnessed, in an imperial expansion that covered a quarter of the earth's surface area and ruled over more than 500 million people.

Queen Victoria lived to celebrate her Diamond Jubilee in 1897, but died four years later aged 81 and was laid to rest in Windsor. Her reign is seen as the climax of Britain's world supremacy, when London was the de facto capital of the world.

**1348**
The Black Death (a bubonic plague) wipes out two-thirds of London's population.

**1599**
The Globe Theatre opens in Southwark; *Macbeth, King Lear* and *Hamlet* premiere.
Shakespeare's Globe

MASSIMO SALA/DREAMSTIME ©

# The World Wars

What became known as the Great War (WWI) broke out in August 1914, and the first German bombs fell from zeppelins near the Guildhall a year later, killing 39 people. Planes were soon dropping bombs on the capital, killing in all some 650 Londoners (half the national total of civilian casualties).

After the war the population of London rose to nearly 7.5 million by 1921. Prime Minister Neville Chamberlain's policy of appeasing Adolf Hitler during the 1930s fatally misjudged Germany's ambitions. When Nazi Germany invaded Poland on 1 September 1939, Britain declared war, having signed a mutual-assistance pact with Poland only a few days previously. World War II (1939–45), considered Europe's darkest hour, had begun.

Winston Churchill, who was prime minister from 1940, orchestrated much of the nation's war strategy from the Cabinet War Rooms deep below Whitehall, lifting the nation's spirit from here with his stirring wartime speeches. By the time Nazi Germany capitulated in May 1945, up to a third of the East End and the City had been flattened, 32,000 Londoners had been killed and a further 50,000 had been seriously wounded.

The Monument (p105), a memorial to the 1666 Great Fire of London

MARTIN BEDDALL/ALAMY ©

**1666**
The Great Fire of London burns for five days, leaving the city in smoking ruins.

**1807**
Parliament abolishes the slave trade, after a long campaign led by William Wilberforce.

**1838**
Queen Victoria is crowned at Westminster Abbey, ushering in the greatest period in London's history.

## Postwar London

Once the celebrations of Victory in Europe (VE) day had died down, the nation began to count the cost of war. The years of austerity followed, with rationing of essential items and high-rise residences rising up from bombsites. Rationing of most goods ended in 1953, the year Elizabeth II was crowned following the death of her much-loved father King George VI the year before.

Immigrants from around the world – particularly the former British colonies – flocked to postwar London, where a dwindling population had generated labour shortages, and the city's character changed forever. The place to be during the 1960s, London became the epicentre of cool in fashion and music, its streets awash with colour and vitality. The ensuing 1970s brought glam rock, punk, economic depression and the country's first female prime minister in 1979.

Ruling for the entire 1980s and pushing an unprecedented program of privatisation, Margaret Thatcher is easily the most significant of Britain's postwar leaders. Opinions about 'Maggie' still polarise British opinion today. While poorer Londoners suffered under Thatcher's significant trimming back of the welfare state, things had rarely looked better for the wealthy as London underwent explosive economic growth.

Blitz monument near St Paul's Cathedral (p102)

**1901**
Queen Victoria dies after a reign of more than 63 years – the longest (so far) in British history.

**1940**
The Blitz begins, although miraculously St Paul's Cathedral escapes the bombing unscathed.

**1953**
Queen Elizabeth II's coronation is held, for which many English families bought their first TVs.

# The Blitz

The Blitz (from the German '*blitzkrieg*', meaning 'lightning war') struck England between September 1940 and May 1941, when London and other parts of Britain were heavily bombed by the German Luftwaffe. Londoners responded with legendary resilience and stoicism. The Underground was converted into a giant bomb shelter, although this was not always safe – one bomb rolled down the escalator at Bank station and exploded on the platform, killing more than 100 people.

In 1992, to the astonishment of most Londoners, the Conservatives were elected for a fourth successive term in government, despite Mrs Thatcher being jettisoned by her party shortly beforehand. By 1995 the writing was on the wall for the Conservatives, as the Labour Party, apparently unelectable for a decade, came back with a new face.

## London in the New Century

Invigorated by its sheer desperation to return to power, the Labour Party elected the thoroughly telegenic Tony Blair as its leader, who in turn managed to ditch some of the more socialist-sounding clauses in its party credo and reinvent the brand as New Labour, leading to a huge landslide win in the May 1997 general election. The Conservatives atomised nationwide; the Blair era began in earnest.

Most importantly for London, Labour recognised the demand the city had for local government, and created the London Assembly and the post of mayor. In Ken Livingstone London elected a mayor who introduced a congestion charge and sought to update the ageing public transport network. In 2008, he was defeated by Conservative and arch-rival Boris Johnson, while the 2012 mayoral election promises a thrilling rematch between the two powerful, but wildly different, personalities.

**1997**
Tony Blair rides into office with one of the biggest electoral landslides in British history.

**2005**
On 7 July, 52 people are killed by Muslim suicide bombers attacking the London transport network.

**2012**
London hosts its third Olympic Games, the first city in history to do so.

# Family Travel

Ice skating outside the Natural History Museum (p153)

*The idea that children should be seen and not heard vanished with the Victorians. London is becoming increasingly child-friendly every year, with bundles of new activities and special events for kids at museums and sights. Just remember that children are easily exhausted by the crowds and long walks – don't plan too much, and build in some rest time in London's fantastic public parks.*

## Museums

London's museums are particularly child friendly. You'll find storytelling at the National Gallery for children aged three years and over, arts and crafts workshops at the Victoria & Albert Museum, train-making workshops at the Transport Museum, tons of finger-painting opportunities at Tate Modern and Tate Britain, and performance and creative workshops at Somerset House. And what's better, they're all free (check websites for details).

Other excellent activities for children include sleepovers at the Science Museum or Natural History Museum, though you'll need to book months ahead; the Natural History Museum offers fantastic free explorer backpacks for under-sevens.

The Science Museum is the definitive children's museum, with interactive displays as well as a basement play area. The British Museum is another hit with kids.

## Other Attractions

Kids love London Zoo, the London Eye, the London Dungeon and Madame Tussauds. Ice rinks glitter around London in winter at the Natural History Museum, Somerset House, Hampton Court Palace, Kew Gardens and the Tower of London.

There's also the exciting climbs up St Paul's Cathedral or the Monument, feeding the ducks in St James's Park and watching the performers at Covent Garden Piazza. Many arts and cultural festivals aimed at adults also cater for children. London's parks burst with possibilities: open grass, playgrounds, wildlife, trees and ice-cream vans (in summer).

Most attractions offer family tickets and discounted entry for kids under 15 or 16 years (children under five are usually free).

## Eating & Drinking with Kids

Restaurants in London are generally highly accommodating of young children and many have children's menus. High chairs are usually available, but it's good to call ahead to check. You may feel rather less welcome bringing younger children out to smarter restaurants in the evenings. Babysitting services are widely available.

The one place that isn't traditionally very child-friendly is the pub. By law, minors aren't allowed into the main bar (though walking through is fine), but many pubs have areas where children are welcome, usually a garden or outdoor space.

### Not for Parents

For an insight into London aimed directly at kids, pick up a copy of Lonely Planet's *Not for Parents: London*. Perfect for children aged eight and up, it opens up a world of intriguing stories and fascinating facts about London's people, places, history and culture.

## Getting Around with Kids

When it comes to getting around, buses are much more child-friendly than the tube, which is often very crowded and hot in summer. As well as being big, red and iconic, buses in London are usually the famous 'double decker' type; kids love to sit on the top deck and get great views of the city. Another excellent way to get around is to walk.

## Need To Know

○ **Public transport** Under-16s travel free on buses, under-11s travel free on the tube, and under-fives ride free on trains.

○ **Babysitters** Find a babysitter or nanny at Greatcare (www.greatcare.co.uk).

○ **Cots** Available in most hotels, but always request them in advance.

# Food & Drink

Roast beef

HAJE JAN KAMPS/ALAMY

*Once the laughing stock of the cooking world, London has got its culinary act together over the last 20 years to become an undisputed dining destination. There are plenty of fine, Michelin-starred restaurants, but it is the sheer diversity on offer that is extraordinary: from Afghan to Vietnamese, London is a virtual A to Z of world cuisine.*

## Gastropubs

The culinary revolution began with the advent of the so-called 'gastropub' – a smattering of savvy central London pubs that replaced their stodgy microwave meals with freshly prepared contemporary cuisine, bringing little-known ingredients to the plates of many locals for the first time. The gastropub may be old hat, but you'll still find them across the city, signposting an area's 'up-and-coming' status and providing meeting places for the young urban professionals slowly colonising London's less-expensive boroughs.

## Food
### English & British Food

England may have given the world beans on toast, mushy peas and chip butties (French fries between two slices of buttered, untoasted white bread), but that's hardly the whole story. When well prepared – be it a Sunday lunch of roast beef and Yorkshire pudding (light batter baked until fluffy and eaten with gravy) or a cornet of lightly battered fish and chips sprinkled with salt and malt vinegar – English food has its moments. And nothing beats a fry-up (or full English breakfast) with bacon, sausages, beans, eggs and mushrooms the morning after a big night out. Some devotees insist it's the perfect hangover cure.

Modern British food, however, has become a cuisine in its own right, by championing traditional (and sometimes underrated) ingredients such as root vegetables, smoked fish, shellfish, game and other meats such as sausages and black pudding (a rich kind of sausage stuffed with oatmeal, spices and blood). Dishes can be anything from game served with Jerusalem artichoke to seared scallops with orange-scented black pudding, or roast pork with chorizo on rosemary mash.

## The Best... Restaurants

1 Providores & Tapa Room (p81)

2 Wapping Food (p191)

3 Gordon Ramsay (p158)

4 Gaucho Grill (p210)

**IN FOCUS FOOD & DRINK**

## Food from Everywhere

One of the joys of eating out in London is the profusion of choice. For historical reasons Indian cuisine is widely available (curry has been labelled a national dish), but Asian cuisines in general are extraordinarily popular: you'll find umpteen Chinese, Thai, Japanese and Korean restaurants, as well as elaborate fusion establishments blending flavours from different parts of Asia. The best Indian – or, more accurately, Bangladeshi and Pakistani – food is found out east around Commercial and Whitechapel Rds.

Cuisine that originated in continental Europe – French, Italian, Spanish, Greek, Scandinavian – is another favourite, with many classy Modern European establishments. Restaurants serving other cuisines tend to congregate where their home community is based; for example Eastern European restaurants are found in Shepherd's Bush, Turkish in Dalston.

You'll find lots of other cuisines – from Eritrean to Burmese – elsewhere in the capital, and part of the joy of London is trying dishes you've never had before.

## Seafood

Many who travel to England comment on the fact that, for an island, Brits seem to make surprisingly little of their seafood, with the exception of the ubiquitous fish and chips. Modern British restaurants have started catching up, however, and many now offer local specialities such as Dover sole, Cornish oysters, Scottish scallops, smoked Norfolk eel, Atlantic herring and mackerel. There are some excellent restaurants specialising in seafood, as well as fish-and-chips counters trading in battered cod, haddock and plaice.

# Dining Out
## World-Class Dining

Food-wise, London has an embarrassment of riches, with 55 Michelin-starred restaurants, including two three-star restaurants, the most famous of which is Gordon Ramsay (p158) in Chelsea. The picks in the city today are therefore nothing short

of sublime if you want to have a memorable meal (and especially if you don't mind splashing out – as with almost everything in London, you'll get what you pay for). For top tables, you'll always need to reserve in advance, and for the very best you'll need to book several months ahead.

But it's not all about Michelin stars and three-month waiting lists for reservations. Some of London's most glorious treats are both easily accessible and not too expensive.

## Vegetarians & Vegans

London has been one of the best places for vegetarians to dine out since the 1970s. Initially due to the many Indian restaurants which, for religious reasons, always cater for people who don't eat meat, a number of dedicated vegetarian restaurants have since cropped up, offering imaginative, filling and truly delicious meals. Most non-vegetarian places generally offer a couple of dishes for those who don't eat meat; vegans, however, will find it harder outside Indian or dedicated restaurants.

## Supper Clubs

If you think restaurants are so last season, you'll love supper clubs: half restaurant and half dinner party. They're run by average Joes with a penchant for cooking and generally cater for 10 to 20 people; meals are set three- or four-course menus (£20 to £40), and the clientele couldn't be more eclectic.

The difficulty is that these underground restaurants are rarely permanent, so recommending a supper club can be tricky. The following will help:

○ Supper club hostess **Ms Marmite** (http://supperclubfangroup.ning.com) has set up an excellent directory of London supper clubs.

○ Food blog **The London Foodie** (www.thelondonfoodie.co.uk) features regular supper club reviews.

Draught beer

● Facebook is the way forward; hosts post details of their forthcoming events on their pages.

● Another place to look is newspapers: all the broadsheets regularly write about new ventures.

## Food Markets

The boom in London's eating scene has extended to its markets. As well as being found at farmers markets, food stalls are now a part of broader markets (eg Spitalfields, Borough or Camden) and appeal to visitors keen to soak up the atmosphere.

# Pubs & Bars

At the heart of London social life, the pub (public house) is one of the capital's great social levellers.

You can order almost anything you like, but beer is the staple. Some specialise, offering drinks from local microbreweries, fruit beers, organic ciders and other rarer beverages; others proffer strong wine lists, especially gastropubs. Some pubs have delightful gardens – crucial in summer.

Unless otherwise stated all pubs and bars reviewed in this book open at 11am and close at 11pm from Monday to Saturday and close at 10.30pm on Sunday. Some pubs and bars stay open longer; most close around 2am or 3am at the latest.

Generally open later than pubs, but closing earlier than clubs, bars tempt those keen to skip bedtime at 11pm but not up for clubbing. They may have DJs and a small dance floor and door charges after 11pm.

## Need to Know

● **Opening Hours** In this book opening hours are listed in individual reviews only when they significantly differ from standard opening hours:

**Chain restaurants** noon-11pm

**Most restaurants** noon-2.30pm and 6-11pm

● **Price Ranges** The symbols below indicate the average cost per main course at the restaurant in question.

**£** less than £10

**££** £10–20

**£££** more than £20

● **Reservations** Make reservations for weekends if you're keen on a particular place or if you're in a group of more than four people. Top-end restaurants often run multiple sittings, with allocated time slots (generally two hours); pick a late slot if you don't want to be rushed.

# Architecture

Houses of Parliament (p58)

MATHEW LODGE/ALAMY

*Some cities have a unifying architectural style, but London is a glorious architectural mongrel, with a heritage forged from 2000 years of conflict, expansion and reinvention.*
*If there was such a thing as a distinctive London building, it would have to be the tall Georgian town house, seen all over the West End. These handsome homes are a monument to a city on the up-and-up, when even residential housing was given that extra flourish.*

## Ancient London Architecture

Considering over a million German bombs rained down on London during WWII, it's miraculous that any ancient architecture survived, but London remains awash with historical treasures. Traces of medieval London are hard to find thanks to the devastating Great Fire of 1666 (p248), but several works by the celebrated Inigo Jones (1573–1652) have endured through the centuries, including Covent Garden Piazza in the West End, Banqueting House and the gorgeous Queen's House in Greenwich, south of the River Thames.

There are a few even older treasures scattered around – including the mighty Tower of London in the City, parts of which date back to the 11th century. Westminster Abbey and Temple Church are 12th- to 13th-century creations, while even more historic ruins include the remains of the Roman Temple of Mithras in the City, which dates back to the 3rd century. Stretches of the Roman wall remain as foundations to a medieval wall outside Tower Hill tube station and in a few sections below Bastion highwalk, next to the Museum of London, all in the City. The best place to see *in situ* what the Saxons left behind is the church of All Hallows-by-the-Tower, northwest of the Tower of London, which boasts an important archway, the walls of a 7th-century Saxon church and fragments from a Roman pavement.

Noteworthy medieval secular structures include the 1365 ragstone Jewel Tower, opposite the Houses of Parliament, and nearby Westminster Hall, both surviving chunks of the medieval Palace of Westminster.

## After the Great Fire

After the fire, renowned architect Sir Christopher Wren was commissioned to oversee reconstruction, but his grand scheme for a new city layout of broad, symmetrical avenues never made it past the planners. His legacy lives on, however, in the stunning 300-year-old St Paul's Cathedral, the maritime precincts at Greenwich and some of the churches dotted around the City.

Wren-protégé Nicholas Hawksmoor joined contemporary James Gibb in creating a new style known as English Baroque, which found its greatest expression in Spitalfields' Christ Church and St Martin-in-the-Fields on Trafalgar Square. However, remnants of Inigo Jones' classicism endured, morphing into neo-Palladianism in the Georgian era.

Like Wren before him, Georgian architect John Nash aimed to impose some symmetry on unruly London, and was slightly more successful in achieving this through grand creations such as Trafalgar Square and the elegantly curving arcade of Regent St. Built in similar style, the surrounding squares of St James's remain some of the finest public spaces in London – little wonder then that Queen Victoria decided to move into the recently vacated Buckingham Palace in 1837.

## Towards Modernity

Pragmatism replaced grand vision with the Victorians, who desired ornate civic buildings that reflected the glory of empire but were open to the masses, not just the privileged few. The highly decorative neo-Gothic style found champions in George Gilbert Scott (1811–78), Alfred Waterhouse (1830–1905), Augustus Pugin (1812–52)

## Open House London

To stick your nose inside buildings you aren't normally able to see, September is the time to visit. One weekend that month (usually the third), the charity **Open House London** ( ☎ 3006 7008; www.londonopenhouse.org) arranges for owners of more than 700 private buildings to throw open their front doors and let in the public free of charge. Major buildings, including 30 St Mary Axe and Lloyd's of London, have participated. The full program becomes available in August. An architectural London Night Hike winds its way through London during the same period and three-hour, architect-led tours are run on Saturdays year-round.

and Charles Barry (1795–1860). The turrets, towers and arches of the style are best exemplified by the flamboyant Natural History Museum (Waterhouse), St Pancras Chambers (George Gilbert Scott) and the Houses of Parliament (Pugin and Barry), the latter replacing the Palace of Westminster which largely burned down in 1834. The Victorians and Edwardians were also ardent builders of functional and cheap terraced houses, many of which became miserable slums but today house London's mortgaged-to-the-hilt middle classes.

A flirtation with art deco and the great suburban residential building boom of the 1930s was followed by a utilitarian modernism after WWII, as the city rushed to build new housing to replace terraces lost in the Blitz. Low-cost developments and unattractive high-rise housing were thrown up on bomb sites and many of these blocks still fragment the London horizon today. Brutalism – a hard-edged and uncompromising architectural school that flourished from the 1950s to the 1970s, favouring concrete and reflecting socialist utopian principles – worked better on paper than in real life but made significant contributions to London's architectural melange. Denys Lasdun's (1914–2001) National Theatre, begun in 1966, is representative of the style.

## Postmodernism & Beyond

The next big wave of development arrived in the derelict wasteland of the former London docks, which were razed of their working-class terraces and warehouses and rebuilt as towering skyscrapers and 'loft' apartments for Thatcher's yuppies. Taking pride of place in the Docklands was Cesar Pelli's 244m-high 1 Canada Square (1991), commonly known as Canary Wharf and easily visible from central London. The City was also the site of architectural innovation, including the centrepiece 1986 Lloyd's of London, Sir Richard Rogers' 'inside-out' masterpiece of ducts, pipes, glass and stainless steel.

30 St Mary Axe, aka the Gherkin (p108), designed by Norman Foster
RICHARD I'ANSON/LONELY PLANET IMAGES ©

# Contemporary Architecture

There followed a lull in new construction until 2000, when a glut of millennial projects unveiled new structures and rejuvenated others: the London Eye, Tate Modern and the Millennium Bridge all spiced up the South Bank, while Norman Foster's iconic 30 St Mary Axe, better known as the 'Gherkin', marked the start of a new wave of skyscraper construction. Even the once-mocked Millennium Dome won a new lease of life as the 02 concert and sports hall.

The 2012 Olympics has seen a massive redevelopment program for East London, by far London's poorest area and one that has desperately needed investment for decades. Even in the shadow of the global economic turndown, London's third games has retained its £9 billion budget and has thrown up some big must-see new structures, including the 80,000-capacity Olympic Stadium, the Aquatics Centre, the Velodrome and Anish Kapoor's ArcelorMittal Orbit, aka the 'Hubble Bubble Pipe'.

The spotlight may be shining over East London, but parts of South London are undergoing energetic and perhaps even visionary renewal, despite the economic gloom. The highlight of the commercial, business and transport regeneration scheme known as the **London Bridge Quarter** (www.londonbridgequarter.com), in Borough, is the Shard, a glass-clad spike-like tower that will poke dramatically into Borough skies from 2012, its sharp form visible from across London. The new Tate Modern Project extension will achieve a dramatically modern and inspirational add-on to the southern facet of the Tate Modern when it opens in 2016.

## The Best...
## Modern
## Architecture

1 30 St Mary Axe (p108).

2 Lloyd's of London (p108)

3 The Shard (p261)

4 Tate Modern (p124)

5 Millennium Bridge (p129)

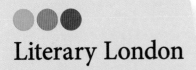

# Literary London

Sherlock Holmes Museum (p76)

LUDOVIC MAISANT/HEMIS/CORBIS

*London has been endlessly captured in prose; a history of London writing has become a history of the city itself. The capital has been the inspiration for the masterful imaginations of Shakespeare, Defoe, Dickens, Thackeray, Wells, Orwell, Conrad, Eliot, Greene and Woolf, to name but a few. Ever changing, yet somehow eerily consistent, London has left its mark on some of the most influential writing in the English language.*

## Old Literary London

London's ever-changing zeitgeist and appearance has been explored by literary minds since quill first met parchment, making it hard to reconcile Chaucer's bawdy London with Dickens' bleak hellhole in *Oliver Twist*, let alone Daniel Defoe's plague-ravaged metropolis in *A Journal of the Plague Year* with Zadie Smith's multi-ethnic romp, *White Teeth*. The first literary reference to London is indeed in Chaucer's *Canterbury Tales*, written between 1387 and 1400, where the pilgrims gather for their trip at the Tabard Inn in Southwark.

### Shakespeare to Defoe

William Shakespeare spent most of his life as an actor and playwright in London around the turn of the 17th century. He trod the boards of Southwark theatres, writing his greatest tragedies, including *Hamlet*, *Othello*, *Macbeth* and *King Lear*, for the original Globe theatre.

Living in and writing about the city during the early 18th century, Daniel Defoe is most famous for *Robinson Crusoe* (1720) and *Moll Flanders* (1722), which he wrote while living in Church St in Stoke Newington. Defoe's *Journal of the Plague Year* documents the horrors of the Great Plague in London during the summer and autumn of 1665, when the author was a child.

## Dickensian & 19th-Century London

Two early 19th-century poets drew inspiration from London: John Keats wrote *Ode to a Nightingale* while living near Hampstead Heath in 1819 and *Ode on a Grecian Urn* after inspecting the Portland Vase in the British Museum. William Wordsworth visited in 1802, discovering inspiration for the poem *On Westminster Bridge*.

Charles Dickens (1812–70) was the definitive London author. When his father and family were imprisoned for not paying their debts, the 12-year-old Charles was forced to fend for himself on the streets. His family was released three months later, but that grim period provided a font of experiences on which he would later draw. His novels most closely associated with London are *Oliver Twist, Little Dorrit,* and *Our Mutual Friend.*

Sir Arthur Conan Doyle (1858–1930) portrayed a very different London, with his pipe-smoking, cocaine-snorting sleuth, Sherlock Holmes, coming to exemplify a cool and unflappable Englishness.

London at the end of the 19th century appears in numerous books including HG Wells' *The War of the Worlds,* W Somerset Maugham's first novel, *Liza of Lambeth* and his *Of Human Bondage,* an engaging portrait of late-Victorian London.

## The Best... Literary Sites

1 Shakespeare's Globe (p138)

2 Dickens House Museum (p61)

3 Sherlock Holmes Museum (p76)

4 Gordon Square (p60)

# 20th-Century Writing

## American Writers & London

Of Americans writing about London at the turn of the century, Henry James, who settled and died here, stands supreme with *Daisy Miller* and *The Europeans. The People of the Abyss,* by American socialist writer Jack London, is a sensitive portrait of poverty and despair in the East End. And we couldn't forget Mark Twain's *The Innocents Abroad,* in which the inimitable humorist skewers both the Old and New Worlds. St Louis–born TS Eliot settled in London in 1915, where he published his poem *The Love Song of J Alfred Prufrock* almost immediately and moved on to his seminal epic *The Waste Land*.

## Interwar Developments

Between the wars, PG Wodehouse (1881–1975) depicted London high life with his hilarious lampooning of the English upper classes in the Jeeves stories. George Orwell's experience of living as a beggar in London's East End coloured his book *Down and Out in Paris and London* (1933), while the sternly modernist Senate House on Malet St, Bloomsbury, was the inspiration for the Ministry of Truth in his classic dystopian 1949 novel *Nineteen Eighty-Four.*

## The Modern Age

*The End of the Affair,* Graham Greene's novel chronicling a passionate and doomed romance, takes place in and around Clapham Common just after WWII.

Colin MacInnes described the bohemian, multicultural world of 1950s Notting Hill in *City of Spades* and *Absolute Beginners,* while Doris Lessing captured the political mood of 1960s London in *The Four-Gated City* and also provided some of the funniest and most vicious portrayals of 1990s London in *London Observed.* Nick Hornby found himself the voice of a generation, nostalgic about his days as a young football fan in *Fever Pitch* and vinyl-obsessive in *High Fidelity.*

Hanif Kureishi explored London from the perspective of ethnic minorities, specifically young Pakistanis, in *The Black Album* and *The Buddha of Suburbia,* while Timothy Mo's *Sour Sweet* is a poignant and funny account of a Chinese family in the 1960s trying to adjust to English life.

The late 1970s and 1980s were strong for British literature, introducing a dazzling new generation of writers, including Martin Amis *(Money, London Fields)*, Julian Barnes *(Metroland, Talking it Over)*, Ian McEwan *(Atonement, Enduring Love)*, Salman Rushdie *(Midnight's Children, The Satanic Verses)*, AS Byatt *(Possession, Angels & Insects)* and Alan Hollinghurst *(The Swimming Pool Library, The Line of Beauty).*

## Millennium London & the Current Scene

Helen Fielding's *Bridget Jones's Diary* effectively founded the 'chick lit' genre and Will Self has long been the toast of London. His *Grey Area* is a superb collection of short stories, while *The Book of Dave* is both hilarious and surreal.

Peter Ackroyd's *London: The Biography* is his inexhaustible paean to the capital, while *Thames: Sacred River* stands as his fine monument to the muck, magic and mystery of the river through history, displaying an ambitious sense of exploration further revealed in his *London Under,* in which the subterranean city comes to life.

Gordon Square, Bloomsbury (p60)
PAUL CARSTAIRS/ALAMY ©

# Literary Readings, Talks & Events

A host of literary events are regularly held across London, ranging from book and poetry readings to talks, open-mic performances, writing workshops and other occasions.

Covent Garden's **Poetry Café** (☎7420 9880; www.poetrysociety.org.uk; 22 Betterton St WC2; ⊖Covent Garden) is a favourite for lovers of verse, with almost daily readings and performances by established poets, open-mic evenings and writing workshops.

The **Institute of Contemporary Arts** (ICA; ☎information 7930 6393, bookings 7930 3647; www.ica.org.uk; Nash House, the Mall SW1; ⊖Charing Cross or Piccadilly Circus) has excellent talks every month, with well-known writers from all spectrums.

Bookshops, particularly Waterstone's and Foyle's, often stage readings. Some major authors also now appear at the Southbank Centre. Many are organised on an ad-hoc basis, so keep an eye on the listings in *Time Out*.

Held in the first two weeks of July, the **London Literary Festival** (www.londonlitfest.com) at the Southbank Centre hosts talks and events from writers and literati.

Iain Sinclair's acclaimed and ambitious *London Orbital,* a journey on foot around the M25, is required London reading; *Hackney, That Rose Red Empire,* is an exploration of London's most notorious borough, one that underwent enormous changes in the approach to 2012, a subject Sinclair revisited in *Ghost Milk*.

Other new London talent in recent years ranges from Monica Ali, who brought the East End to life in *Brick Lane,* to Jake Arnott's intelligent Soho-based gangster yarn *The Long Firm* and Gautam Malkani's much-hyped *Londonstani.*

# The Arts

Compañía Aída Goméz perform *Carmen*, Sadler's Wells (p177)

JANE HOBSON/ALAMY ©

*The streets of London are virtually paved with creativity: the cultural life here is the richest and most varied in the English-speaking world. The London theatre scene is also the world's most diverse, while dance in London executes some gorgeous moves. Music and London are almost synonymous, and you'll find something to applaud, whatever your genre. Film is celebrated in a host of festivals and cracking cinemas.*

## Art

London today is the art capital of Europe, with a vibrant gallery scene and some of the world's leading modern art collections. Many of the world's greatest artists have spent time here, including Monet and Van Gogh. Although Britain's artists have historically been eclipsed by their European confrères, some distinctly innovative artists have emerged from London.

An impressive list of artists have been associated with the city, including the German Hans Holbein the Younger (1497–1543), landscapist Thomas Gainsborough (1727–88), William Hogarth (1697–1764), poet, engraver and watercolourist William Blake (1757–1827) and John Constable (1776–1837). JMW Turner (1775–1851) embodied the pinnacle of 19th-century British art, while the brief but splendid flowering of the pre-Raphaelite Brotherhood (1848–54) took its inspiration from the Romantic poets.

In the early 20th century, Cubism and Futurism helped generate the short-lived Vorticists, a modernist London group of artists and poets, centred on the dapper Wyndham Lewis (1882–1957), which sought to capture dynamism in artistic form.

Sculptors Henry Moore and Barbara Hepworth both typified the modernist movement in British sculpture, and Irish-born painter Francis Bacon (1909–92) spooked the art world with his repulsive yet mesmerising visions. Other big names include Lucian Freud (1922–2011), David Hockney (b 1937) and suited duo Gilbert and George.

In more recent years, Brit Art was a dominant and highly marketable aesthetic, launching names such as Damien Hirst and Tracey Emin. The areas of Shoreditch, Hoxton and Whitechapel – where many artists lived, worked and hung out – became the epicentre of the movement, and a rash of galleries moved in.

The biggest date on the art calendar is the controversial Turner Prize at the Tate Britain. Any British artist under the age of 50 is eligible, although there is a strong preference for conceptual art (a sound installation from Susan Philipsz won in 2010, attracting considerable cynicism from the general public) rather than painting.

London continues to generate talent across a range of artistic media, keeping critics on their toes. Among the biggest-name artists working in contemporary London are Banksy (the anonymous street artist whose work has become a worldwide phenomenon), Antony Gormley (best known for the 22m-high sculpture, *Angel of the North*), Anish Kapoor (an Indian sculptor working in London since the 1970s) and Marc Quinn (whose work includes *Self,* a sculpture of his head made from the artist's own frozen blood, at the National Portrait Gallery).

# The Best... London Artworks

1 *Sunflowers* by Vincent Van Gogh (National Gallery)

2 *Fighting Temeraire* by JMW Turner (National Gallery)

3 *Whaam!* by Roy Lichtenstein (Tate Modern)

4 *Ophelia* by Sir John Everett Millais (Tate Britain)

5 *Three Studies for Figures at the Base of a Crucifixion* by Francis Bacon (Tate Britain)

# Theatre

London has more theatrical history than almost anywhere else on the globe, and it's still being made nightly on the stages of the West End, the South Bank and the epic London fringe. No visit to the city is complete without taking in a show, and just an evening walk through 'theatreland' in the West End is an electrifying experience.

Nowhere else, with the possible exception of New York, offers such a diversity of high-quality drama, first-rate musical theatre and such a sizzling fringe. Whether it's Hollywood A-listers gracing tiny stages and earning Equity minimum for their efforts or lavish West End musicals, London remains an undisputed theatrical world leader and innovator.

There's something for all dramatic tastes here, from contemporary political satire to creative reworking of old classics and all shades in between. In recent years the mainstream West End has re-established its credentials, with extraordinary hits, while the smarter end of the fringe continues to shine with risky and controversially newsworthy productions. The hottest tickets are still for the National Theatre, which has gone from strength to strength under Nicholas Hytner, with productions enjoying both huge box-office success and critical acclaim. If innovation and change are too much for you, drop by St Martin's Theatre, where the same production of *The Mousetrap* has been running since 1952!

Shakespeare's Globe on the South Bank is a magnificent recreation of the Elizabethan theatre experience. Artistic director Dominic Dromgoole, having taken over the reins at the start of 2006, has ensured that Shakespeare's plays remain at the core of the theatre's program, but at the same time has produced a wider range of European and British classics, as well as new material.

# The Best... Theatres

## Dance

Contemporary, classical or crossover, London will have the right dance moves for you. As one of the world's great dance capitals, London's artistic habitat has long created and attracted talented choreographers with both the inspiration and aspiration to fashion innovative dance.

The Place in Euston was the original birthplace of modern British dance, and the training school Laban has emerged strongly for cutting-edge performances. Revamped Sadler's Wells – the birthplace of English classical ballet in the 19th century – continues to stage an exciting program of various styles from leading national ballets and international troupes.

Covent Garden's redeveloped Royal Opera House is the stunning home of London's leading classical-dance troupe, the world-famous Royal Ballet. The company largely sticks to the traditional, but more-contemporary influences occasionally seep into productions. The Royal Ballet has also made itself more accessible by dropping some ticket prices to £10 (as at the National Theatre).

For more cutting-edge work, the innovative Rambert Dance Company (www.rambert.org.uk) is the UK's foremost contemporary dance troupe. The dance company is possibly the most creative force in UK dance and although currently based in Chiswick, will move to purpose-built premises in Doon St (behind the National Theatre in the far more creative milieu of the South Bank) in 2013.

Also a leading UK dance company and one of the world's best, the English National Ballet (www.ballet.org.uk) is a touring company that can often be seen at various venues in London, but most principally at the London Coliseum.

Another important venue for experimental dance is the Barbican; for the latest of what's on, check www.londondance.com. Running for six weeks from early October, Dance Umbrella is one of the world's leading dance festivals of its kind.

## Music

Drawing upon a deep and sometimes gritty reservoir of talent, the modern music scene is one of London's greatest sources of artistic energy and a magnet for bands and hopefuls from all musical hemispheres. Periodically a world-leader in musical fashion and innovative soundscapes, London blends its home-grown talent with a continuous influx of styles and cultures, keeping currents flowing and inspiration percolating upwards. Classical music can be found here at the very highest level.

## Classical

The modern-day London classical calendar peaks with the annual Proms, which has expanded its repertoire in recent years to appeal to a broader audience; the festival mainly focuses on the grand Royal Albert Hall in Kensington. Beyond this, classical music and opera are celebrated and performed within a host of world-class venues across town.

## Opera

With one of the world's leading opera companies at the Royal Opera House in Covent Garden, and impressive direction from Edward Gardner at the English National Opera (the Coliseum), as well as other operatic venues and events, London has more than enough for opera goers. It's not just the classics that are produced, as innovative productions bring operatic expression to a host of modern-day subjects. Holland Park in Kensington is the summer venue for operatic productions. Opera is expensive to produce and, consequently, tickets can be pricey.

## Rock

From the Kinks, the Rolling Stones, the Who, T Rex and David Bowie to Coldplay, Goldfrapp, Lily Allen, Adele, Mumford and Sons, Amy Winehouse and Tinie Tempah, London is an unimpeachable roll-call of musical talent. But it didn't just start in the 20th century: London has been generating cutting-edge music for centuries – George Frideric Handel wrote some of his most famous oratorios from his home in Mayfair between 1723 and 1759.

London is virtually synonymous with indie rock, and thumping venues in the West End, Shoreditch and Camden dangle the tempting baubles of stardom in front of hopeful makeshift bands taking to the stage.

## Jazz

If jazz floats your boat, spend time with fellow enthusiasts at Ronnie Scott's, the 606 Club and other great jazz venues in the West End and central London. Check the pulse of the contemporary London music scene in weekly listings mag *Time Out* and select any one of dozens of gigs in a range of genres playing each night across the capital.

## Cinematic Festivals

A host of London festivals celebrating cinema across the film spectrum entertains film enthusiasts from the popcorn crowd to art-house buffs.

**London Film Festival** (www.bfi.org.uk/lff) Held in October, this is the highlight of London's many festivals celebrating cinema.

**Raindance Festival** (www.raindance.co.uk) Europe's leading independent filmmaking festival. It's a terrific celebration of independent cinema from across the globe, screening just before the London Film Festival.

**Portobello Film Festival** (www.portobellofilmfestival.com) Held in September, it features largely independent works by London filmmakers and international directors. It is free to attend.

**London Lesbian & Gay Film Festival** (www.bfi.org.uk/llgff) One of the best of its kind with hundreds of independent films from around the world shown over a fun, party-intensive fortnight at the BFI Southbank.

## Film

Londoners have a passion for all things celluloid and digital, from the vast BFI IMAX in Waterloo, to the huge screen at the Empire Leicester Square, to small 40-seater cinemas, to a host of art-house and independent cinemas, and local pub film clubs that cram in beer-quaffing film buffs. For back-catalogue classics, turn to the BFI at South Bank, but keep an eye out for film festivals at independent cinemas, which bring in reels of foreign movies. For further eclectic tastes, shorts, foreign cinema as well as mainstream movies, London's independent cinemas allow you to put your feet up, sip a glass of wine and feel right at home. You can catch monthly seasons and premieres, as well as actors and directors chatting about their work and answering questions. Cinemas such as the Prince Charles (www.princecharlescinema.com) in Leicester Pl have cheap tickets, run minifestivals and screen popular sing-along classics. Many major premieres are held in Leicester Square, the priciest part of London for cinema tickets. Outdoor cinema is rolled out in London in the warmer months at Somerset House Summer Screen (www.somersethouse.org.uk/film), where films can be enjoyed in a sublime setting.

Scottish Symphony Orchestra performance at BBC Proms, Royal Albert Hall (p159)
CHRISTER FREDRIKSSON/LONELY PLANET IMAGES ©

# Shopping

Harrods (p160)

*London's sights are the main draws but visitors are also in town to shop. You'll be bumping into big chain stores everywhere, but London has some legendary department stores and inspiring independent shops. Even world-famous designers like Stella McCartney and Matthew Williamson have one-off boutiques where ordinary mortals can browse the latest in high fashion away from the snobbery of the big couture houses.*

## Shopping in London

From charity-shop finds to designer 'it bags', there are thousands of ways to get through your hard-earned cash in London. Fashion may be London's biggest retail commodity and the city has been setting trends ever since Mary Quant dreamt up miniskirts. Big designers' ideas are translated into high-street fashion faster than you can say Yves Saint Laurent. Mayfair may cater to the high end of the market, but low priced high street outlets such as Primark and Topshop offer catwalk style on a shoestring.

For street fashion and London's famous cutting edge, head to Shoreditch in East London, where magazine-ready looks appear even before you exit Old St tube station. Wander the boutiques of Spitalfields, Brick Lane, Rivington St and the surrounding area to discover the looks that will soon be heading worldwide.

## High Fashion

High fashion is squarely located between Oxford Circus and Knightsbridge. The two big designer streets are Bond St in Mayfair and Sloane St in Knightsbridge, where you'll find nothing but big international names and prices to match.

An alternative place to shop for top brands is in one of London's world-famous department stores. Harrods (p160), Harvey Nichols (p161), Selfridges (p91) and Liberty (p90) are the top four to prioritise. If you're planning a splurge, aim for the sales in June and July or January.

## Markets

One of the biggest draws for visitors is the capital's famed markets. A treasure trove of small designers, unique jewellery pieces, original framed photographs and posters, colourful vintage pieces and bric-a-brac, they are the antidote to impersonal, carbon-copy high-street shopping.

The most popular markets are Camden, Spitalfields and Portobello Rd, in full swing at the weekend. Although they're all more or less outdoors (Spitalfields is now covered, as are the Stables in Camden), they are always busy, rain or shine.

London also has some excellent food markets – Borough Market (p129), in particular – and dozens of smaller local farmers markets and delis stocked with fine cheeses, charcuterie and artisanal ingredients.

## Other Treats

The West End offers plenty of nonsartorial choice, from the great furniture and electronics shopping of Tottenham Court Rd to the small independent bookshops of Charing Cross Rd. For exotic flavours head to Ridley Rd in Hackney or Whitechapel High St in the East End, while for antiques and art Mayfair and St James's are your best bet.

Don't miss splendid Fortnum & Mason (p89), on Piccadilly for all your Anglophile paraphernalia, and, if you're with kids, Hamleys (p90), London's famous toy store.

Charity shops in areas such as Chelsea, Notting Hill and Kensington often have cheap designer wear (usually, the richer the area, the better the secondhand shops).

## The Best...
## Shopping
## Strips

1 Oxford St

2 Brick Lane (p172)

3 Knightsbridge

4 Spitalfields Market (p177)

5 Regent St

# Survival Guide

The Strand, the West End (p47)
LUCIANO MORTULA/DREAMSTIME ©

# Sleeping

Finding the right accommodation is integral to your London experience, and there's no shortage of choice. But just because London is a city that never sleeps doesn't mean it doesn't go to bed: rooms in popular hotels often need to be booked well in advance. There are some fantastic hotels about, whatever the price tag, but plan ahead.

## Accommodation Types

### Hotels

London has some stunning hotels and many are experiences in their own right. The lead-up to 2012 has seen some big-profile openings, while others remain under development. Standards across the top end and much of the boutique bracket are high, but so are prices. A host of more budget-friendly boutique hotels has explored a profitable niche, while midrange chain hotels generally offer good locations and dependable comfort, even if a rung or two down in overall quality and charm. Demand can often outstrip supply, especially at the bottom end of the market, so book ahead,

particularly during holiday periods and in summer.

### B&Bs

Bed and breakfasts dwell a tier below hotels, but often have boutique-style charm, are housed in lovely old buildings and offer a personal level of service. B&B clusters can be found in South Kensington, Victoria and Bloomsbury.

### Hostels

After B&Bs the cheapest forms of accommodation are hostels, both the official Youth Hostel Association (YHA) ones and the (usually) hipper, more party-orientated independent ones. Hostels vary in quality so select carefully; most offer twins as well as dorms.

### Apartments

If you're in London for a week or more, a short-term or serviced apartment such as **196 Bishopsgate** (✆ 621 8788; www.196bishopsgate. com; studio £232-245, 1-bed apt £276-288, cheaper after 6 nights; ❋ ☎ ; ⊖ Liverpool St) or **Number 5 Maddox Street** (✆ 7647 0200; www.5maddoxstreet.com; 5 Maddox St W1; ste £270-650; ❋ ☎ ; ⊖ Oxford Circus) may make sense; rates at the bottom end are comparable to a B&B.

## Costs

Deluxe hotel rooms will cost from around £350 per double but there's plenty of variety at the top end, so you should be able to find a room from about £180 offering superior comfort without the prestige. Some boutique hotels also occupy this bracket. There's a noticeable dip in quality below £180 for a double, but we have listed the best in this range. Under £100 and you're at the more serviceable, budget end of the market. Look out, though, for weekend deals that can put a better class of hotel within reach. Rates often slide in winter. Book through the hotels' websites for the best online deals or promotional rates. Unless otherwise indicated, accommodation prices quoted in this book include breakfast. International Youth Hostel Federation (IYHF) members net discounts on YHA accommodation. Be aware that room prices will skyrocket to unspecified heights during the 2012 Olympic Games.

## Useful Websites

**Lonely Planet** (www.hotels. lonelyplanet.com) Bookings.

**YHA central reservations system** ( ☎ 0800 019 1700; www.yha.org.uk) Hostel room bookings.

**Visit London** (www. visitlondon.com) London tourist organisation's website, offering special deals and list of gay-friendly accommodation.

**LondonTown** ( ☎ 7437 4370; www.londontown.com)

# Where to Stay

| NEIGHBOURHOOD | FOR | AGAINST |
| --- | --- | --- |
| THE WEST END | Close to main sights; ubercentral; great transport links; wide accommodation range in all budgets and great restaurants. | Busy, tourist area and expensive. |
| THE CITY | St Paul's and the Tower of London; good transport links; handy central location; quality hotels; some cheaper weekend rates. | Very quiet at weekends, a business district so prices are high during week. |
| SOUTH BANK | Near Tate Modern, London Eye and Southbank Centre; cheaper than West End; excellent pubs and views. | Many chain hotels, and choice and transport limited. |
| KENSINGTON & HYDE PARK | Excellent for South Kensington museums and shopping; great accommodation range; stylish area with good transport. | Quite expensive, drinking and nightlife options are limited. |
| CLERKENWELL, HOXTON & SPITALFIELDS | Trendy area with great bars and nightlife; excellent for boutique hotels. | Few top sights and transport options are limited. |
| THE EAST END & DOCKLANDS | Well positioned for Olympic Park, markets, great restaurants and traditional pubs; has a multicultural feel. | Rather limited sleeping options and some areas are less safe at night. |
| HAMPSTEAD & NORTH LONDON | Leafy feel; vibrant and energetic nightlife; pockets of village charm; excellent boutique hotels and hostels; great gastropubs; quiet during week. | Non-central and away from main sights. |
| GREENWICH | Ace boutique options; leafy escapes; near top Greenwich sights. | Sights spread out beyond Greenwich and transport is limited. |

# Best Places to Stay

| NAME | NEIGHBOURHOOD | REVIEW |
| --- | --- | --- |
| HAYMARKET £££ | The West End | Opulently beautiful with hand-painted Gournay wallpaper, signature fuchsia and green designs, sensational 18m pool, and exquisite library lounge. |
| HAZLITT'S £££ | The West End | Three Georgian houses with bedrooms furnished with antiques, mahogany four-poster beds, sumptuous fabrics and modern creature comforts. |
| DEAN STREET TOWNHOUSE ££ | The West End | Soho gem with gorgeous boudoir atmosphere, Georgian furniture, retro black-and-white tiled bathroom floors and beautiful lighting. |
| NO 10 MANCHESTER STREET £££ | The West End | Wonderful Edwardian townhouse with print wallpaper, high-tech must haves and impeccable service. |
| FIELDING HOTEL ££ | The West End | Pretty, tucked away 24-room Covent Garden hotel refurbished to a very high standard with pleasant air-conditioned rooms. No breakfast. |
| ARRAN HOUSE HOTEL ££ | The West End | Welcoming, good-value 28-room Bloomsbury hotel with simple dorm-style rooms, bright, well-furnished doubles, a cosy lounge and gorgeous gardens. |
| ONE ALDWYCH £££ | The West End | Hotel in grand Edwardian building with spacious and stylish rooms and great views from circular suites. |
| CLARIDGE'S £££ | The West End | Claridge's is one of the greatest of London's five-star hotels, well known for its art deco features. |
| YHA OXFORD ST £ | The West End | Centrally located YHA hostel, intimate and attractive with excellent facilities and bright, funky lounge. |
| THREADNEEDLES £££ | The City | Wonderfully anonymous with grand circular lobby, and 69 pleasantly attired rooms with dark, sleek furnishings. |
| ANDAZ LIVERPOOL STREET £££ | The City | Hyatt-branded London flagship for its youth-oriented Andaz chain. Black-clad staff check you in on laptops; rooms are cool and spacious. |
| BERMONDSEY SQUARE HOTEL ££ | South Bank | Hip, purpose-built, 80-room boutique hotel with smallish rooms but very stylish suites, each unique and named after iconic '60s songs. |
| PARK PLAZA WESTMINSTER BRIDGE £££ | South Bank | Snazzy new hotel with contemporary, stylish rooms. Pricier studio and penthouse rooms have great views of Westminster Bridge and Big Ben. |
| B+B BELGRAVIA ££ | Kensington & Hyde Park | Spiffing six-floor Georgian B&B, remodelled with contemporary flair. Rooms aren't huge but there are studio rooms nearby. Pleasant courtyard garden. |
| ASTER HOUSE £££ | Kensington & Hyde Park | Award-winning, lovely house with welcoming staff, comfortable rooms, sparkling bathrooms, delightful orangery and charming garden. |

| PRACTICALITIES | BEST FOR |
| --- | --- |
| 7470 4000; www.haymarkethotel.com; 1 Suffolk Pl SW1; r £260-340, ste from £410; ⊖Piccadilly Circus; ❄ 🛜 ⛵ | A special treat. |
| 7434 1771; www.hazlittshotel.com; 6 Frith St W1; s £185, d £230-360, ste £550-850; ⊖Tottenham Court Rd; ❄ 🛜 | Old-school charm and modern comfort. |
| 7434 1775; www.deanstreettownhouse.com; 69-71 Dean St W1; r £160-310; ⊖Tottenham Court Rd; ❄ 🛜 | Style and romance. |
| 7317 5900; www.tenmanchesterstreethotel.com; 10 Manchester St W1; d £225; ❄ 🛜; ⊖Baker St | Top-notch elegance. |
| 7836 8305; www.the-fielding-hotel.co.uk; 4 Broad Ct, Bow St WC2; s/d from £90/140; ❄ 🛜; ⊖Covent Garden | Great value, hyper central. |
| 7636 2186; www.arranhotel-london.com; 77-79 Gower St WC1; dm £30-35, s/d £80/120, with shared bathroom £70/97; @ 🛜; ⊖Goodge St | Cosy home away from home. |
| 7300 1000; www.onealdwych.co.uk; 1 Aldwych WC2; d £275-370, ste from £585; ❄ 🛜 ⛵; ⊖Covent Garden or Charing Cross or Temple | Luxury, class and grandeur. |
| 7629 8860; www.claridges.co.uk; 55 Brook St W1; r/ste from £299/555; ❄ @ 🛜; ⊖Bond St | Art deco classic. |
| 0845 371 9133; www.yha.org.uk; 3rd fl, 14 Noel St W1; dm £16-28, d £51-74; @ 🛜; ⊖Oxford Circus or Tottenham Court Rd | Central, budget, very dependable. |
| 7657 8080; www.theetoncollection.com; 5 Threadneedle St EC2; r/ste from £390/606, weekend rate r/ste from £222/390, breakfast £15; ❄ 🛜; ⊖Bank | Smart boutique elegance. |
| 7961 1234; www.andaz.com; 40 Liverpool St EC2; r/ste from £234/396, breakfast £20; ❄ 🛜; ⊖Liverpool St | Business class, boutique sophistication. |
| 7378 2450; www.bermondseysquarehotel.co.uk; Bermondsey Sq, Tower Bridge Rd SE1; r £120-250, ste £300-500; ❄ @ 🛜; ⊖London Bridge | Swinging '60s escapism. |
| 0844 415 6780; 200 Westminster Bridge Rd, London SE1; d £238; ❄ 🛜 ⛵ | Snappy, fresh, great location. |
| 7259 8570; www.bb-belgravia.com; 64-66 Ebury St SW1; s/d/tw/tr/q £99/135/145/165/175; @ 🛜; ⊖Victoria | For a snappy and stylish stay. |
| 7581 5888; www.asterhouse.com; 3 Sumner Pl SW7; s £144, d & tw £216-300, ste £300; ❄ @; ⊖South Kensington | Traditional English charm. |

| NUMBER SIXTEEN ££ | Kensington & Hyde Park | Stunning, with 42 individually designed rooms, cosy drawing room and idyllic garden. |
|---|---|---|
| BLAKES £££ | Kensington & Hyde Park | Five Victorian houses cobbled into one hotel, incomparably designed. Each room is distinctive: four-poster beds, rich fabrics and antiques. |
| GORE £££ | Kensington & Hyde Park | Charismatically kooky palace of polished mahogany, oriental carpets, antique-style bathrooms, potted aspidistras, and portraits and prints. |
| MEININGER £ | Kensington & Hyde Park | Efficient German-run 'city hostel and hotel' opposite the Natural History Museum, with clean rooms, dorms and private rooms. Roof terrace. |
| PORTOBELLO HOTEL £££ | Kensington & Hyde Park | Beautifully appointed boutique hotel has been a favourite with rock-and-rollers and movie stars. |
| YHA EARL'S COURT £ | Kensington & Hyde Park | On a quiet street in Earl's Court, this is a cheerful, recently upgraded place with clean, airy dormitories. |
| ROOKERY £££ | Clerkenwell, Hoxton & Spitalfields | Absolute charmer within a row of 18th-century Georgian houses; antique furniture, original wood panelling and much whimsy. |
| ZETTER HOTEL £££ | Clerkenwell, Hoxton & Spitalfields | A temple of cool with an overlay of kitsch, small but perfectly formed rooms and lovely rooftop studios with commanding views. |
| HOXTON HOTEL ££ | Clerkenwell, Hoxton & Spitalfields | Sleek Shoreditch hotel aiming for continually full occupancy with loads of freebies and excellent deals. Small but stylish rooms. |
| 40 WINKS ££ | The East End | Short on space, not on style; a two-room boutique guesthouse in an old townhouse oozing charm. |
| TOWN HALL HOTEL & APART-MENTS £££ | The East End | An erstwhile Edwardian town hall, updated with art deco features and cutting-edge art. No rooms are identical; apartments are well equipped. |
| OLD SHIP ££ | The East End | Bright and good value 10-room spot above a Hackney pub with surprisingly cheerful rooms and public areas. |
| YORK & ALBANY £££ | Hampstead & North London | Luxurious yet cosy, this place oozes Georgian charm with feature fireplaces, antique furniture plus all mod-cons. Five minutes' walk from Camden. |
| CLINK78 £ | Hampstead & North London | Fab hostel in a 19th-century courthouse with heritage features, pod beds and superb kitchen. |
| CLINK261 £ | Hampstead & North London | Refurbished in 2010; a top-notch hostel with bright, funky dorms, a brilliant kitchen and TV lounge. |
| ROUGH LUXE £££ | Hampstead & North London | Half rough, half luxury, all unique: scraps of old newspaper adorn the walls along with works of art. |
| ST PANCRAS RENAISSANCE HOTEL £££ | Hampstead & North London | Gothic, red-brick stunner with a fully-restored interior from grand staircase to Victorian-tiled pool (most rooms not in the original building, though). |

📞 7589 5232; www.numbersixteenhotel.co.uk; 16 Sumner Pl SW7; s £168, d £222-360, breakfast £16-17.50; ❄@🛜; ⊖South Kensington

For a gorgeous boutique getaway.

---

📞 7370 6701; www.blakeshotels.com; 33 Roland Gardens SW7; s £195, d £295-395, ste from £695, breakfast £12.50-19.50; 🅿❄@🛜; ⊖Gloucester Rd

Classic style.

---

📞 7584 6601; www.gorehotel.com; 190 Queen's Gate SW7; s £140-180, d £180-280, ste from £440, breakfast £12.95-16.95; ❄@🛜; ⊖Gloucester Rd or High St Kensington

Gorgeously indulgent.

---

📞 7590 6910; www.meininger-hostels.com; 65-67 Queen's Gate SW7; dm £15-27, s/tw/tr from £75/70/96; ❄@🛜; ⊖Gloucester Rd or South Kensington

Kensington location, non-central prices.

---

📞 7727 2777; www.portobello-hotel.co.uk; 22 Stanley Gardens W11; s/d from £174/234, feature r from £288; ❄@🛜; ⊖Notting Hill Gate

Exclusive boutique charm.

---

📞 7373 7083; www.yha.org.uk; 38 Bolton Gardens SW5; dm from £19.65, tw/d from £48.50/50.50; @🛜; ⊖Earl's Court

Great location, budget bracket.

---

📞 7336 0931; www.rookeryhotel.com; 12 Peter's Lane, Cowcross St EC1; s £222, d £276-300, ste £420-612, breakfast £11.95; ❄🛜; ⊖Farringdon

Mellow elegance.

---

📞 7324 4444; www.thezetter.com; 86-88 Clerkenwell Rd EC1; r £222-294, studio £294-438, breakfast £13.50-17.50; ❄🛜; ⊖Farringdon

Neat, nifty, exemplary.

---

📞 7550 1000; www.hoxtonhotels.com; 81 Great Eastern St EC2; r incl breakfast £1-199; ❄🛜; ⊖Old St

Fine value and stylish stay.

---

📞 7790 0259; www.40winks.org; 109 Mile End Rd E1; s/d £95/140; 🛜; ⊖Stepney Green

Exquisite, delicious fun.

---

📞 7871 0460; www.townhallhotel.com; Patriot Square E2; d £348-384, apt £402-546, breakfast £15; ❄🛜🏊; ⊖Bethnal Green

Period style and vintage charms.

---

📞 8986 1641; www.urbaninns.co.uk; 2 Sylvester Path E8; s/d from £79.95/99.95; 🛜; ®Hackney Central, ⛍38 or 55

Boutique comfort, downstairs pub.

---

📞 7387 5700; www.gordonramsay.com/yorkandalbany; 127-129 Parkway NW1; r from £186; ❄🛜; ⊖Camden Town

Gorgeously charming with modern touches.

---

📞 7183 9400; www.clinkhostels.com; 78 King's Cross Rd WC1; dm £17-27, d £75; @🛜; ⊖King's Cross/St Pancras

History, heritage and budget value.

---

📞 7833 9400; www.clinkhostels.com; 261-265 Gray's Inn Rd WC1; dm £18-22, d with shared bathroom £55; @🛜; ⊖King's Cross/St Pancras

Great value, perky and popular.

---

📞 7837 5338; www.roughluxe.co.uk; 1 Birkenhead St WC1; r from £200, with shared bathroom £177; 🛜; ⊖King's Cross/St Pancras

Trendily different.

---

📞 7841 3540; www.stpancrasrenaissance.co.uk; Euston Rd NW1; r from £228; ❄🛜🏊; ⊖King's Cross/St Pancras

Sumptuous magnificence.

# Transport

## Getting to London

Most passengers arrive in London by air. The city has five airports: Heathrow, which is the largest, to the west; Gatwick to the south; Stansted to the northeast; Luton to the northwest; and London City in the Docklands.

Most trans-Atlantic flights land at Heathrow (average flight time is about seven to eight hours from the east coast, and 10 to 11 hours from the west coast; slightly more on the way back).

Visitors from Europe are more likely to arrive in Gatwick, Stansted or Luton (the latter two are used exclusively by low-cost airlines such as easyJet and Ryanair).

Check any of the websites below for good deals on airline tickets:

o www.cheapflights.co.uk

o www.ebookers.com

o www.lastminute.com

o www.opodo.co.uk

o www.skyscanner.net

o www.expedia.com

Or try the following for rail bookings:

o www.raileurope.co.uk

o www.eurostar.com

Flights, tours and rail tickets can be booked online at lonelyplanet.com/bookings.

## Heathrow Airport

Some 15 miles west of central London, **Heathrow** (LHR; www.heathrowairport.com), with five terminals (although Terminal 2 is closed for refurbishment until 2014), is the world's busiest international airport.

### Train

**Underground** (www.tfl. gov.uk) Three Piccadilly line stations serve the airport: one for Terminals 1, 2 and 3, another for Terminal 4, and a third for Terminal 5. The Underground, commonly referred to as 'the tube' (one way £5, from central London one hour, every three to nine minutes) is the cheapest way of getting to Heathrow.

**Heathrow Express** (www. heathrowexpress.com) This ultramodern train (one way/ return £16.50/32, 15 minutes, every 15 minutes) whisks passengers from Heathrow Central station (serving Terminals 1, 2 and 3) and Terminal 5 to Paddington. Terminal 4 passengers should take the free shuttle train available to Heathrow Central and board the Heathrow Express there.

**Heathrow Connect** (www. heathrowconnect.com) Travelling to Paddington station, this modern passenger train service (one way £8.50, 25 minutes, every 30 minutes) has five stops en route including Southall and Ealing Broadway.

### Taxi

A metered black cab trip to/ from central London will cost between £45 and £65 (£55 from Oxford St) and takes 45 minutes to an hour, depending on your departure point.

### Bus

**National Express** (www. nationalexpress.com) coaches (one way/return from £5/9, tickets valid three months, 45 minutes to 90 minutes, every 30 minutes to one hour) link the Heathrow Central Bus Station with **Victoria coach station** (164 Buckingham Palace Rd SW1; ⊖ Victoria) about 45 times per day.

At night the N9 bus (£1.30, 1¼ hours, every 20 minutes) connects Heathrow with central London.

## Gatwick Airport

Located some 30 miles south of central London, **Gatwick** (LGW; www.gatwickairport.com) is smaller than Heathrow. The North and South Terminals are linked by a 24-hour shuttle train, with the journey time about three minutes.

### Train

Regular **trains** (www.national-rail.co.uk) run to/from London Bridge (30 minutes, every 15 to 30 minutes), King's Cross (45 minutes, every 15 to 30 minutes) and London Victoria (30 minutes, every 10 to 15 minutes). Fares vary depending on the time of travel and the train company, but allow £7 to £10 for a single.

**Gatwick Express** (www.gatwickexpress.com) train services (one way/return £17.90/30.80, 30 minutes, every 15 minutes) link the station near the South Terminal with Victoria station in central London.

## Bus

**National Express** (www.nationalexpress.com) coaches (one way/return £7.50/15, tickets valid three months, 65 minutes to 90 minutes) run from Gatwick to Victoria coach station about 18 times per day.

**easyBus** (www.easybus.co.uk) runs 19-seater minibuses (one way £10, from £2 online, 70 minutes, every 20 minutes) from Earl's Court/West Brompton to Gatwick from 3am to 11.30pm daily.

## Taxi

A metered trip to/from central London costs about £90 and takes just over an hour.

# Stansted Airport

**Stansted** (STN; www.stanstedairport.com) is 35 miles northeast of central London, heading towards Cambridge.

## Train

**Stansted Express** (www.standstedexpress.com) rail service (one way/return £21/29.70, 45 minutes, every 15 to 30 minutes) links the airport and Liverpool St station.

## Bus

**National Express** (www.nationalexpress.com) coaches run around the clock, offering some 120 services per day. The A6 runs to Victoria coach station (one way/return £10.50/17.50, 85 to 110 minutes, every 10 to 20 minutes) via North London. The A9 runs

to Stratford (£8.50/15, 45 minutes to one hour, every 30 minutes), from where you can catch a Jubilee line tube (20 minutes) into central London.

**easyBus** (www.easybus.co.uk) minibuses (one way £10, from £2 online, 75 minutes, every 20 to 30 minutes) from Baker St to Stansted run 24 hours a day.

**Terravision** (www.terravision.eu) coaches (one way/return £9/14) link Stansted to both Liverpool St rail station (bus A51; 55 minutes) and Victoria coach station (bus A50; 75 minutes) every 20 to 40 minutes between 6am and 1am.

## Taxi

A metered trip to/from central London costs around £90.

# Luton Airport

A smallish airport 32 miles northwest of London, **Luton** (LTN; www.london-luton.co.uk) caters for cheap charter flights and discount airlines.

## Train

**Services** (www.nationalrail.co.uk) run from London Bridge and King's Cross/St Pancras stations to Luton Airport Parkway station (off-peak one way/return £12.50/21.50, 30 to 40 minutes, every six to 15 minutes, from 7am to 10pm), from where an airport shuttle bus will take you to the airport in eight minutes.

## Bus

**easyBus** (www.easybus.co.uk) minibuses run from Victoria coach station (one way £10, online from £2, 80 minutes, every 30 minutes) to Luton via Marble Arch, Baker St and Finchley Rd tube stations

every half-hour round the clock, with the same frequencies coming from the airport.

**Green Line bus 757** (www.greenline.co.uk) buses to Luton (one way/return £16/22, tickets valid three months, 60 to 90 minutes) run from Buckingham Palace Rd just south of Victoria station, leaving approximately every half-hour round the clock.

## Taxi

A metered trip to/from central London costs about £90.

# London City Airport

Its proximity to central London, which is just six miles to its west, as well as to the commercial district of the Docklands, means **London City Airport** (LCY; www.londoncityairport.com) is predominantly a gateway for business travellers, although it does also serve holidaymakers with its two dozen continental European and seven national destinations.

## Train

**Docklands Light Railway** (DLR; www.tfl.gov.uk/dlr) stops at the London City Airport station (one way £4, with an Oyster card £2.20 to £2.70).

## Taxi

A metered trip to or from the City/Oxford St/Earl's Court costs about £25/30/40.

# St Pancras International

**Eurostar** (www.eurostar.com) high-speed rail links Gare du Nord in Paris (or Bruxelles Midi in Brussels) and St Pancras International, with up to two dozen arrivals daily.

The main national rail routes are served by InterCity trains, which are neither cheap nor particularly punctual. Check **National Rail Enquiries** (www.nationalrail.co.uk) for timetables and fares.

## Victoria Coach Station

**Eurolines** (www.eurolines.com; 52 Grosvenor Gardens SW1) has National Express–operated buses arriving from continental Europe at **Victoria coach station** (164 Buckingham Palace Rd SW1; ⊖ Victoria).

**National Express** (www .nationalexpress.com), the main coach operator, has comfortable and reliable services.

# Getting Around London

Public transport in London is excellent, if pricey. It is managed by **Transport for London** (www.tfl.gov.uk), which has a really helpful, multilingual website with live updates on traffic, a journey planner, maps and detailed information on every mode of transport in the capital.

The cheapest way to travel is with an Oyster card, which is a smart card.

## 🚇 Underground, DLR & Overground

Despite the never-ending upgrades and weekend closures, the London Underground ('the tube', 11 colour-coded lines), Docklands Light Railway (DLR, a driverless train operating in the eastern part of the city) and Overground network (mostly outside of Zone 1) are overall the quickest and easiest way of getting around the city, if not the cheapest.

The first trains operate around 5.30am Monday to Saturday and 7am Sunday. The last trains leave around 12.30am Monday to Saturday and 11.30pm Sunday.

**Fares**

◉ London is divided in nine concentric fare zones.

◉ It will always be cheaper to travel with an Oyster card (p282) than a paper ticket.

◉ Children under the age of 10 travel free.

## 🚌 Bus

London's iconic double-decker Routemaster was phased out in 2005 except for two 'heritage routes' (No 9 and 15). Bus services normally operate from 5am to 11.30pm.

**Night Bus**

◉ More than 50 night bus routes (prefixed with the letter 'N') run from midnight to 4.30am.

◉ There are also another 60 bus routes operating 24 hours; the frequency decreases between 11pm and 5am.

**Fares**

◉ Oyster cards are valid on all bus services, including night buses, and are cheaper than cash fares. Bus journeys cost a flat fare (non-Oyster/Oyster £2.20/1.30) regardless of how far you go.

◉ At bus stops with a yellow background, if you don't have an Oyster card, you must buy your ticket at the stop's ticket machine before boarding the bus (you will need the exact amount in coins).

◉ Children aged under 11 years travel free; those aged 11 to 18 years do as well but require an Oyster photocard.

## 🚕 Taxi

The London **black cab** (www.londonblackcabs.co.uk) is as much a feature of the cityscape as the red double-decker bus.

---

# Oyster Card

The Oyster card is a smart card on which you can store credit towards so-called 'prepay' fares, as well as Travelcards. Oyster cards are valid across the entire public transport network in London. All you need to do when entering a station is touch your card on a reader (which has a yellow circle with the image of an Oyster card on it) and then touch again on your way out. For bus journeys, you only need to touch once upon boarding.

The benefit lies in the fact that fares for Oyster-users are lower than standard ones.

Oyster cards can be bought (£5 refundable deposit) and topped up at any Underground station, travel info centre or shop displaying the Oyster logo.

# Barclays Cycle Hire Scheme

Following the success of cycling hire schemes in Paris and other European cities, London got in on the act in 2010, and unveiled its very own Barclays bikes.

The idea is simple: pick up a bike from one of the 400 docking stations dotted around the capital. Cycle. Drop it off at another docking station.

The access fee costs £1/5 per 24 hours/week. All you need is a credit or debit card.

Hire rates:

○ Up to 30 minutes: free

○ Up to one hour: £1

○ Up to two hours: £4

○ Up to three hours: £15

○ Up to 24 hours (max): £50

You can take as many bikes as you like during your access period (24 hours or one week), leaving five minutes between each trip.

You must be over 18 years old to buy access and at least 14 to ride a bike.

For more information, check www.tfl.gov.uk.

○ Cabs are available for hire when the yellow sign above the windscreen is lit; just stick your arm out to signal one.

○ Fares are metered, with the flag-fall charge of £2.20 (covering the first 336m during a weekday), rising by increments of 20p for each subsequent 168m.

○ Fares are more expensive in the evenings and overnight.

##  Boat

There are a number of companies operating along the Thames. However, only the **Thames Clippers (www.thamesclippers.com)** really offers commuter services.

The route goes from London Eye Millennium Pier to Woolwich Arsenal Piers, serving London Eye, Tate Modern, Shakespeare's Globe, Borough Market, Tower Bridge, Canary Wharf, Greenwich and the O2.

## 🚗 Car & Motorcycle

As a visitor, it's unlikely you'll need to drive in London. Mayors Ken Livingstone (2000–2008) and Boris Johnson (elected in 2008 and in office until 2012) have done everything in their power to encourage Londoners to get out of their car and into public transport (or on their bikes!) and the same disincentives should keep you firmly off the road: extortionate parking charges, congestion charge, traffic jams, high price of petrol, fiendishly efficient traffic wardens and wheel clampers etc.

## Congestion Charge

London was the world's first major city to introduce a congestion charge to reduce the flow of traffic into its centre. For full details log on to www.tfl.gov.uk/roadusers/congestioncharging.

## Hire

There is no shortage of car rental agencies in London. The following agencies have several branches across the capital:

**easyCar** (www.easycar.com)

**Avis** (www.avis.com)

**Hertz** (www.hertz.com)

# Tours

## ⛴ Boat

**Circular Cruise (**  **7936 2033; www.crownriver.com; adult/child/family £11/5.50/33;** ⊙ **11am-6.30pm late May-early Sep, to 5pm early Apr-late May & early Sep-Oct, to 3pm Nov-early Apr)** Vessels travel east from Westminster Pier to St Katharine's Pier near the Tower of London and back, calling at Embankment, Festival, Bankside and London Bridge Piers.

**Thames River Services (** ☑ **7930 4097; www.westminsterpier.co.uk; Westminster Pier, Victoria Embankment SW1; adult/child one way £8.40/4.20, return £11/5.50, family £28;** ⊙ **tours every 30min 10am-4pm or 5pm Apr-Oct)** These cruise boats leave Westminster Pier for Greenwich, stopping at the Tower of London.

## ℹ Practicalities

o **Weights & Measures** The UK uses a confusing mix of metric and imperial systems.

o **Smoking** Forbidden in all enclosed public places in England. Most pubs have a smoking area outside.

**Thames River Boats**
( 🕿 7930 2062; www.wpsa. co.uk; Westminster Pier, Victoria Embankment SW1; Kew adult/child/family one way £12/6/30, return £18/9/35, Hampton Court adult/child/family one way £15/7.50/37.50, return £22.50/11.25/56.25; ⏰ departs 10.30am, 11.30am, noon & 2pm Apr-Oct) These boats head upriver from Westminster Pier to the Royal Botanic Gardens at Kew (1½ hours) and some go on to Hampton Court Palace (another 1½ hours; noon boat only).

### 🚌 Bus

**Big Bus Tours** (www. bigbustours.com; adult/child £27/12; ⏰ departs every 15min 8.30am-6pm) Informative commentaries in eight languages.

### Specialist

**London Duck Tours**
( 🕿 7928 3132; www. londonducktours.co.uk; adult/child/family from £21/14/62; ⊖ Waterloo) These bright yellow, amphibious craft, which are based on D-Day landing vehicles, depart from behind the London Eye and cruise the streets of central London before making a dramatic descent into the Thames at Vauxhall for a 30-minute cruise.

# A-Z
# Directory

# Business Hours

Following are standard opening hours. Reviews in this book won't list opening hours unless they significantly differ from these standards.

**Information** 9am-5pm Mon-Fri

**Sights** 10am-6pm

**Banks** 9am-5pm Mon-Fri

**Shops** 9am-7pm Mon-Sat, 11am-5pm Sun

**Restaurants** Noon-2.30pm & 6-11pm

**Pubs & bars** 11am-11pm

# Customs Regulations

The UK distinguishes goods bought duty-free outside the EU and those bought in another EU country where taxes and duties have already been paid.

For European goods, there is officially no limit to how much you can bring but customs have guidelines to distinguish between personal and commercial use.

# Discount Cards

Possibly of most interest to visitors who want to take in lots of sights during their stay is the **London Pass** (www. londonpass.com). Prices for the London Pass start at £16.50 per day (for six days), although the pass can be altered to include use of the Underground and buses. The London Pass offers free entry and queue-jumping to all major attractions; check the website for details.

# Electricity

230V/50Hz

# Emergency

Dial 999 to call the police, fire brigade or ambulance in an emergency.

# Holidays

Most attractions and businesses close for a couple of days over Christmas.

**New Year's Day** 1 January

**Good Friday** Late March/April

**Easter Monday** Late March/April

**May Day Holiday** First Monday in May

**Spring Bank Holiday** Last Monday in May

**Summer Bank Holiday** Last Monday in August

**Christmas Day** 25 December

**Boxing Day** 26 December

# Internet Access

Most hotels now provide wi-fi, although many, particularly top end places, charge for the service.

A large number of cafes now offer free wi-fi, including chains such as Starbucks, Pret a Manger, McDonalds and Le Pain Quotidien.

The City of London is one big wi-fi zone (see www.thecloud.net); it's free to use for iPhone users but not for other devices.

## Import Restrictions

| ITEM | DUTY-FREE | TAX & DUTY PAID |
|------|-----------|-----------------|
| Tobacco | 200 cigarettes or 100 cigarillos or 50 cigars or 250g tobacco | 3200 cigarettes, 200 cigars, 400 cigarillos, 3kg tobacco |
| Spirits & liqueurs | 1L spirit or 2L of fortified wine | 10L spirit, 20L fortified wine |
| Beer & wine | 16L beer, 4L still wine | 110L beer, 90L still wine |
| Other goods | Up to a value of £390 | n/a |

Most major train stations and airport terminals also have wi-fi access, but it can be quite pricey.

# Maps

The *London A-Z* series produces a range of excellent maps and hand-held street atlases.

# Medical Services

EU nationals can obtain free emergency treatment on presentation of a **European Health Insurance Card** (www.ehic.org.uk).

Reciprocal arrangements with the UK allow Australian residents, New Zealand nationals, and residents and nationals of several other countries to receive free emergency medical treatment and subsidised dental care through the **National Health Service** (NHS; 0845 4647; www.nhsdirect.nhs.uk).

## Dental Services

For emergency dental care, call into **University College Hospital** ( 3456 7890; 253 Euston Rd NW1; Euston Sq).

## Hospitals

The following hospitals have 24-hour accident and emergency departments. However, in an emergency just call 999 and an ambulance will normally be dispatched from the hospital nearest to you.

**Charing Cross Hospital** ( 3311 1234; Fulham Palace Rd W6; Hammersmith)

**Chelsea & Westminster Hospital** ( 8746 8000; 369 Fulham Rd SW10; South Kensington, then 14 or 414)

**Guy's Hospital** ( 7188 7188; Great Maze Pond SE1; London Bridge)

# Money

**o** Despite being a member of the EU, the UK has not signed up to the euro and has retained the pound sterling (£) as its unit of currency.

## Post

The **Royal Mail** (www.royalmail.co.uk) is generally very reliable.

| POSTCARDS & LETTERS | PRICE | DELIVERY |
| --- | --- | --- |
| Domestic 1st class | 46p | Next working day |
| Domestic 2nd class | 36p | 3 working days |
| Europe | 68p | 3-5 working days |
| North America, Asia, Oceania | £1.10 | 5 working days |

○ One pound sterling is made up of 100 pence (called 'pee', colloquially).

○ Notes come in denominations of £5, £10, £20 and £50, while coins are 1p, 2p, 5p, 10p, 20p, 50p, £1 and £2.

○ Unless otherwise noted, all prices in this book are in pounds sterling.

### ATMs

ATMs are everywhere and generally accept Visa, MasterCard, Cirrus or Maestro cards, plus more obscure ones. There is usually a transaction surcharge for cash withdrawals with foreign cards. There are nonbank ATMs that charge £1.50 to £2 per transaction.

### Changing Money

○ The best place to change money is in any local post office branch, where no commission is charged.

○ You can also change money in most high-street banks and some travel-agent chains, as well as at the numerous bureaux de change throughout the city.

## Credit & Debit Cards

Londoners live off their debit cards, which can be used to get 'cash back' from supermarkets. Visitors should know that:

○ Credit and debit cards are accepted almost universally in London, from restaurants and bars to shops and even some taxis.

○ American Express and Diner's Club are less widely used than Visa and MasterCard.

## Taxes & Refunds

Value-added tax (VAT) is a 20% sales tax levied on most goods and services except food, books and children's clothing. Restaurants must, by law, include VAT in their menu prices, although VAT is not always included in hotel room prices so make sure you ask when booking accommodation to avoid surprises at bill time.

It's sometimes possible for visitors to claim a refund of VAT paid on goods. You're eligible if you have spent fewer than 365 days out of the two years prior to making the purchase living in the UK, and if you're leaving the EU within three months of making the purchase.

Not all shops participate in the VAT refund scheme, called the Retail Export Scheme or Tax-Free Shopping, and different shops will have different minimum purchase conditions (normally around £75 in any one shop). On request, participating shops will give you a special form (VAT 407). This must be presented with the goods and receipts to customs when you depart the country (VAT-free goods can't be posted or shipped home).

## Telephone

British Telecom's (BT's) famous red phone boxes survive in conservation areas only (notably Westminster).

Some phones will still accept coins, but most of them take phonecards (available from retailers, including most post offices and some newsagents) or credit cards.

Useful phone numbers (charged calls):

**Directory enquiries, international** (📞 118 661, 118 505)

**Directory enquiries, local & national** (📞 118 118, 118 500)

**Operator, international** (📞 155)

Phone codes worth knowing:

**International dialling code** (📞 00)

**Local call rate applies** (📞 08457)

**National call rate applies** (📞 0870, 0871)

**Premium rate applies** (📞 09) From 60p per minute.

**Toll-free** (📞 0800)

## Calling London

○ London's area code is 📞020, followed by an eight-digit number beginning with 📞7 (central London), 📞8 (Greater London) and 📞3 (nongeographic).

○ You only need to dial the 📞020 when you are calling London from elsewhere in the UK or if you're calling from a mobile.

○ To call London from abroad, dial your country's international access code, then 📞44 (the UK's country code), then 📞20 (dropping the initial 0), followed by the eight-digit phone number.

## International Calls & Rates

○ International direct dialling (IDD) calls to almost anywhere can be made from nearly all public telephones. Direct dialling is cheaper than making a reverse-charge (collect) call through the international operator (📞155).

○ Many private firms offer cheaper international calls than British Telecom (BT). In such shops you phone from

a metered booth and then pay the bill. Some cybercafes and internet shops also offer cheap rates for international calls.

○ International calling cards with a PIN (usually denominated £5, £10 or £20), which you can use from any phone by dialling a special access number, are usually the cheapest way to call abroad. These calling cards are available at most corner shops.

## Local & National Call Rates

○ Local calls are charged by time alone; regional and national calls are charged by both time and distance.

○ Daytime rates apply from 6am to 6pm Monday to Friday.

○ The cheap rate applies from 6pm to 6am Monday to Friday; weekend rates apply from 6pm Friday to 6am Monday.

## Mobile Phones

○ The UK uses the GSM 900 network, which covers Europe, Australia and New Zealand. However, it is not compatible with the North American GSM 1900 or Japanese mobile technology.

○ If you have a GSM phone, check with your service provider about using it in the UK and enquire about roaming charges.

○ It's usually better to buy a local SIM card from any mobile phone shop, though in order to do that you must ensure your handset is unlocked before you leave home.

# Time

Wherever you are in the world, the time on your watch is measured in relation to the time at Greenwich in London – Greenwich Mean Time (GMT). British Summer Time, the UK's form of daylight-saving time, muddies the water so that even London is ahead of GMT from late March to late October.

○ Paris: GMT +1

○ New York: GMT -5

○ San Francisco: GMT -8

○ Sydney: GMT +10

# Tourist Information

**Britain Visitor Centre** (www.visitbritain.com; 1 Regent St SW1; ⏰ 9.30am-6pm Mon, 9am-6pm Tue-Fri, 9am-4pm Sat, 10am-4pm Sun & bank holidays Sep-May, plus to 5pm Sat Jun-Sep; ⊖ Piccadilly Circus) London's main tourist office has comprehensive information, in eight languages, on London and the whole of the UK. It can arrange accommodation, tours, and train, air and car travel.

**Visit London** (📞 0870 156 6366; www.visitlondon.com) Can fill you in on everything from tourist attractions and events (such as the Changing of the Guard) to river trips and tours, accommodation, eating, theatre, shopping, children's London, and gay and lesbian venues.

## Visa Requirements

| COUNTRY | TOURISM | WORK | STUDY |
| --- | --- | --- | --- |
| European Economic Area (except Romania & Bulgaria) | X | X | X |
| Australia, Canada, New Zealand, South Africa, USA | X (up to 6 months) | √ | √ |
| Other nationalities | √ | √ | √ |

**Heathrow Airport** (Terminal 1, 2 & 3 Underground station; ⏰7.15am-9pm)

**King's Cross/St Pancras station** (⏰7.15am-9.15pm Mon-Sat, 8.15am-8.15pm Sun)

**Liverpool Street station** (⏰7.15am-9.15pm Mon-Sat, 8.15am-8.15pm Sun)

**Victoria train station** (⏰7.15am-9.15pm Mon-Sat, 8.15am-8.15pm Sun)

## Travellers with Disabilities

For disabled travellers London is an odd mix of user-friendliness and downright disinterest. New hotels and modern tourist attractions are legally required to be accessible to people in wheelchairs, but many historic buildings, B&Bs and guesthouses are in older buildings, which are hard (if not impossible) to adapt.

Transport is equally hit and miss, but slowly improving:

Only 62 of London's tube stations have step-free access; the rest have escalators or stairs.

The DLR is fully accessible for wheelchair users.

All buses are low-floor vehicles: they are lowered to street level when the bus stops; wheelchair users travel free.

Guide dogs are universally welcome on public transport, in hotels, in restaurants and at attractions.

The local government Transport for London publishes the *Getting Around London* guide, which contains the latest information on accessibility for passengers with disabilities. Download it from www.tfl.gov.uk.

## Visas

The table indicates who will need a visa for what, but make sure you check www.ukvisas.gov.uk or with your local British embassy for the most up-to-date information.

### Visa Extensions

Tourist visas can only be extended in clear emergencies (eg an accident, death of a relative). Otherwise you'll have to leave the UK (perhaps going to Ireland or France) and apply for a fresh one. To extend (or attempt to extend) your stay in the UK, ring the **Visa & Passport Information Line** (☏ 0870 606 7766; Home Office's Immigration & Nationality Directorate, Lunar House, 40 Wellesley Rd, Croydon CR9 2BY; ⏰8am-4pm Mon-Fri; 🚇East Croydon) before your current visa expires.

## Women Travellers

In general, London is a fairly laid-back place, and you're unlikely to have too many problems provided you take the usual city precautions. And if you feel unsafe, you should hang the expense and take a taxi. Archway-based **Lady Mini Cabs** (☏ 7272 3300) has women drivers.

# Behind the Scenes

## Author Thanks

### DAMIAN HARPER

I would like to thank Daisy Harper, Bill Moran, Daniel Hands, Matthew Scudamore and George Whitman, plus Jo Cooke and all the staff at Lonely Planet. Thanks as always to Timothy and Emma for everything.

## Acknowledgments

Illustrations p100-1 and p126-7 by Javier Zarracina. Cover photographs: Front: Houses of Parliament, Peter Adams/Photolibrary. Back: red telephone boxes outside building near the Inns of Court, Rick Gerharter/Lonely Planet Images ©.

Many of the images in this guide are available for licensing from Lonely Planet Images: www.lonelyplanetimages.com.

## This Book

This 2nd edition of Lonely Planet's *Discover London* was written and coordinated by Damian Harper, and researched and written by Emilie Filou, Sally Schafer, Vesna Maric and Steve Fallon. The previous edition was written by Tom Masters, Vesna Maric, Steve Fallon and Joe Bindloss. This guidebook was commissioned in Lonely Planet's London office, and produced by the following:

**Commissioning Editor** Joanna Cooke
**Coordinating Editors** Victoria Harrison, Lauren Hunt
**Coordinating Cartographer** Andrew Smith
**Coordinating Layout Designer** Frank Deim
**Managing Editors** Barbara Delissen, Susan Paterson, Martine Power
**Managing Cartographers** Alison Lyall, Mandy Sierp
**Managing Layout Designer** Chris Girdler
**Assisting Editor** Joanne Newell
**Cover Research** Naomi Parker
**Internal Image Research** Rebecca Skinner
**Thanks to** Jessica Boland, Laura Crawford, Janine Eberle, Ryan Evans, Jane Hart, Liz Heynes, Carol Jackson, Laura Jane, Yvonne Kirk, Annelies Mertens, Kylie McLaughlin, Wayne Murphy, Jarvis Nolan, Trent Paton, Mik Ruff, Laura Stansfeld, Gerard Walker, Clifton Wilkinson, Juan Winata

## SEND US YOUR FEEDBACK

We love to hear from travellers – your comments keep us on our toes and help make our books better. Our well-travelled team reads every word on what you loved or loathed about this book. Although we cannot reply individually to postal submissions, we always guarantee that your feedback goes straight to the appropriate authors, in time for the next edition. Each person who sends us information is thanked in the next edition, the most useful submissions are rewarded with a selection of digital PDF chapters.

Visit **lonelyplanet.com/contact** to submit your updates and suggestions or to ask for help. Our award-winning website also features inspirational travel stories, news and discussions.

NOTES

NOTES

292

**Index**

See also separate subindexes for:

⚔ Eating p300

🍷 Drinking & Nightlife p301

⭐ Entertainment p302

🔒 Shopping p302

Sights 000
Map pages 000

Sights 000
Map pages 000

Sights 000
Map pages 000

Sights 000
Map pages 000

# How to Use This Book

**These symbols will help you find the listings you want:**

- ◉ Sights
- ✪ Entertainment
- ✖ Eating
- 🔒 Shopping
- 🍷 Drinking & Nightlife
- ✦ Sports & Activities

**These symbols give you the vital information for each listing:**

- ♪ Telephone Numbers
- ☉ Opening Hours
- P Parking
- ⊖ Nonsmoking
- ✳ Air-Conditioning
- @ Internet Access

- 🛜 Wi-Fi Access
- ✉ Swimming Pool
- ✔ Vegetarian Selection
- 📋 English-Language Menu
- ⟆ Family-Friendly
- 🐾 Pet-Friendly

- 🚌 Bus
- 🛳 Ferry
- Ⓜ Metro
- Ⓢ Subway
- ⊖ London Tube
- 🚃 Tram
- 🚆 Train

**Reviews are organised by author preference.**

## Look out for these icons:

 No payment required

 A green or sustainable option

*Our authors have nominated these places as demonstrating a strong commitment to sustainability – for example by supporting local communities and producers, operating in an environmentally friendly way, or supporting conservation projects.*

# Map Legend

## Sights
- 🏖 Beach
- 🔵 Buddhist
- 🏰 Castle
- ✝ Christian
- 🕉 Hindu
- ☪ Islamic
- ✡ Jewish
- ❗ Monument
- 🏛 Museum/Gallery
- 🔴 Ruin
- 🍇 Winery/Vineyard
- 🦁 Zoo
- ◉ Other Sight

## Activities, Courses & Tours
- 🤿 Diving/Snorkelling
- 🛶 Canoeing/Kayaking
- ⛷ Skiing
- 🏄 Surfing
- 🏊 Swimming/Pool
- 🚶 Walking
- 🏄 Windsurfing
- ✦ Other Activity/ Course/Tour

## Sleeping
- 🛏 Sleeping
- ⛺ Camping

## Eating
- ✖ Eating

## Drinking
- 🍷 Drinking
- ☕ Cafe

## Entertainment
- ✪ Entertainment

## Shopping
- 🔒 Shopping

## Information
- 📧 Post Office
- ℹ Tourist Information

## Transport
- ✈ Airport
- ✖ Border Crossing
- 🚌 Bus
- 🚡 Cable Car/ Funicular
- 🚲 Cycling
- ⛴ Ferry
- Ⓜ Metro
- 🚝 Monorail
- P Parking
- Ⓢ S-Bahn
- 🚕 Taxi
- 🚉 Train/Railway
- 🚊 Tram
- ⊖ Tube Station
- Ⓤ U-Bahn
- • Other Transport

## Routes
- Tollway
- Freeway
- Primary
- Secondary
- Tertiary
- Lane
- Unsealed Road
- Plaza/Mall
- Steps
- )⸬( Tunnel
- Pedestrian Overpass
- Walking Tour
- Walking Tour Detour
- Path

## Boundaries
- ─ ─ International
- ─ ─ ─ State/Province
- ─ ─ Disputed
- Regional/Suburb
- Marine Park
- Cliff
- Wall

## Population
- 🟢 Capital (National)
- ◉ Capital (State/Province)
- ● City/Large Town
- • Town/Village

## Geographic
- 🛖 Hut/Shelter
- 🚩 Lighthouse
- 👁 Lookout
- ▲ Mountain/Volcano
- 🌴 Oasis
- 🅿 Park
- )( Pass
- 🍽 Picnic Area
- 💧 Waterfall

## Hydrography
- River/Creek
- Intermittent River
- Swamp/Mangrove
- Reef
- Canal
- Water
- Dry/Salt/ Intermittent Lake
- Glacier

## Areas
- Beach/Desert
- Cemetery (Christian)
- Cemetery (Other)
- Park/Forest
- Sportsground
- Sight (Building)
- Top Sight (Building)

## Our Story

A beat-up old car, a few dollars in the pocket and a sense of adventure. In 1972 that's all Tony and Maureen Wheeler needed for the trip of a lifetime – across Europe and Asia overland to Australia. It took several months, and at the end – broke but inspired – they sat at their kitchen table writing and stapling together their first travel guide, *Across Asia on the Cheap*. Within a week they'd sold 1500 copies. Lonely Planet was born.

Today, Lonely Planet has offices in Melbourne, London and Oakland, with more than 600 staff and writers. We share Tony's belief that 'a great guidebook should do three things: inform, educate and amuse'.

# Our Writers

### DAMIAN HARPER

**Coordinating Author, The South Bank; Kensington & Hyde Park; Greenwich** Born off the Strand within earshot of Bow Bells (favourable wind permitting), Damian grew up in Notting Hill way before it was discovered by Hollywood. A Wykehamist, former Shakespeare and Company bookseller, and linguist with two degrees, Damian has been authoring guidebooks for Lonely Planet since the late 1990s. Damian currently lives in South London with his China-born wife and two kids.

### STEVE FALLON

**Day Trips from London** After more than a decade of living in the centre of the known universe (east London), Steve cockney-rhymes in his sleep, eats jellied eel for brekkie, drinks lager by the bucketful and dances round the occasional handbag. For this edition he went bush and is happy to report that there is life – and lots of it – beyond the M25. Steve is a newly qualified Blue Badge London guide.

### EMILIE FILOU

**The West End, Hampstead & North London** Emilie was born in Paris, where she lived until she was 18. Following her three-year degree and three gap years, she found herself in London, fell in love with the place and never really left. She now works as a journalist, specialising in Africa. Emilie also wrote Transport and Directory.

Read more about Emilie at:
lonelyplanet.com/members/emiliefilou

### SALLY SCHAFER

**The City, Clerkenwell, Hoxton & Spitalfields, East End & Docklands** Having lived in east London for over 10 years, in the shadow of the emerging Olympic Park for four, and worked in Clerkenwell and Old St for the last six, Sally had a whale of a time re-exploring her own backyard. She usually goes by the title of Associate Publisher in Lonely Planet's London office but has also written about London, Spain and Portugal on previous office flits.

## Contributing Writer

**Vesna Maric** wrote the Family Travel chapter and has lived in London for 15 years. She has been delighted to discover an entirely new side of the city since having her daughter Frida, a year and a half ago. She looks forward to showing her the city's wonderful array of offerings in the years to come.

**Published by Lonely Planet Publications Pty Ltd**
ABN 36 005 607 983
2nd edition – June 2012
ISBN 978 1 74220 585 4
© Lonely Planet 2012  Photographs © as indicated 2012
10 9 8 7 6 5 4 3 2 1
Printed in China

Although the authors and Lonely Planet have taken all reasonable care in preparing this book, we make no warranty about the accuracy or completeness of its content and, to the maximum extent permitted, disclaim all liability arising from its use.